Rudiments of Music

A DETAILED STUDY IN MUSIC ESSENTIALS

by

JEANNETTE CASS

UNIVERSITY OF KANSAS

PRENTICE-HALL, INC., Englewood Cliffs, New Jersey

Printed in the United States of America

ISBN: 0-13-783654-6

10 9 8 7 6 5 4 3 2 1

PRENTICE-HALL INTERNATIONAL, INC., *London*
PRENTICE-HALL OF AUSTRALIA, PTY. LTD., *Sydney*
PRENTICE-HALL OF CANADA, LTD., *Toronto*
PRENTICE-HALL OF INDIA PRIVATE LIMITED, *New Delhi*
PRENTICE-HALL OF JAPAN, INC., *Tokyo*

To

My students and friends whose questions concerning the essentials of music notation have given me the inspiration to compile this knowledge into book form.

PREFACE

The purpose of this book is to provide the student with the background in music essentials that is prerequisite to the study of four-part writing, playing, and singing. Its content has been presented and tested over a period of ten years in a six-weeks' course, called "Rudiments of Music Theory," offered to students attending the Mid-Western Music Camp during summer school sessions at the University of Kansas.

The book may be used in many ways. Sight-singing, ear-training, and keyboard drills are interwoven with the presentation of written rudiments, and it is suggested that the best results may be obtained by teaching all of these aspects of the subject more or less simultaneously, as they appear in the text. However, any one aspect may be segregated for a course of study. The book can be successfully used for self-guided study.

Because they bear upon the name and degree of intervals and upon the analysis of some twentieth-century compositions, the unusual sharp and flat signatures and scales are presented in full. Each of the seven sharp and seven flat scales is written out, together with its respective minor scales in all forms. The author has found that many students are extremely confused regarding the minor scales, and she hopes that this method of approach will eliminate some of the mystery so often surrounding the minor scales. The minor scales, properly understood, are no more difficult to use than the major scales. Similarly, with sufficient drill and understanding of the keys beyond four sharps and four flats, the student will gain facility in their use; he will no longer shudder at the signatures of five or more sharps or flats.

All of the seven clefs are represented in the sight-singing exercises. This not only reflects the great amount of interest in the pre-Bach period of music; it helps students gain facility in transposing music by changing clef signs, a method recognized as the most reliable one.

The sight-singing examples have been drawn from a wide field of well-known musical literature and are placed in various keys. All are within the range of the average singing voice. Each musical example is specifically identified as to source, brief biographical notes are supplied, and the instrument for which the example was scored is indicated.

The tests and worksheets which appear at the end of most lessons have been used by hundreds of students and have been found to be very practicable. The students themselves have praised the effectiveness of these sheets, and the grades obtained by average students in each class indicate that the worksheets and tests are well within the capabilities of first-year college students. All necessary blank music paper is included in the book.

The author's thanks are due to all those who have helped make this book possible: to the hundreds of students in the Mid-Western Music Camp who have used the tests and worksheets; to Mr. Raymond Verrey and Mr. Jack Newcomb, without whose interest this book would not have materialized.

J. C.

CONTENTS

LESSON 1
Clefs

There seems to be no adequate definition of the term *music*. Perhaps, in a general way, one can say that music is an art that has as its elements rhythm and sound.

PROPERTIES OF A MUSICAL SOUND

There are four properties of a musical sound or tone: pitch, duration, quantity (intensity), and quality.

1. *Pitch* is the rate of vibration of a wave generated by a sounding body which creates in the ear a sensation of highness or lowness of tone. The pitch of a tone is determined by the number of vibrations per second. The fewer the number of vibrations per second, the lower the pitch; and the greater the number of vibrations per second, the higher the pitch.
2. *Duration* is the length of time that a sound continues.
3. *Quantity* (intensity) is the amount of tone produced (loud or soft). In more scientific terminology, it might be said that it is the amplitude of a sound wave which creates in the air a sensation of loudness or softness.
4. *Quality* is determined by the instrument or voice producing the sound (piano, violin, and so on). Technically, it is the shape of the sound wave produced that determines quality.

THE STAFF AND THE CLEFS

When one first approaches a musical composition, he is conscious of the music paper and the staff upon it. This staff (plural, staves) consists of five lines and four spaces:

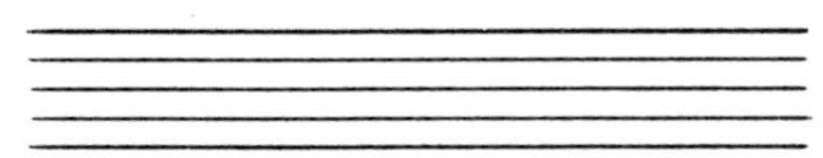

The notes that are placed on the lines and in the spaces of the staff represent musical tones. Upon the staff is placed a *clef sign*. This determines the names of the lines and spaces of the staff.

There are seven different clefs. The most familiar one is the *treble clef* (treble means high). This clef is made by drawing a perpendicular line across the staff, curving from the top of the line to the right, crossing the fourth line of the staff and the perpendicular line, curving left to the first line, circling right to the third line, and then curving left to the second line. (Study the example and draw several treble clef signs for practice.)

Printed *Manuscript*

This sign was derived from the Old English letter G, and it designates that the second line from the bottom of the staff is to be called G. Since only seven letters of the alphabet are used in music (A, B, C, D, E, F, G), the lines of the treble clef are named:

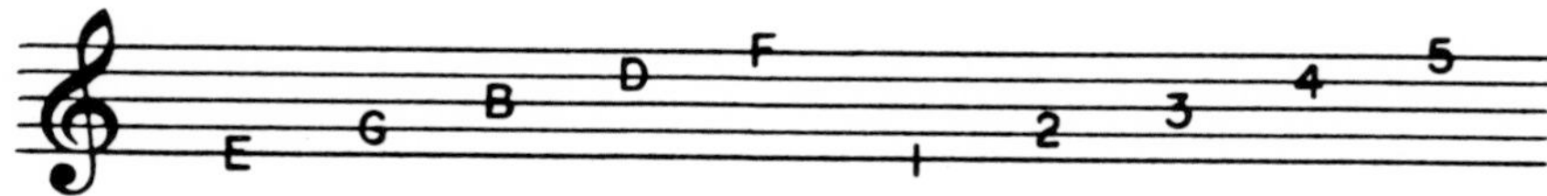

The spaces of the treble clef are named:

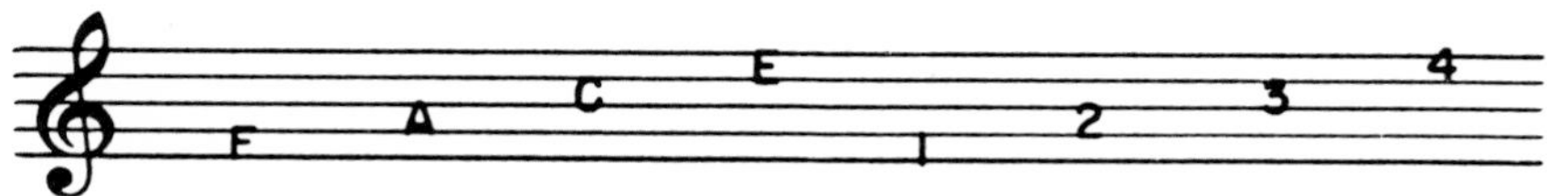

The lines and spaces of the staff are always counted from the bottom to the top.

There are two *F clefs*. The one with which we are most familiar is the *bass clef.* This clef is drawn by starting on the fourth line and almost encircling it, curving downward to the right to the first line. Then a dot is placed on both sides of the fourth line, denoting that the fourth line is to be called F. (Study the example and draw several bass clef signs for practice.) The *most important part* of this clef sign is the correct placement of the two dots. The lines of the bass clef are therefore named:

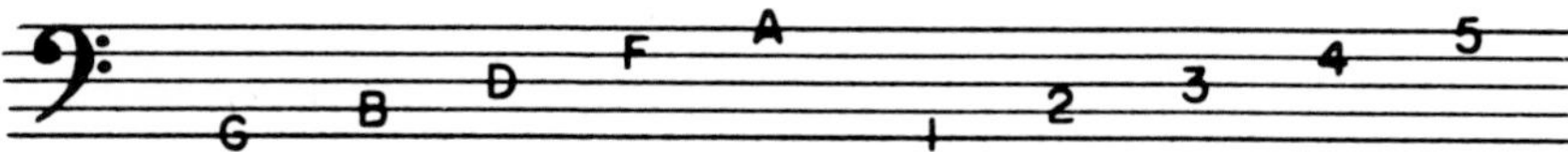

The spaces of the bass clef are named:

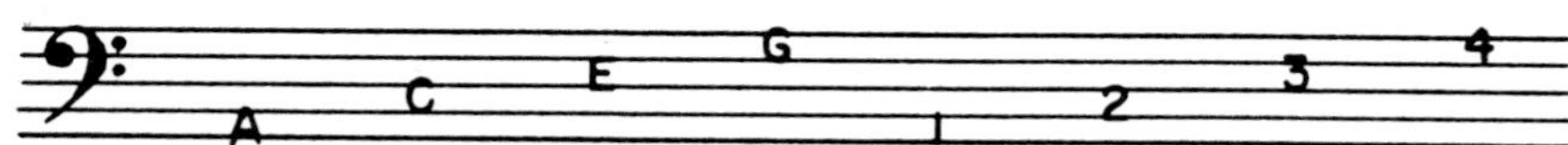

The combination of the treble and bass clefs is known as the *Great Staff,* which is used for keyboard (piano) music:

Originally this was an eleven-line staff; but because it was very confusing to read, the middle line (middle C) has been omitted and is used only when needed.

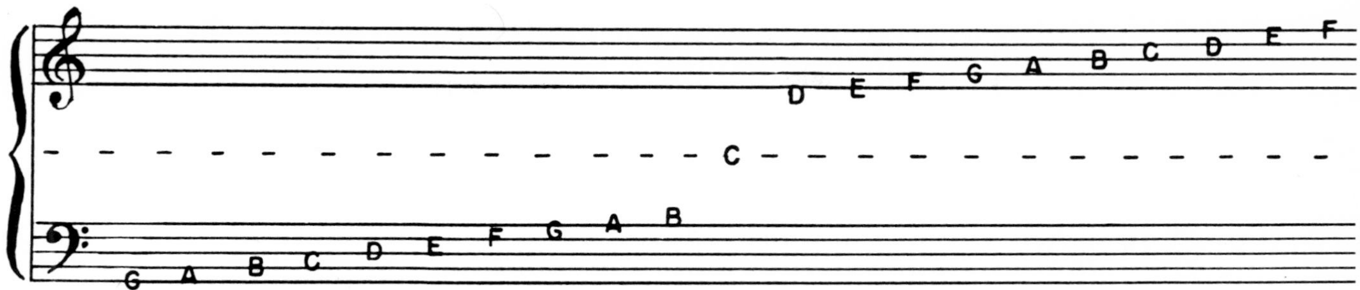

Leger lines and spaces are added lines and spaces above and below the staff. These are necessary because not all of the notes a composer may wish to use can be placed within the limits of the ten lines and eight spaces of the Great Staff.

The other F clef is the *baritone clef.* This clef sign is similar to the bass clef sign, except that it is drawn from the third line and a dot is placed on both sides of this line. The third line thus becomes F, and the names of the lines of the baritone clef are:

The names of the spaces of the baritone clef are:

In viewing these two F clefs, one sees how important the dots of the clef sign become, for these designate the difference between the names of the lines and spaces of the two clefs. It is very necessary, therefore, to place these dots in their correct positions on the staff.

There are four *C clefs.* The vertical center of the C clef sign locates middle C on each of the staves.

1. The *soprano clef,* with middle C on the first line:

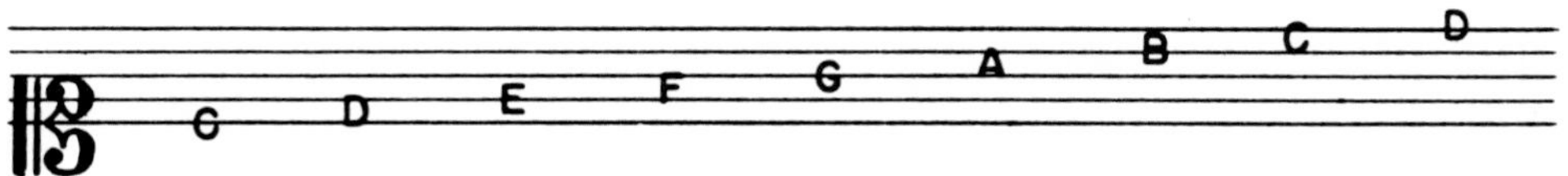

2. The *mezzo-soprano clef* (mezzo, an Italian word, means half), with middle C on the second line:

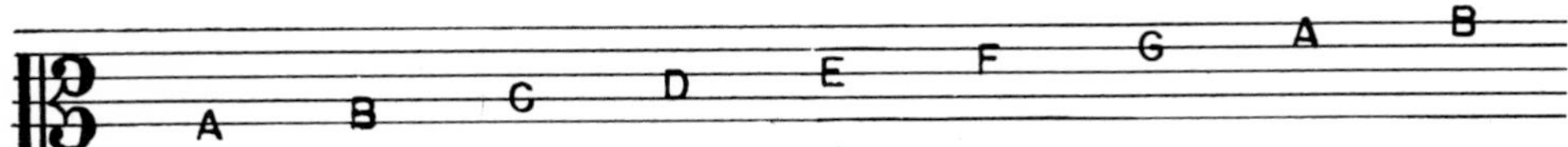

3. The *alto* or *viola clef,* with middle C on the third line:

4. The *tenor* or *cello clef,* with middle C on the fourth line:

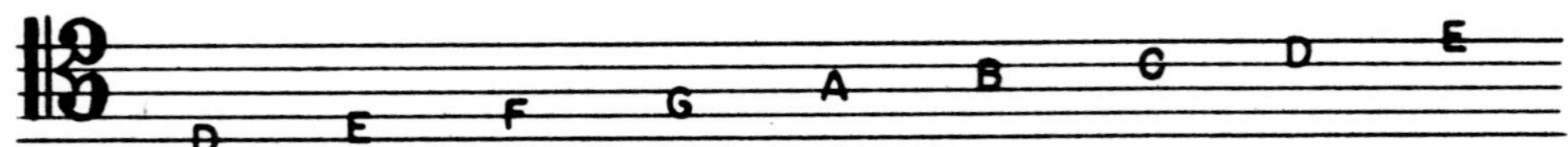

The soprano and mezzo-soprano clefs are not used to any great extent in writing music today. Music for the viola is usually written in the alto clef. When music written for the cello or bassoon would require a number of leger lines if the bass clef were used, it is common practice to use the tenor clef.

One of the outstanding uses of these clefs is in the art of transposition (the performance of the same melody in a different key). If the student would become as skilled in the use of all seven clefs as he is in the two most common ones (treble and bass), all that would be necessary for transposition would be the changing of the clef sign and then reading in the new clef.

Let us assume, for example, that you are given the following notes:

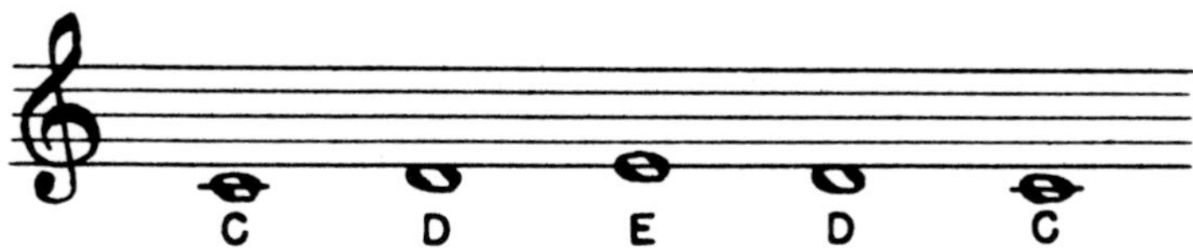

If you desire to sing this melody in the key of E major, just change the clef sign to the bass clef and add the four sharps of the key of E major:

If you want to sing the same melody in the key of G major, just change the clef sign to the baritone clef and place the F♯ in the key signature:

Here is how the melody will look in the remaining clefs:

OCTAVE GROUPS

For convenience in determining the location or register of tones, and in learning the names of the lines and spaces, the Great Staff is divided into octave groups.

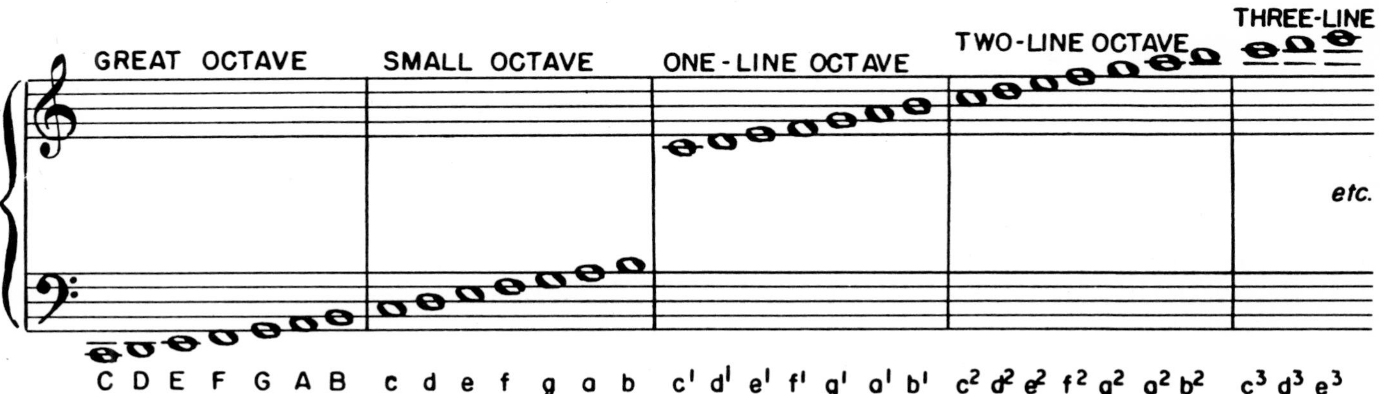

Name .... Date ....

WORKSHEET FOR LESSON 1: Clefs

1. Make each of the clef signs and write the two names for each clef.
   In making the C clef sign in manuscript, use the form shown at the right.

.... clef .... clef .... clef .... clef

.... clef .... clef .... clef .... clef

.... clef .... clef .... clef

.... clef .... clef .... clef

2. Write the clef signs again and name the lines of each clef.

3. Write the clef signs again and name the spaces of each clef.

What clef is used if:

(1) A is on the fifth line of the staff? ....

(2) B is on the third line? ....

(3) C is on the fourth line? ....

(4) D is on the fourth line? ....

(5) E is in the second space? ....

(6) F is on the first line? ....

(7) G is on the fourth line? ....

(8) A is in the second space? ....

(9) B is in the third space? ....

(10) C is on the first line? ....

5. Write in the *treble* clef (be sure to place the clef sign at the beginning of each staff): a^2, e^1, small b, d^3, small g, f^2, c^1, a^1, b^2, c^2.

6. Write in the *bass* clef: Great A, small g, e^1, Great D, small f, g^1, small b, c^1, Great B, Great C.

7. Add the appropriate clef signs for the six clefs not supplied and write the letter name under each note.

Name ....   Date ....

Alto 

Tenor 

8. Place the following notes on the Great Staff: d^2, small b, Great F, e^3, small g, Great A, b^2, a^1, c^3, c^1.

9. What are the four properties of a tone?

How is pitch determined?

What explains the difference between a high tone and a low tone?

Name ....   Date ....

SAMPLE TEST FOR LESSON 1: Clefs

1. Name the four properties of a tone.

2. What is the plural of *staff?*

3. Place the seven clefs on the staff. Give two names for each clef. Name the lines and spaces of each clef, placing the letters on the staff in their proper places.

4. On the Great Staff, write: g^1, c^2, Great B, small a, f^3, Great D, e^2, small g, b^1, a^2.

5. Place the following in C major by changing the clef sign and key signature. (C major does not have any sharps or flats in the signature.)

There are 100 points on this test. Each point equals 1 per cent.

LESSON 2

Major Scales in Sharp Keys

Directly following the clef sign on the staff, the *key signature* is located. The key signature, which indicates the notes that are normally to be sharped or flatted, is determined by the scale used in a composition. In this lesson the major scales of the sharp keys will be presented.

All major scales conform to the same pattern, an arrangement of whole and half-steps within the scale. On a piano keyboard, between any two adjacent white keys that are separated by a black key, there is an interval of a whole step. (Later, in our study of intervals, we will call this a major second.) Between E and F, and between B and C, where no black key exists, there is an interval of a half-step. (Later we will call this a minor second.) The interval between any white key and an adjacent black key is a half-step.

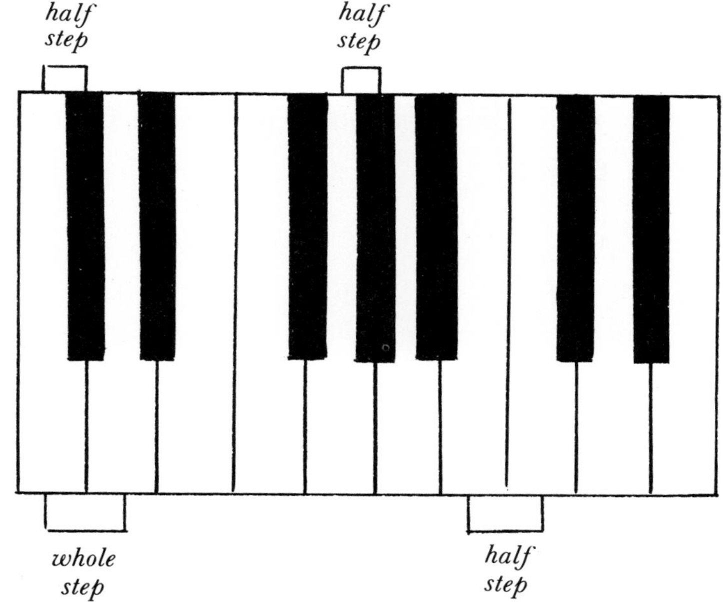

PATTERN OF THE MAJOR SCALE

As an example of a major scale, let us take the scale of C major. This scale is first divided into two tetrachords (*tetra* means four; a *chord* is a group of three or more notes):

C D E F G A B C

Analyzing the scale of C major, we find:

Scale — C D E F G A B C
Steps — 1 1 ½ 1 1 1 ½

We see now that the two tetrachords contain the same intervals in the same sequence. Each contains two whole steps and a half-step, and the two tetrachords are separated by a whole step.

CONSTRUCTING MAJOR SCALES IN SHARP KEYS

To find the beginning note (keynote) of the scale containing one sharp, count *up* to the fifth note of the C major scale:

C D E F G A B C
1 2 3 4 5

Following the established pattern of whole steps and half-steps, the new scale will be spelled as follows:

G A B C D E F♯ G
1 1 ½ 1 1 1 ½

Note that the F must be raised to F♯ to conform to the pattern. When any natural letter is raised a half-step, we say that it is sharped (♯). The center of the sharp symbol must be *in* the space or *through* the line it affects:

Now we see why the scale of G major has one sharp, and why that sharp is F♯ rather than some other.

Counting up to the fifth note of the G major scale, one finds D:

G A B C D E F♯ G
1 2 3 4 5

and counting up successively by fives from the keynote of each new scale, one finds:

D E F♯ G A B C♯ D
1 1 ½ 1 1 1 ½

A B C♯ D E F♯ G♯ A
1 1 ½ 1 1 1 ½

E F♯ G♯ A B C♯ D♯ E
1 1 ½ 1 1 1 ½

B C♯ D♯ E F♯ G♯ A♯ B
1 1 ½ 1 1 1 ½

F♯ G♯ A♯ B C♯ D♯ E♯ F♯
1 1 ½ 1 1 1 ½

C♯ D♯ E♯ F♯ G♯ A♯ B♯ C♯
1 1 ½ 1 1 1 ½

Each of these scales above contains one more sharp than its predecessor. Placing these scales on the staff with their respective key signatures (the key signature, as already noted, is placed on the staff immediately following the clef sign), we have:

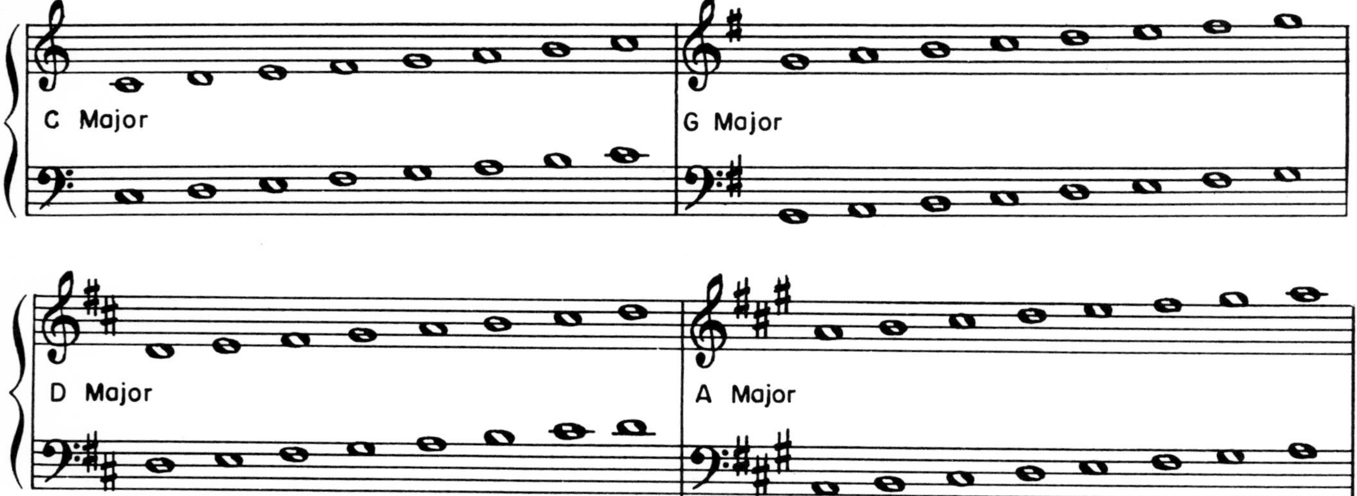

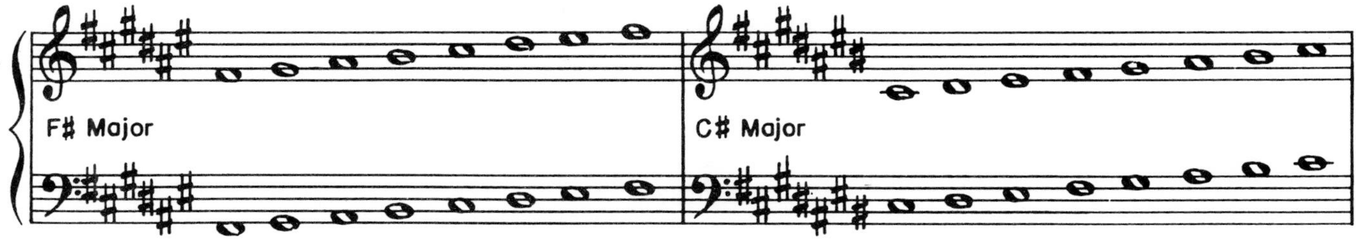

In memorizing these scales there are three helpful points to remember:

1. Memorize thoroughly the C♯ major signature in both the bass and treble clefs. The sharps always appear in this order next to the clef sign. Thus, if you desire six sharps, omit the seventh sharp; for five sharps, omit the last two, and so on.
2. The last sharp to the right is always one half-step down from the tonic, or keynote, of the scale. You therefore count up one half-step from the last sharp to the right to get the name of the keynote. The name of the scale is taken from the keynote.
3. Given the keynote of the scale, you go down one half-step from the keynote to find the last sharp to the right, and then fill in the correct sharps back to the clef sign.

The sharp scales are built in a Circle of Fifths formation:

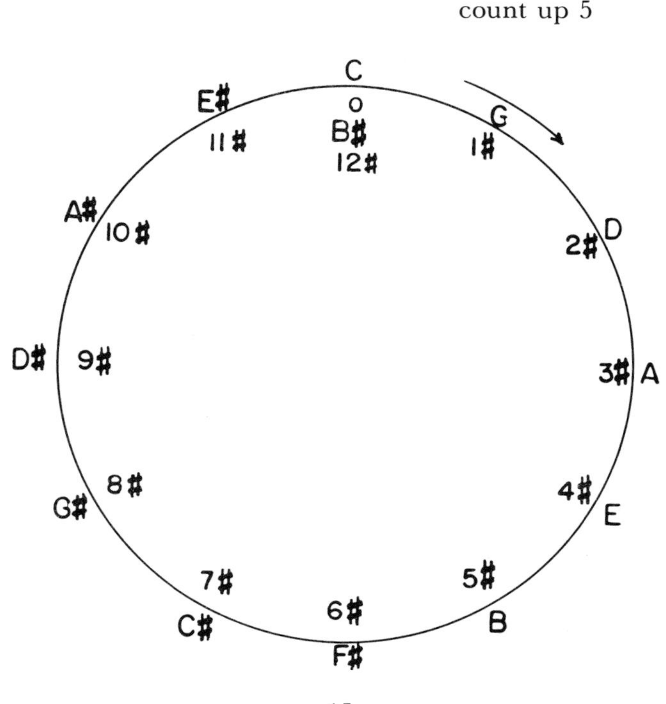

SOME DEFINITIONS

When a note is *sharped,* it does not always mean that the symbol of a sharp (♯) will be placed in front of that note. When a note that is natural is raised a half-step, then the sharp is used. When a sharp is raised a half-step, then a double sharp (𝄪) is used. When a flat is raised a half-step, then a natural sign (♮) is used.

Enharmonic means the same sound with a different name. For example, C and B♯ are enharmonic. Thus, proceeding around the Circle of Fifths to the right, one is back to C major when the circle is completed. The only practical scales in this circle are the scale of C major and those bearing from one to seven sharps. Beyond seven sharps, double sharps must be employed; and since these are quite difficult to read, the enharmonic equivalents in flat keys are used. There is such a thing as a triple sharp (♯ 𝄪), which raises a double sharp one half-step. In some modern compositions a triple sharp is used, but the instances are very rare.

MAJOR SCALES IN UNUSUAL SHARP KEYS

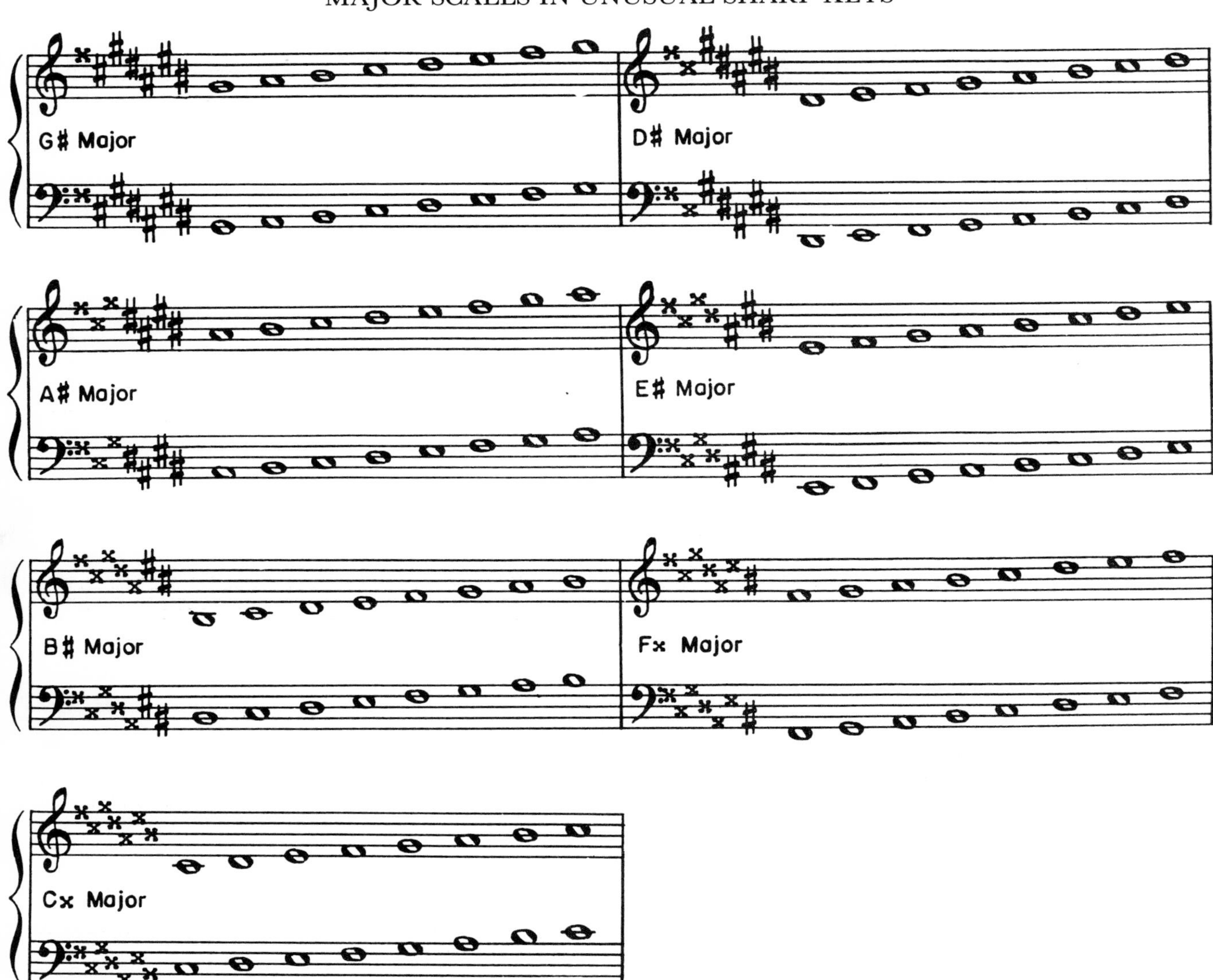

Of course, these scales are impractical for use, but theoretically they are possible; and the knowledge that they do exist is often helpful to the student. The sharps of the first seven sharp scales are now double sharps, and then the remainder of the sharps through B♯ are used in the key signature.

Name .... Date ....

WORKSHEET FOR LESSON 2: Major Scales in Sharp Keys

1. In the treble clef, write the key signature and scale of A major.

   Method of finding key signature of the A major scale:

   1. Down one half-step from A is G♯.
   2. Therefore G♯ is the last sharp to the right in the key signature.
   3. Before you can have G♯ in the signature, you must have F♯ next to the clef sign, and then then C♯.
   4. Therefore A major has three sharps: F♯, C♯, G♯.

2. In the bass clef, write the key signature and the scale of five sharps.

   Method of finding keynote of the scale with five sharps:

   1. The first five sharps of a major scale are, in order, F♯, C♯, G♯, D♯, A♯.
   2. Place these sharps on the staff in the bass clef.
   3. Go up one half-step from the last sharp to the right, which is A♯.
   4. B is the keynote.

3. In the treble clef, write the major scale which has no flats or sharps.

   This scale must be memorized, for there is no way of finding the answer.

4. In the treble clef, write the key signature and scale of D major.

5. In the bass clef, write the key signature and scale of E major.

6. In the bass clef, write the key signature and the scale of six sharps.

7. In the treble clef, write the key signature and scale of F♯ major.

8. In the bass clef, write the key signature and the scale of three sharps.

9. In the treble clef, write the key signature and scale of B major.

10. In the bass clef, write the key signature and the scale of C♯ major.

Name ....   Date ....

SAMPLE TEST FOR LESSON 2: Major Scales in Sharp Keys

On the staves below, write the following scales with their respective key signatures:

1. Treble clef—B major

2. Bass clef—C♯ major

3. Bass clef—scale with one sharp

4. Treble clef—scale with three sharps

5. Treble clef—E major

6. Bass clef—C major

7. Treble clef—scale with five sharps

8. Bass clef—F♯ major

9. Bass clef—A major

10. Treble clef—scale with two sharps

Each scale equals 5 per cent; each key signature equals 5 per cent.

LESSON 3

Rest and Active Tones in Sharp Scales

The rest tones of any scale are the keynote (tonic), the third note of the scale, and the fifth note. They are so called because they give an impression of stability. All other notes in the scale are known as active tones, for they seem to lead naturally (resolve) to the rest tones.

Active tones resolve as follows:

2 to 1 or 3 (preferably to 1)

4 to 3

6 to 5

7 to 8

DRILL ON REST TONES

From the keynote of C major and every sharp major scale, sing the rest tones 1-3-5-8-5-3-1 (these groups form the tonic chord in every major scale).

The following are the tonic chords in C major and in each of the major sharp keys:

Sing the following numbers with their proper pitches in the key of C major; and then substitute letter names for the numbers:

1-3-5-8	1-8-5-3-1	3-5-8-5-3-8-1
8-5-3-1	1-5-8-5-1	3-1-3-5-8-5-3-1
1-3-5-3-1	1-3-5-5-8	3-5-8-5-3-8-1
1-8-5-1-8	8-5-3-5-8	3-1-3-5-8-1-5-3-1
1-3-8-3-1	5-3-5-5-1-3-1-8	5-8-5-1-3-8
1-5-3-5-1	8-5-3-5-1	5-3-1-3-5-5-8
8-5-1-5-8	1-3-5-3-5-3-1	5-3-5-1-5-3-8
1-8-5-8-1	8-5-3-5-3-5-1	5-8-5-1-8-5-3-1
1-5-1-5-8	8-5-5-3-3-1-8	5-1-5-8-5-3-3-1
8-5-1-8-5-8	3-5-8-5-3-1	5-1-1-3-3-5-1-8
8-5-1-5-1	3-1-3-5-8-5-3-1	

Sing in the keys of G major, D major, A major, E major, B major, and F♯ major, the letter names that correspond to the numbers above.

DICTATION FOR DRILL ON REST TONES

The instructor plays the following exercises, or similar ones, and the student places on the staff the notes heard. Dictation should be in the major keys of C, G, D, A, E, B, and F♯.

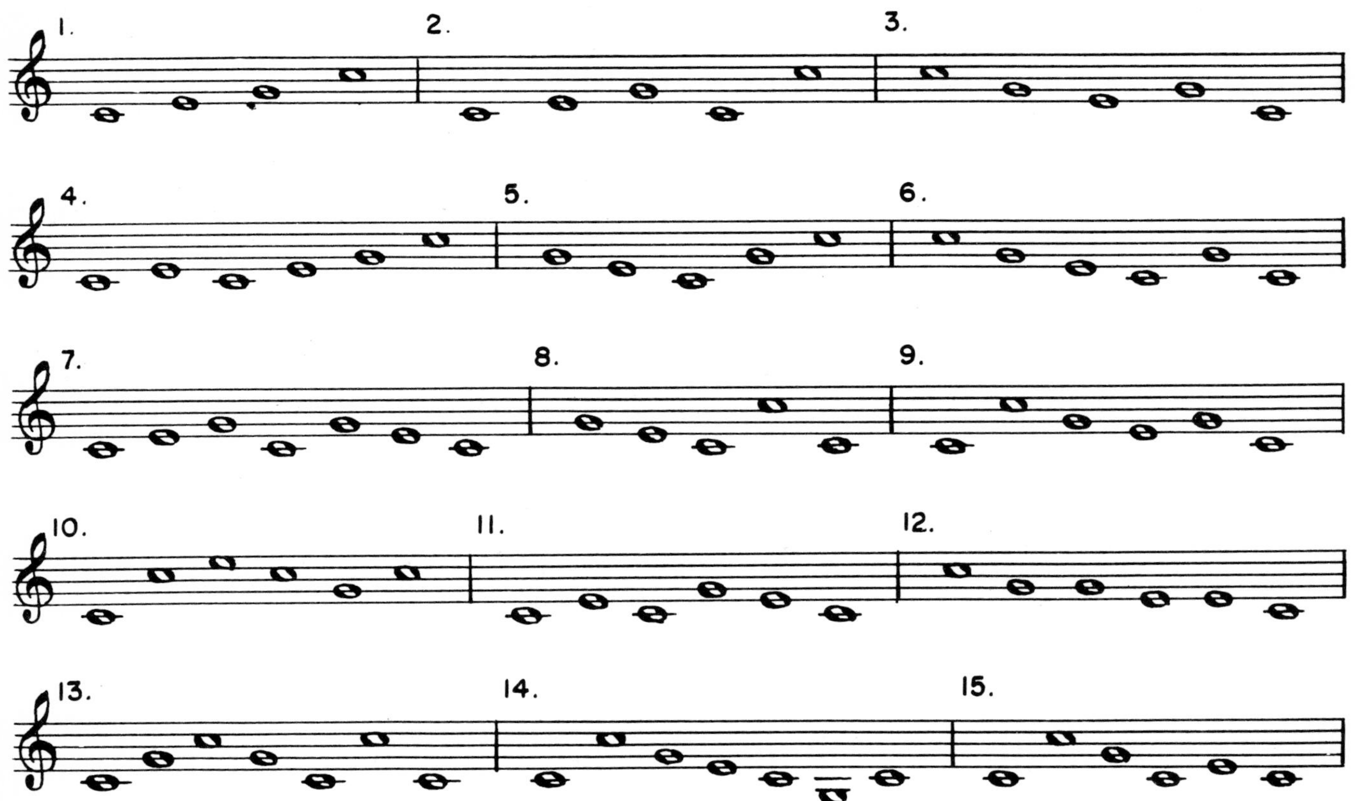

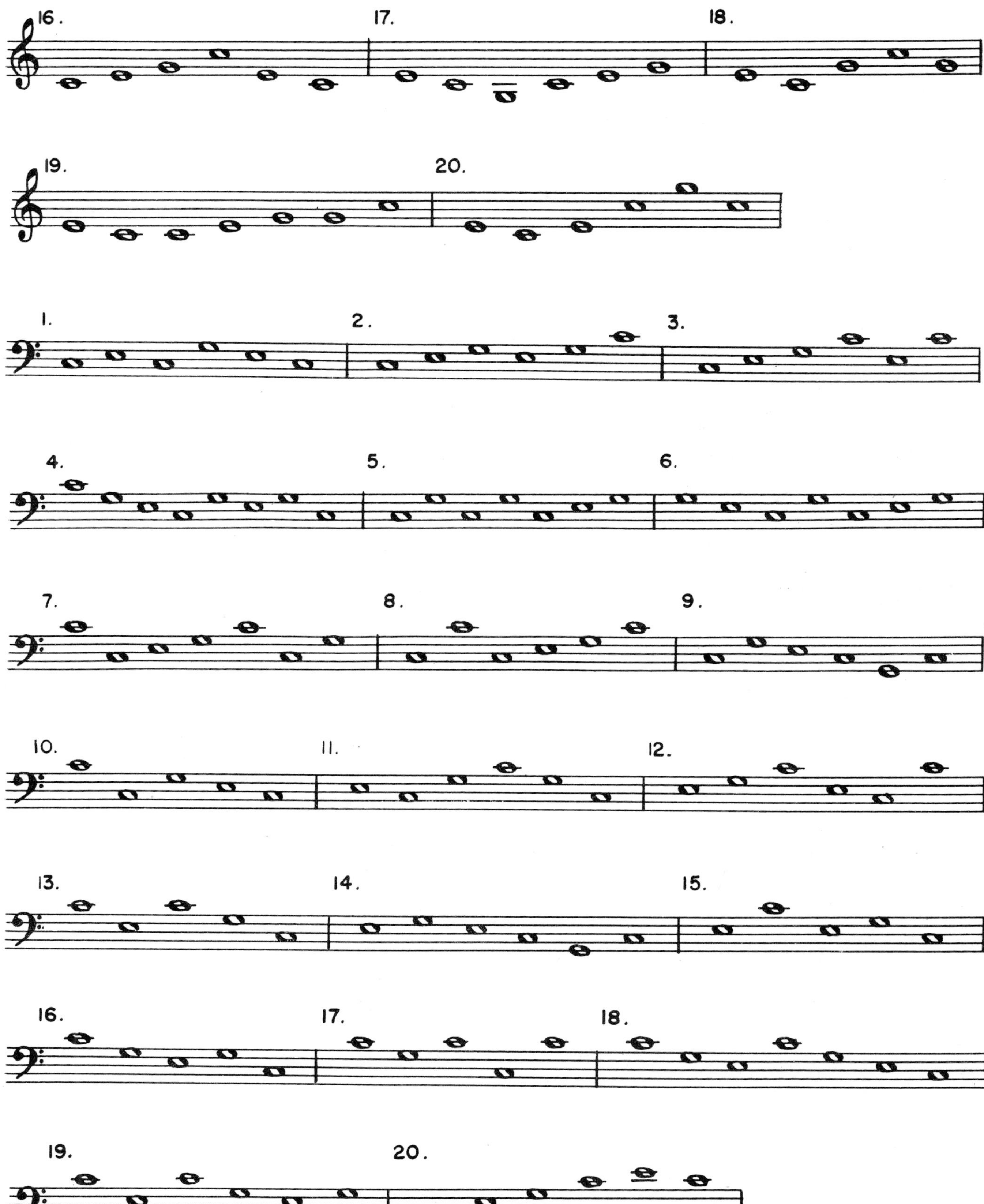
16.
17.
18.
19.
20.
1.
2.
3.
4.
5.
6.
7.
8.
9.
10.
11.
12.
13.
14.
15.
16.
17.
18.
19.
20.

DRILL IN SINGING ACTIVE AND REST TONES

Perform these in C major, singing first the numbers with their correct pitches and then substituting the correct letter names:

1-2-1-3-4-3-5-6-5-6-7-8
8-7-8-3-5-4-3-1-2-1
3-5-6-5-3-2-1-5-7-8
1-4-3-2-1-3-5-6-5-7-8
1-2-3-5-6-5-7-8
1-2-3-5-8-6-5-7-8
1-2-3-5-8-7-8
1-2-3-3-5-6-5-8-1
1-2-3-1-3-4-3-5-8-1
1-2-3-5-3-5-6-7-8
1-2-3-5-3-2-1-8
1-2-3-5-8-5-6-5-3-2-1
1-3-2-1-5-4-3-2-1
1-8-3-2-1-5-3-4-3-2-1
3-4-5-8-5-4-3-2-3-2-1
3-4-5-1-3-6-5-7-8

3-4-5-1-5-8-7-8-1
3-4-5-8-1-5-5-4-3-1
3-8-5-4-3-1-8
5-4-5-3-2-1-5-7-8
5-6-7-8-1-3-2-1
5-6-7-8-1-3-5-3-2-1
5-6-7-8-1-5-8-3-2-1
5-6-7-8-7-8-3-5-1-2-1
5-6-7-8-1-5-4-3-8-1
5-1-8-5-7-8-3-2-1
5-1-3-5-6-7-8-3-2-1
8-7-6-5-3-5-1-2-1
8-7-6-5-3-8-3-2-1
8-5-8-7-6-5-1-3-2-1
8-3-8-7-6-5-1-8-1-2-1

Sing in the major keys of G, D, A, E, B, and F♯, the letter names that correspond to the numbers above.

Utilizing the same method of dictation used for rest tones, the instructor dictates the following exercises or similar ones. These are to be dictated in the major keys of C, G, D, A, E, and F♯.

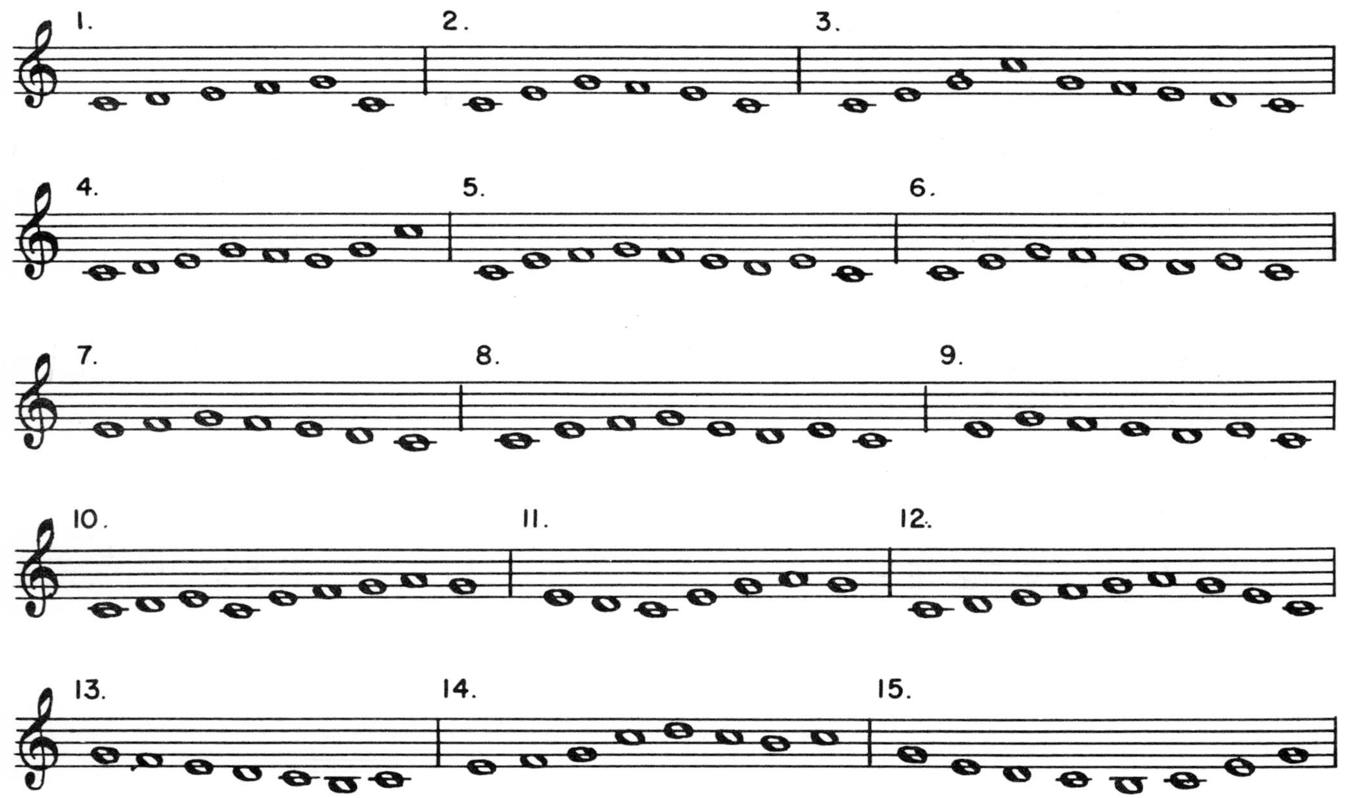

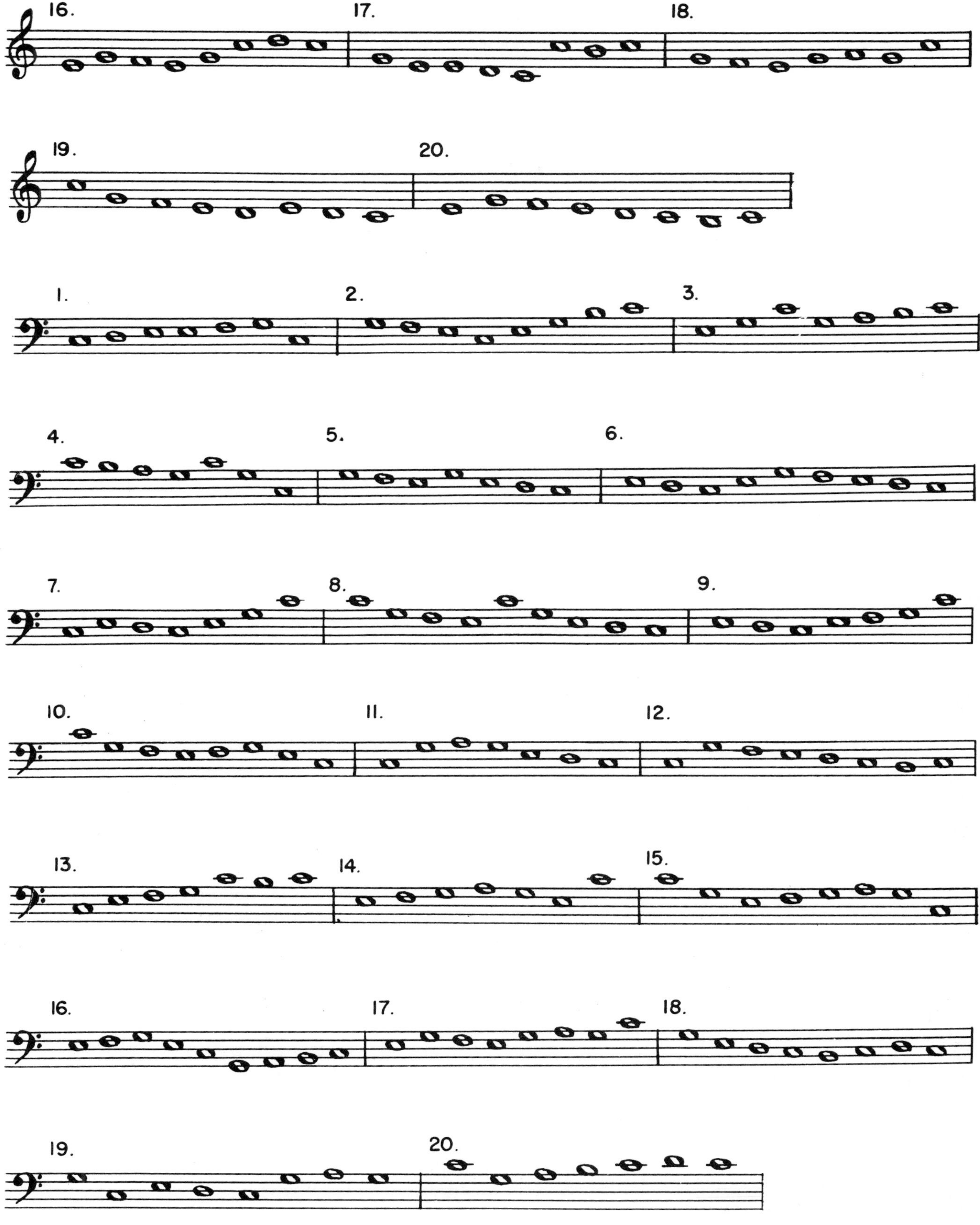
16.
17.
18.
19.
20.
1.
2.
3.
4.
5.
6.
7.
8.
9.
10.
11.
12.
13.
14.
15.
16.
17.
18.
19.
20.

KEYBOARD DRILL FOR MAJOR SCALES AND REST AND ACTIVE TONES IN SHARP KEYS

1. Play the major scale beginning on each of the following tones:

   C G D A E B F♯ C♯

   Play with the right hand alone first, using the following fingering (the thumb is considered the first finger of the hand, and the little finger is the fifth finger):

ascending (scales C, G, D, A, E, B)	:	1-2-3-1-2-3-4-5
scale F♯	:	2-3-4-1-2-3-1-2
scale C♯	:	2-3-1-2-3-4-1-2
descending (scales C, G, D, A, E, B)	:	5-4-3-2-1-3-2-1
scale F♯	:	2-1-3-2-1-4-3-2
scale C♯	:	2-1-4-3-2-1-3-2

   Play with the left hand alone, using this fingering:

ascending (scales C, G, D, A, E)	:	5-4-3-2-1-3-2-1
scale B	:	4-3-2-1-4-3-2-1
scale F♯	:	4-3-2-1-3-2-1-2
scale C♯	:	3-2-1-4-3-2-1-2
descending (scales C, G, D, A, E)	:	1-2-3-1-2-3-4-5
scale B	:	1-2-3-4-1-2-3-4
scale F♯	:	2-1-2-3-1-2-3-4
scale C♯	:	2-1-2-3-4-1-2-3

2. Play the rest tones, right hand only, in the major keys of C, G, D, A, E, B, F♯, C♯. (Fingering: 1-2-3-5-3-2-1)
3. Play and resolve, making each of the following the second degree of a major scale, and name the key to which it belongs (right hand only): D, A, E, B, F♯, C♯, D♯, G♯.
4. Play and resolve, making each of the following the fourth degree of a major scale, and name the key to which it belongs (right hand only): F, C, G, D, A, E, B, F♯.
5. Play and resolve, making each of the following the sixth degree of a major scale, and name the key to which it belongs (right hand only): A, E, B, F♯, C♯, G♯, D♯, A♯.
6. Play and resolve, making each of the following the seventh degree of a major scale and name the key to which it belongs (right hand only): B, F♯, C♯, G♯, D♯, A♯, E♯, B♯.

Name .... Date ....

WORKSHEET FOR LESSON 3: Rest and Active Tones in Sharp Scales

1. Write the rest tones on the staff in these keys:

2. Resolve the following active tones and state the key to which each belongs. Identify the rest and active tones by number (for example, 2 to 1, 4 to 3, and so on).

Name .... Date ....

SAMPLE TEST FOR LESSON 3: Rest and Active Tones in Sharp Scales

I. (1) In the treble clef, write the signature and the tonic chord of E major, C♯ major, A major, F♯ major, C major, D major, and B major.

(2) In the bass clef, write the signature and the tonic chord of F♯ major, B major, G major, C♯ major, A major, D major, C major.

II. (1) Write the following on the staff in D major (treble clef), as the teacher dictates the actual notes on the piano. Use key signature and whole notes to indicate the pitches heard.

(a) 1-3-5-3-8
(b) 5-3-5-8-1
(c) 3-1-8-5-1
(d) 8-5-8-3-8
(e) 8-1-5-3-5-1
(f) 5-8-3-5-1

(2) Write the following on the staff in C major (bass clef) as the teacher dictates the actual notes on the piano. Use key signature and whole notes to indicate the pitches heard.

(a) 5-8-5-3-5-1
(b) 3-5-1-8-1
(c) 1-8-5-3-5-1
(d) 1-5-1-3-5-8
(e) 3-1-5-3-5-8
(f) 1-3-1-8-5-1

III. (1) Write the active tones, with their resolutions, in the following keys (treble clef):

(2 stands for second step of scale, 4 stands for fourth step of scale, etc.)

(a) 2—B major
(b) 4—C♯ major
(c) 2—G major
(d) 4—A major
(e) 6—E major
(f) 7—F♯ major

(2) Write the active tones with their resolutions in the following keys (bass clef):

(a) 6—C major
(b) 7—B major
(c) 2—C♯ major
(d) 4—D major
(e) 6—A major
(f) 7—G major

IV. (1) Write the following on the staff in B major (treble clef), as the teacher dictates the actual pitches on the keyboard.

(a) 3-4-3-5-6-5-8
(b) 3-2-1-5-6-5-8
(c) 1-3-2-1-6-5-3-1
(d) 8-5-6-5-3-2-1
(e) 1-5-4-3-2-1-5-1
(f) 3-4-5-3-2-1-5-1

(2) Write the following on the staff in G major (bass clef), as the teacher dictates the actual pitches on the keyboard.

(a) 8-7-8-5-6-5-1
(b) 1-3-5-3-4-3-2-1
(c) 8-7-8-5-6-5-3-2-1
(d) 3-5-4-3-8-7-8
(e) 5-6-5-8-3-2-1
(f) 3-5-6-5-8-7-8

There are 50 points on this test. Each point, therefore, equals 2 per cent.

LESSON 4

Major Scales in Flat Keys

The major scales in flat keys must follow the same sequence of whole and half-steps set forth for the sharp keys. To find the keynote of the scale containing one flat, we count *down* five steps from the keynote of the C major scale. (Note how this differs from finding the keynote in sharp scales.)

C D E F G A B C
5 4 3 2 1

The new scale of F major will be spelled:

F G A B♭ C D E F
1 1 ½ 1 1 1 ½

Note that the B must be lowered a half-step to conform to the established pattern. When a natural note is lowered a half-step, we say that it is flatted (♭). By its position, the loop of the flat symbol indicates which line or space is to be affected.

Successively counting *down* by fives from the keynote of each newly derived scale, we find:

F G A B♭ C D E F
5 4 3 2 1

B♭ C D E♭ F G A B♭
1 1 ½ 1 1 1 ½

E♭ F G A♭ B♭ C D E♭
1 1 ½ 1 1 1 ½

A♭ B♭ C D♭ E♭ F G A♭
1 1 ½ 1 1 1 ½

D♭ E♭ F G♭ A♭ B♭ C D♭
1 1 ½ 1 1 1 ½

G♭ A♭ B♭ C♭ D♭ E♭ F G♭
1 1 ½ 1 1 1 ½

C♭ D♭ E♭ F♭ G♭ A♭ B♭ C♭
1 1 ½ 1 1 1 ½

CONSTRUCTING MAJOR SCALES IN FLAT KEYS

Each of the scales above contains one more flat than its predecessor. Placing these scales on the staff with their respective key signatures, we have:

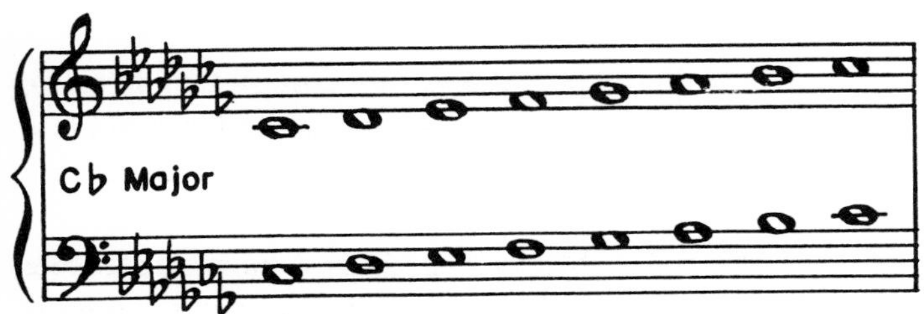

In memorizing these scales, there are three helpful points to remember.

1. Memorize thoroughly the C♭ major signature, for it shows the order in which flats are added to the right of the clef sign. Thus, if you desire the scale of six flats, omit the last flat to the right. If you desire the scale of three flats, omit the last four flats to the right, and so on.

2. The next to the last flat from the right always indicates the keynote of the scale. The scale of F major, having but one flat, cannot qualify under this rule; and it is necessary to memorize its key signature.

3. When you are given the keynote and wish to find the key signature, consider the keynote as the next to the last flat on the right; then add one more flat. When you are given the key signature and wish to find the keynote, take the next to the last flat as the keynote.

The flat scales can be arranged in a Circle of Fifths. Note that when a flat is flatted, it becomes a double flat (♭♭).

count down five

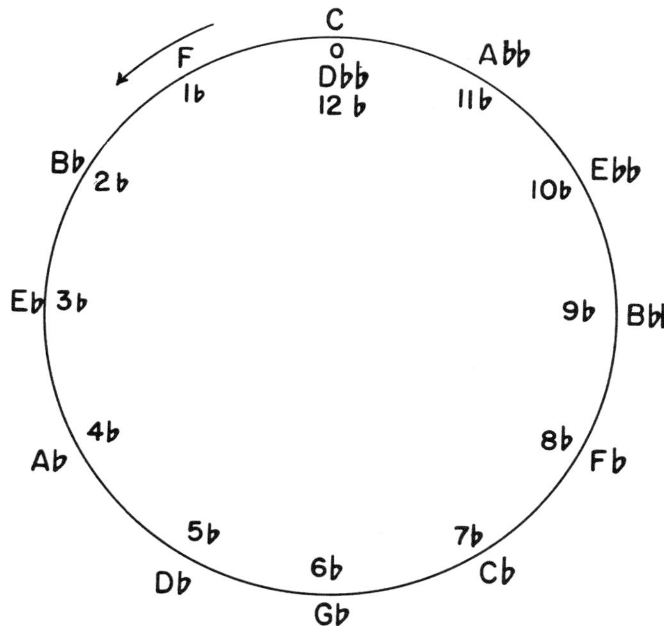

Starting from C major and proceeding around the Circle of Fifths to the left, one completes the circle by arriving at D♭♭, which is the enharmonic of C. The only practical scales in the circle are the key of C and those with the first seven flats. Beyond this point, double flats are employed; so the enharmonic scales with sharp signatures are the most practical to use.

When we flat a note, we do not always use the symbol of the flat. When flatted;(1) a natural becomes a flat; (2) a sharp becomes a natural; (3) a double sharp becomes a single sharp; (4) a flat becomes a double flat; and (5) a double flat becomes a triple flat. The effect of sharping or flatting a note which already bears a symbol is shown in the following pattern:

Sharps ⟶ ♭♭♭ | ♭♭ | ♭ | ♮ | ♯ | 𝄪 | ♯𝄪 |

Flats ⟵ ♭♭♭ | ♭♭ | ♭ | ♮ | ♯ | 𝄪 | ♯𝄪 |

MAJOR SCALES IN UNUSUAL FLAT KEYS

E♭♭ Major
A♭♭ Major

D♭♭ Major
G♭♭ Major

C♭♭ Major

Name ....   Date ....

WORKSHEET FOR LESSON 4: Major Scales in Flat Keys

1. In the treble clef, write these major scales with their key signatures:

   (a) A♭
   (b) E♭
   (c) scale of five flats
   (d) F

   Method of finding key signature of the A♭ major scale:

   (1) A♭ will be the next to the last flat in the key signature.
   (2) The flats in a key signature appear in this order: B♭, E♭, then A♭. Therefore, add one more flat (D♭) for the key signature of A♭ major.

The E♭ major scale may be worked out in the same manner; the result will be as follows:

Method of finding the keynote for the scale with five flats:

(1) The key of five flats has in its key signature the following flats, reading in order to the right of the clef sign: B♭, E♭, A♭, D♭, and G♭.
(2) The next to the last flat to the right is the keynote. Thus the keynote is D♭.

Method of determining the key signature of F major:

(1) With the scale of F major, you cannot use the rule of taking the next to the last flat to the right, because this key has but one flat (B♭).
(2) The simplest way to learn this scale is simply to memorize it.
(3) You can find the signature by counting up two and one-half steps from the keynote. Since you have already learned that in the flat scales, B♭ is the first flat to the right of the clef sign, you now know that the scale of F major has only one flat.

2. In the bass clef, write these major scales with their key signatures:

   (a) B♭
   (b) D♭
   (c) scale of six flats
   (d) scale of seven flats

   These scales can be worked out using the very same methods as those shown for the treble clef. Place them on the following staves.

Name .... Date ....

SAMPLE TEST FOR ALL MAJOR SCALES — Sharps and Flats

On the staves below, write the following scales with their respective key signatures.

1. Treble clef—three flats
2. Treble clef—A major
3. Bass clef—seven flats
4. Treble clef—B major
5. Bass clef—C♭ major
6. Bass clef—two sharps
7. Treble clef—F major
8. Treble clef—four flats
9. Bass clef—B♭ major
10. Bass clef—C♯ major
11. Treble clef—D♭ major
12. Bass clef—F♯ major
13. Bass clef—six flats
14. Treble clef—G major
15. Bass clef—A♭ major
16. Treble clef—C major
17. Treble clef—D major
18. Bass clef—four sharps
19. Bass clef—G♭ major
20. Treble clef—E major

Each key signature equals 2½ per cent; each scale equals 2½ per cent.

LESSON 5

Rest and Active Tones in Flat Scales

DRILL ON REST AND ACTIVE TONES

Sing from every major flat scale keynote the rest tones 1-3-5-8-5-3-1. The following are the tonic chords in each of the major flat keys.

In all of the major flat keys, sing the following numbers with their proper pitches; and then substitute letter names for the numbers:

1-8-5-1	1-5-3-5-4-3-5-8
1-5-5-8-3-1	1-3-4-3-5-6-5-8
8-5-1-5 8-3-5-1	1-3-5-6-5-7-8
1-5-8-5-1-8-1	1-2-3-5-6-5-7-8
8-5-1-5-8-3-1	1-2-3-5-8-7-8
8-1-5-8-1-3	1-3-5-5-6-7-8
8-5-3-1-8-5-8	1-2-3-2-3-1-4-3
1-8-5-3-1-3-5-8	1-2-3-2-3-1-5-1
1-3-5-5-8-1	1-2-3-5-4-3-5-1
8-1-3-5-8-1	1-2-3-5-1-6-5-7-8
8-5-3-5-8-1	1-2-3-5-4-3-8-1-8
8-5-3-5-1-3-1	1-2-3-5-8-3-2-1
1-3-5-3-1-5-3-1	1-2-3-5-6-5-3-2-1
8-5-3-5-3-5-1	1-2-3-5-6-7-8-1
1-3-3-5-5-8-1	1-2-3-5-4-3-8-7-8
3-5-8-5-3-5-1	3-4-3-5-6-7-8-3-2-1
3-1-3-5-3-5-8	5-6-5-4-3-5-6-7-8
3-5-8-5-8-5-1	5-8-7-6-5-3-2-1-2-1
5-3-1-8-5-3-1	3-2-1-5-6-5-8-7-8
5-1-5-8-3-8-5-1	3-5-6-5-7-8-3-2-3-1

DICTATION FOR DRILL ON REST AND ACTIVE TONES

The instructor plays the following exercises, or similar ones, and the student places on the staff the notes heard. Dictation should be in the major keys of F, B♭, E♭, A♭, D♭, G♭, and C♭.

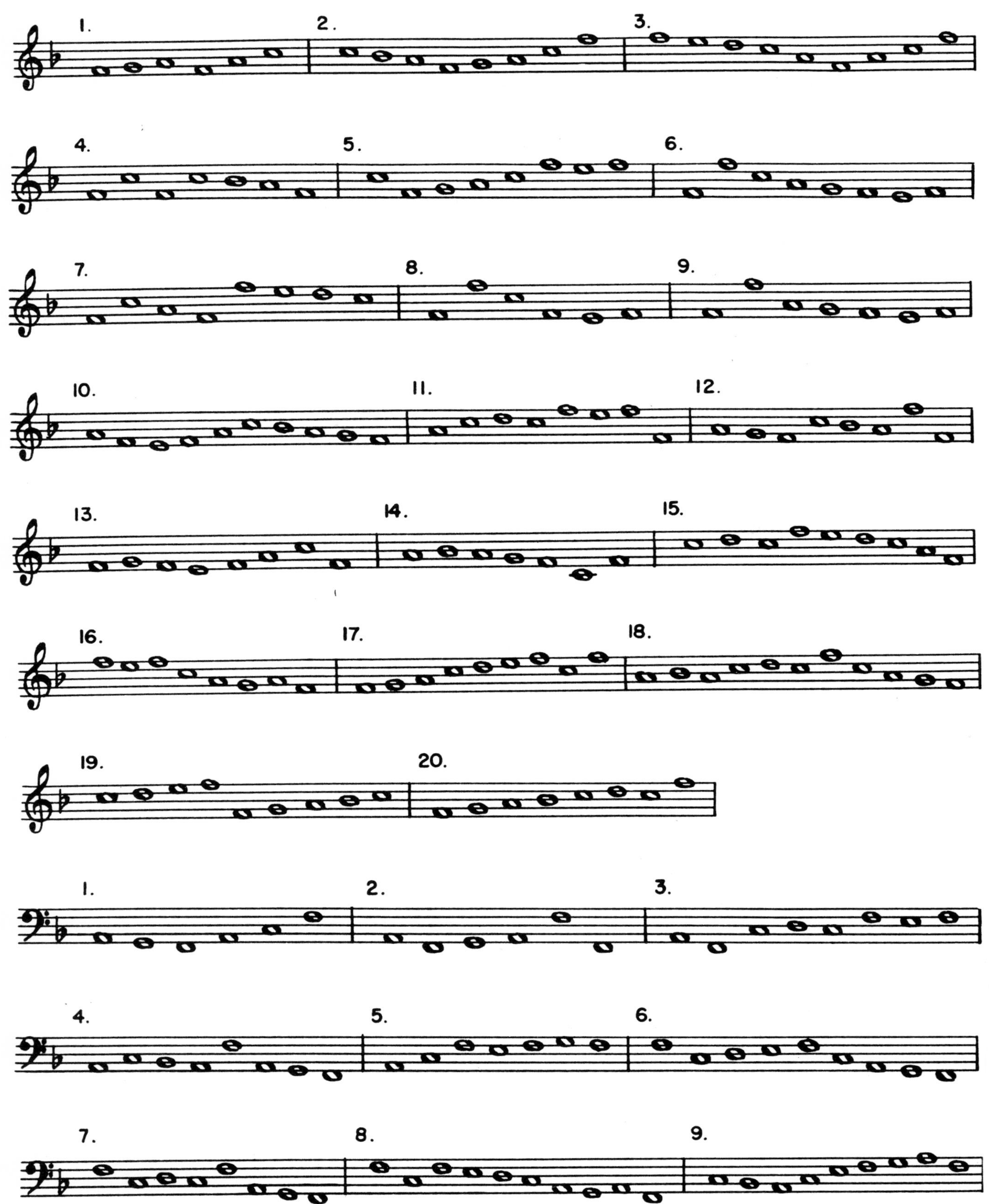
1.
2.
3.
4.
5.
6.
7.
8.
9.
10.
11.
12.
13.
14.
15.
16.
17.
18.
19.
20.
1.
2.
3.
4.
5.
6.
7.
8.
9.

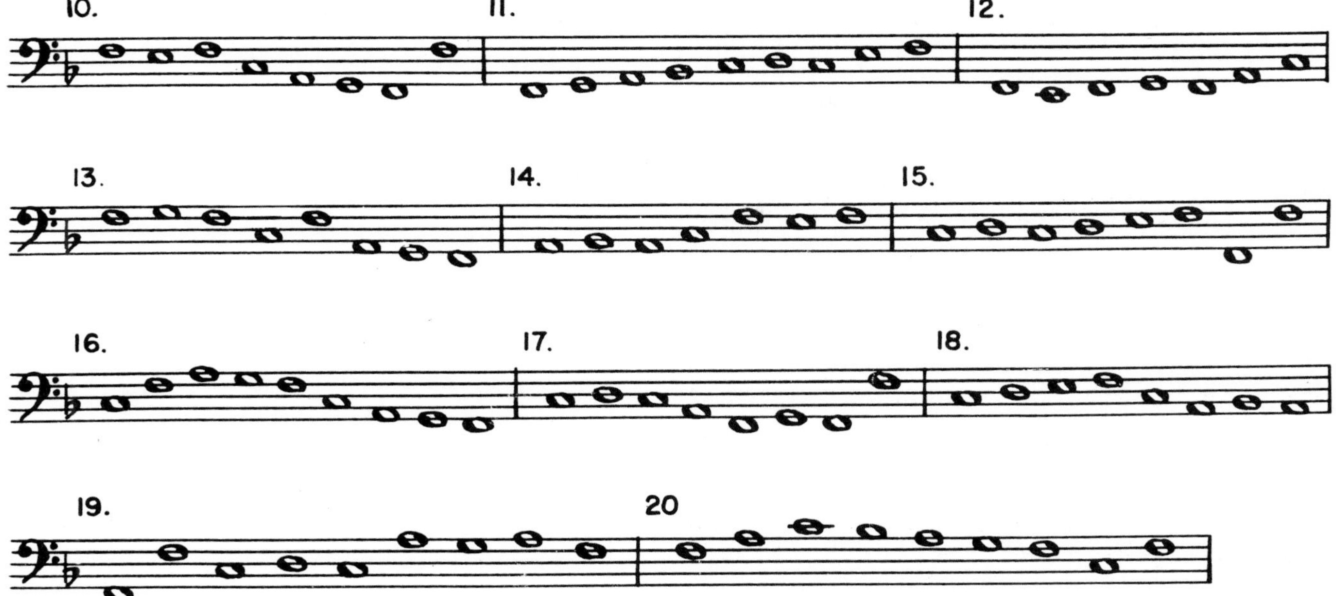

KEYBOARD DRILL FOR MAJOR SCALES IN THE FLAT KEYS

1. Play the major scale beginning on each of the following tones:

F B♭ E♭ A♭ D♭ G♭ C♭

Play with the right hand alone first, using the following fingering:

F : 1-2-3-4-1-2-3-4 ascending
4-3-2-1-4-3-2-1 descending

B♭ : 2-1-2-3-1-2-3-4 ascending
4-3-2-1-3-2-1-2 descending

E♭ : 2-1-2-3-4-1-2-3 ascending
3-2-1-4-3-2-1-2 descending

A♭ : 2-3-1-2-3-1-2-3 ascending
3-2-1-3-2-1-3-2 descending

D♭ : 2-3-1-2-3-4-1-2 ascending
2-1-4-3-2-1-3-2 descending

G♭ : 2-3-4-1-2-3-1-2 ascending
2-1-3-2-1-4-3-2 descending

C♭ : 1-2-3-1-2-3-4-5 ascending
5-4-3-2-1-3-2-1 descending

Play with the left hand alone, using this fingering:

F : 5-4-3-2-1-3-2-1 ascending
1-2-3-1-2-3-4-5 descending

Bb
Eb
Ab
Db
: 3-2-1-4-3-2-1-2 ascending
2-1-2-3-4-1-2-3 descending

Gb : 4-3-2-1-3-2-1-2 ascending
2-1-2-3-1-2-3-4 descending

Cb : 4-3-2-1-4-3-2-1 ascending
1-2-3-4-1-2-3-4 descending

KEYBOARD DRILL ON REST AND ACTIVE TONES

1. Play the rest tones, right hand only, in the major keys of F, Bb, Eb, Ab, Db, Gb, Cb.
2. Play and resolve, making each of the following the second degree of a major scale, and name the key to which it belongs (right hand only): G, C, Bb, Eb, Ab, Db.
3. Play and resolve, making each of the following the fourth degree of a major scale, and name the key to which it belongs (right hand only): Bb, Eb, Ab, Db, Gb, Cb, Fb.
4. Play and resolve, making each of the following the sixth degree of a major scale, and name the key to which it belongs (right hand only): D, G, C, F, Bb, Eb, Ab.
5. Play and resolve, making each of the following the seventh degree of a major scale, and name the key to which it belongs (right hand only): E, A, D, F, G, C, Bb.

EXCERPTS ILLUSTRATING COMPOSERS' USE OF MAJOR SCALES

The following excerpts are from standard compositions, showing how the composer has used an entire major scale in a section of a composition.

1. C major scale found in the first violin part of Haydn's C major String Quartet, Opus 76, No. 3. This excerpt begins the fourth beat of measure seven of the allegro movement.

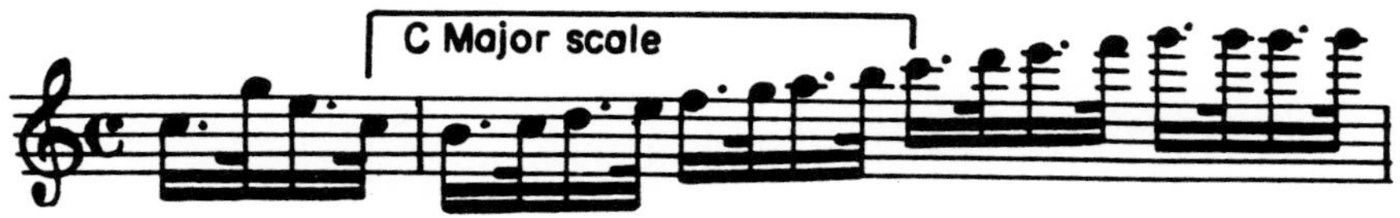

2. This excerpt is from the same quartet: variation II, cello part, fifth from the last measure.

3. This example is taken from Schubert's Symphony No. 8 in B minor *(Unfinished)*, first movement, measure 206. It illustrates the entire string section performing the D major scale. The next measure, not illustrated here, treats the A major scale in the same fashion.

4. This is a measure chosen from Beethoven's Sonata for Piano No. 28 in A major, Op. 101, from the allegro movement, measure 35.

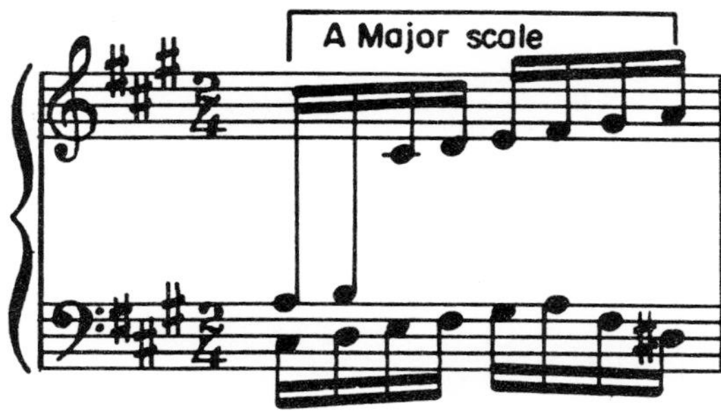

5. This E major scale is taken from the overture to Mendelssohn's *A Midsummer Night's Dream,* Op. 21. It is found in the first and second violin parts (measures 563 through 567).

6. This example is from the same work by Mendelssohn. It is the B major scale played by the second violins and violas in measures 235 through 238.

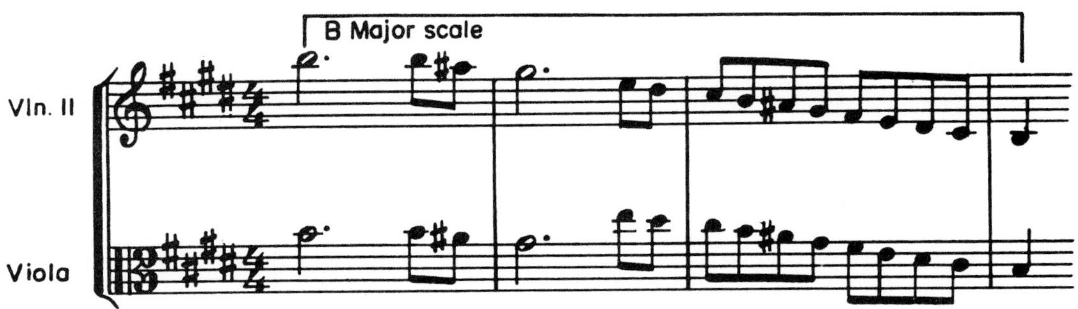

7. This F♯ major scale occurs in Beethoven's Sonata for Piano No. 24 in F♯ major, Op. 78, in the first movement, measures 10 through 12.

8. This example shows how the scale may be used other than as a complete unit. The general direction of the scale is apparent, but the melodic line rises and falls around the scale line. The excerpt is from Bach's *Well-Tempered Clavier:* Book I, Fuga No. 13, the entrance of the second voice.

Name ....

Date ....

WORKSHEET FOR LESSON 5: Rest and Active Tones in Flat Scales

1. Write on the staff the rest tones in the keys illustrated.

2. Resolve the following active tones and state the key to which each belongs. Identify the rest and active tones by number (for example, 2 to 1, 4 to 3, and so on).

Name ....   Date ....

SAMPLE TEST FOR LESSON 5: Rest and Active Tones in Flat Scales

I. (1) In the treble clef, write the signature and the tonic chord of B♭ major, D♭ major, C♭ major, F major, E♭ major, A♭ major, and G♭ major.

(2) In the bass clef, write the signature and the tonic chord of A major, C♭ major, E major, G major, G♭ major, F major, and F♯ major.

II. (1) Write the following on the staff in A♭ major (treble clef) as the teacher dictates the actual notes on the piano. Use key signature and whole notes to indicate the pitches heard. (Note: If the instructor plays another instrument so that the pitches will accurately be heard, it would be advantageous to dictate these pitches on a violin, viola, flute, clarinet, or cornet, as well as on the piano.)

(a) 1-8-5-8-3-8-1
(b) 3-1-3-5-8-5-3-1
(c) 5-3-5-8-5-3-1
(d) 1-3-5-3-5-8-8
(e) 3-3-5-5-8-1-8
(f) 5-8-5-3-5-8-1

(2) Write the following on the staff in G♭ major (bass clef) as the teacher dictates the actual notes on the piano. Use key signature and whole notes to indicate the pitches heard.

(a) 1-3-1-5-3-5-1
(b) 5-3-5-8-8-5-8
(c) 3-5-3-1-1-3-5
(d) 8-1-8-5-3-5-8
(e) 8-3-8-5-8-5-1
(f) 3-5-1-8-5-1-5

III. (1) Write the active tones, with their resolutions, in the following keys (treble clef):
(2 stands for second step of scale; 4 stands for fourth step of scale, etc.)

(a) 2—E♭ major
(b) 4—D♭ major
(c) 2—G♭ major
(d) 4—A♭ major
(e) 6—E major
(f) 7—C♯ major

(2) Write the active tones, with their resolutions, in the following keys (bass clef):

(a) 6—C♭ major
(b) 7—B♭ major
(c) 2—F♯ major
(d) 4—D♭ major
(e) 6—A♭ major
(f) 7—G♭ major

IV. (1) Write the following on the staff in B♭ major (treble clef) as the teacher dictates the actual pitches on the keyboard:

(a) 1-2-1-3-5-6-5-8-7-8
(b) 3-4-3-8-1-2-1
(c) 5-3-4-5-8-7-8-1
(d) 8-1-3-5-6-5-4-3-2-1
(e) 1-2-3-5-6-7-8-1
(f) 3-1-3-4-5-6-5-3-2-1

(2) Write the following on the staff in F major (bass clef) as the teacher dictates the actual pitches on the keyboard.

(a) 1-8-7-6-5-8-1
(b) 5-3-2-1-5-6-7-8
(c) 3-4-3-5-6-5-7-8-1
(d) 3-2-1-8-7-8-1
(e) 1-2-3-1-5-6-5-1
(f) 3-2-1-5-4-3-5-6-7-8

There are 50 points on this test. Each point, therefore, equals 2 per cent.

Name ....

Date ....

MUSIC PAPER for Test

Name ....

Date ....

MUSIC PAPER for Test

LESSON 6
Minor Scales

Minor scales are of two classifications: the *relative minor;* and the *tonic minor,* also known as the corresponding or parallel minor.

The following formulas must be memorized and applied by the student. They are the secret for understanding the minor scales.

1. The *relative minor* has the *same key signature* as the major scale to which it is related but a *different keynote.* By using the sixth step of the major scale as the keynote and ascending the scale degree-wise for an octave (the eight notes of the scale), we produce the relative minor scale in its natural form.
2. The *tonic minor* has the *same keynote* as the major scale but a *different key signature.* The tonic minor scale in its natural form is found by lowering the third, sixth, and seventh degrees of the major scale one half-step each. Place these three "flats" in the key signature in their proper order next to the clef sign. (Bear in mind that flatting a sharp results in a natural. This natural, however, is not placed in the key signature.) More broadly stated, the rule for finding the key signature of a tonic minor is "add three flats" to a major key signature (see page 62 for the method).

It is apparent, then, that for every major scale there are two associated minor scales: the relative minor and the tonic minor.

THREE FORMS OF THE MINOR SCALES

Both the relative minor scale and the tonic minor scale have three forms: natural, harmonic, and melodic.

1. The natural form, also known as the Aeolian or original minor, develops naturally from the associated major scale.

The *natural form* of the *relative minor* results from starting on the sixth degree of the related major scales and ascending degree-wise for eight steps. The interval pattern of whole and half-steps of the natural minor is 1-½-1-1-½-1-1. This scale is the same ascending and descending, just as the major scale is the same ascending and descending.

The *natural form* of the *tonic minor* results from lowering the third, sixth, and seventh degrees of the major scale one half-step each. The interval pattern then becomes the same as that of the natural form of the relative minor scale.

2. The *harmonic form* of either the *relative minor* or the *tonic minor* scales results from raising the seventh degree of the natural minor one half-step. The characteristic interval of the natural minor scale is the whole step between the seventh and eighth degrees. The musicians of the period in which the harmonic scales were created disliked this wide interval, and many preferred to place the seventh degree of the minor scale closer to the eighth degree, as it occurs in the major scale. Thus was produced the harmonic form of the minor scale. The characteristic interval of the harmonic minor scale is the step and a half between the sixth and seventh degrees. (Later we will learn that this interval is called an augmented second.) This interval of a step and a half came to be systematically avoided in the period in which the major and minor scales were the dominant factors in musical composition.

3. One of the best ways of avoiding this interval was to use the *melodic form* of the minor scale. This form, for either the *relative minor* or *tonic minor* scales, will be found by raising the sixth and seventh degrees of the natural minor one half-step each in the ascending scale *only.* In the descending scale, the seventh de-

gree need not be so close to the tonic; hence the descending melodic form is the same as the descending natural form.

Note that the melodic minor is the only scale that changes its form when descending. All other scales stay the same ascending and descending.

C MAJOR SCALE USED TO ILLUSTRATE RELATIVE MINORS

To illustrate how the three forms of the relative minor are obtained, let us begin with the C major scale:

1. To obtain the *relative minor* of the C major scale, take the *same key signature* as the C major scale (no sharps or flats) and use it as the key signature for the relative minor scale. Count up to the sixth step of the major scale, which is A, and use A as the keynote of the relative minor scale. Ascend the scale step-wise until the octave A is reached. The result is the natural form of the relative minor of the C major scale. Since all scales take their name from their own keynote, this scale is the A minor scale in the *natural form.*

2. To change this natural form to the *harmonic form* of the minor scale, raise the seventh degree of the natural form one half-step. In this particular scale the G will become G♯, thus making only a half-step between G♯ and A, the same interval found between the seventh and eighth degrees of the major scale. We now have the A minor scale in the harmonic form.

3. To arrive at the *melodic form* of the minor scale, raise the sixth and seventh steps of the natural form one half-step each. In this particular scale the F will be raised to F♯ and the G will be raised to G♯. Thus we avoid the wide interval between the sixth and seventh degrees of the harmonic form (F to G♯) that met with disfavor among the composers of the "major-minor" period in music history. As mentioned earlier, the melodic minor is the only scale which ascends one way and descends another. In descending, the melodic minor follows the natural minor; the G♯ becomes G♮ and the F♯ becomes F♮. We now have the A minor scale in the melodic form.

C MAJOR SCALE USED TO ILLUSTRATE TONIC MINORS

1. To obtain the *tonic minor* of the C major scale, take the *same keynote* as the major scale, which in this instance is C, and use it as the keynote of the tonic minor scale. Write the C major scale ascending to the octave

C. Lower the third, sixth, and seventh steps of this scale one half-step each. In this particular scale, the E becomes E♭, the A becomes A♭, and the B becomes B♭.

Gather up these three flats and place them in their proper order in the key signature. Since the flat next to the clef sign is always B♭, place this flat first. The next flat in order is E♭. The third flat in order is A♭. Thus, to the major signature of no sharps or flats, three flats have been added; the addition of three flats will give the signature for the tonic minor of any major scale. The flats now occurring in the key signature will not, of course, be placed adjacent to the notes in the scale. The scale we have just produced is the C minor scale in the *natural form*.

2. To change the natural form to the *harmonic form,* raise the seventh degree of the natural form one half-step. In this particular scale, the B♭ will become B♮ (a sharped flat becomes a natural). We now have the C minor scale in the harmonic form.

3. To obtain the *melodic form* of the minor scale, raise the sixth and seventh degrees of the natural form one half-step each. Here the A♭ will be raised to A♮ and the B♭ will be raised to B♮. In the descending scale, the B♮ will go back to B♭ and the A♮ will go back to A♭. The result is now the C minor scale in the melodic form.

SUMMARY: THE MINOR SCALES DERIVED FROM THE MAJOR SCALE, USING C MAJOR AS AN ILLUSTRATION

Major scale (C)

Relative minor (A)

Same key signature (no sharps or flats)
Different keynote (A)

Three forms:

1. Natural
2. Harmonic (raised seventh)
3. Melodic (raised sixth and seventh ascending; natural form descending)

Tonic minor (C)

Different key signature (three flats)
Same keynote (C)

Three forms:

1. Natural
2. Harmonic (raised seventh)
3. Melodic (raised sixth and seventh ascending; natural form descending)

FINDING THE KEY SIGNATURE OF A MINOR SCALE

The key signature of any *relative minor* scale is the same as the signature of the major scale to which it is related. Examples:

C major—no sharps or flats	relative minor—no sharps or flats
G major—one sharp (F♯)	relative minor—one sharp (F♯)
D major—two sharps (F♯,C♯)	relative minor—two sharps (F♯, C♯)
F major—one flat (B♭)	relative minor—one flat (B♭)
B major—two flats (B♭, E♭)	relative minor—two flats (B♭, E♭)

and so on.

The key signature of any *tonic minor* scale is three flats more than the major scale with which it is associated.

Example: To find the key signature of the tonic minor of E major by adding three flats.

1. E major has four sharps in the key signature.

2. The last sharp to the right is D♯. When this is lowered a half-step (flatted), it becomes D♮. (This is flat number 1.)
3. The next to the last sharp to the right is G♯. When this is lowered a half step (flatted), it becomes G♮. (This is flat number 2.)
4. The third from the last sharp is C♯. When this is lowered a half-step (flatted), it becomes C♮. (This is flat number 3.)
5. Now that three flats have been added, there is just one sharp (F♯) left in the original key signature. Therefore the key signature of the tonic minor of E major is one sharp (F♯).

Example: To find the key signature of the tonic minor of A♭ major by adding three flats.

1. A♭ major has four flats in the key signature.

2. To the four flats of the key signature, add three more. The next three flats in the order found in a key signature are G♭, C♭, and F♭.
3. Therefore the key signature of the tonic minor of A♭ major is seven flats.

FINDING THE KEYNOTE OF A MINOR SCALE

The keynote of any *relative minor* scale is the sixth degree of the major scale to which the minor scale is related. The minor scale takes its name from this keynote. For example, in the scale of C major, the sixth step is A. The relative minor of C major is therefore A minor.

Many students will have already learned that the keynote of a relative minor scale may be found by counting down 1½ steps from the keynote of the major scale. This is a perfectly correct method, but the auhor has found that errors in counting down are more common than errors in counting up.

The keynote of any *tonic minor* scale is the same as the keynote of the major scale with which it is associated. For example, the tonic minor of C major has C as its keynote.

RELATIVE MAJOR AND TONIC MAJOR SCALES

Just as every major scale has a relative minor and a tonic minor scale associated with it, so every minor scale has a relative major and a tonic major scale associated with it. In other words, any minor scale can be at the same time the relative minor of one major scale and the tonic minor of another major scale. Perhaps the best way of presenting this is by a diagram:

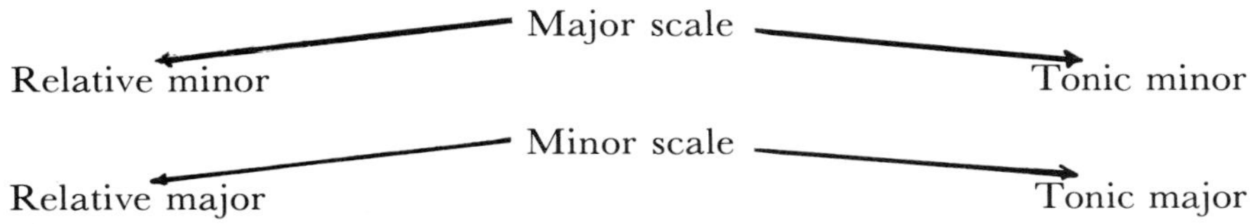

Examining the relationship between C major and its associated minors, we find:

C major has as its relative minor, A minor.

C major has as its tonic minor, C minor.

Each of these minor scales derived from the C major scale has a relative major and a tonic major scale. Examining the relationship between these minor scales and their associated majors, we find:

A minor has as its *relative* major, C major (same key signature results in a relative scale).

A minor has as its *tonic* major, A major (same keynote results in a tonic scale).

C minor has as its *relative* major, E♭ major (same key signature; therefore a relative scale).

C minor has as its *tonic* major, C major (same keynote; therefore a tonic scale).

One point must be made clear to the student. Although any minor scale may be *at the same time* a relative minor of one major scale and the tonic minor of another major scale, the signature of the minor scale *does not* change.

Example: The A minor scale, whether it is a relative minor or a tonic minor scale, always has the signature of no sharps or flats. Let us see why this is true.

1. As the relative minor of the scale of C major (A is the sixth step of the scale of C major), A minor has the same key signature as C major: no sharps or flats.
2. As the tonic minor of the scale of A major (same keynote), A minor is produced by adding three flats to the A major signature of three sharps; the resulting A minor signature is no sharps or flats.

Example: The C♯ minor scale, whether it is a relative minor or a tonic minor scale, always has four sharps in the key signature.

1. As the relative minor of the scale of E major (C♯ is the sixth step of the scale of E major), C♯ minor has the same key signature as E major: four sharps.
2. As the tonic minor of the scale of C♯ major (same keynote), C♯ minor is produced by adding three flats to the C♯ major signature of seven sharps. The last three sharps of the C♯ major signature thus become naturals, and the resulting C♯ minor signature is four sharps.

FINDING THE KEY SIGNATURE OF A RELATIVE MAJOR SCALE

To find the key signature of a relative major scale of a minor scale, use the same key signature as the minor scale.

Example: To find the key signature of the relative major scale of A minor.

1. A minor has no sharps or flats in the key signature. (Note that this is a key signature; many stu-students mistakenly believe that no sharps or flats means no key signature.)
2. The relative major, therefore, will have no sharps or flats in the key signature (C major).

Example: To find the key signature of the relative major scale of G minor.

1. G minor has two flats in the key signature.
2. The relative major, therefore, will have two flats in the key signature (B♭ major).

FINDING THE KEY SIGNATURE OF A TONIC MAJOR SCALE

To find the key signature of a tonic major scale of a minor scale, take the keynote of the minor scale. Consider it as the keynote of a major scale and use the signature of the major scale that has that keynote.

Example: To find the key signature of the tonic major scale of A minor.

1. The keynote of the A minor scale is A.
2. A is therefore the keynote of the tonic major scale (A major).

3. The student has already learned that the scale of A major has three sharps.
4. Thus the key signature of the tonic major scale of A minor has three sharps.

Example: To find the key signature of the tonic major scale of B♭ minor.

1. The keynote of the B♭ minor scale is B♭.
2. B♭ is therefore the keynote of the tonic major scale (B♭ major).
3. The student has already learned that the scale of B♭ major has two flats.
4. Thus the key signature of the tonic major scale of B♭ minor has two flats.

FINDING THE KEYNOTE OF A RELATIVE MAJOR SCALE

To find the keynote of a relative major scale of a minor scale, take the keynote of the major scale that has the same signature as the minor scale.

Example: To find the keynote of the relative major scale of A minor.

1. A minor has no sharps of flats in the key signature.
2. The major scale with no sharps or flats in the key signature is C major.
3. The keynote of C major is C.
4. Therefore the keynote of the relative major scale of A minor is C.

Example: To find the keynote of the relative major scale of F♯ minor.

1. F♯ minor has three sharps in the key signature.
2. The major scale with three sharps in the key signature is A major.
3. The keynote of A major is A.
4. Therefore the keynote of the relative major scale of F♯ minor is A.

FINDING THE KEYNOTE OF A TONIC MAJOR SCALE

To find the keynote of a tonic major scale of a minor scale, take the keynote of the minor scale and consider it as the keynote of the tonic major scale. For example, the keynote of the tonic major scale of E minor is E.

ALL KEY SIGNATURES

It is now necessary for the student to *memorize thoroughly* the signatures of the major and the minor scales, set forth in the following table. The student will use this information as long as he has anything at all to do with music. It is a *must* for every musician. The student must know the table both ways.

MAJOR SCALES

No sharps or flats—C major	C major—no sharps or flats
Sharps	
1♯—G major	G major—1♯
2♯—D major	D major—2♯
3♯—A major	A major—3♯
4♯—E major	E major—4♯
5♯—B major	B major—5♯
6♯—F♯ major	F♯ major—6♯
7♯—C♯ major	C♯ major—7♯

Flats

1♭—F major	F major—1♭
2♭—B♭ major	B♭ major—2♭
3♭—E♭ major	E♭ major—3♭
4♭—A♭ major	A♭ major—4♭
5♭—D♭ major	D♭ major—5♭
6♭—G♭ major	G♭ major—6♭
7♭—C♭ major	C♭ major—7♭

MINOR SCALES

No sharps or flats—A minor	A minor—no sharps or flats

Sharps

1♯—E minor	E minor—1♯
2♯—B minor	B minor—2♯
3♯—F♯ minor	F♯ minor—3♯
4♯—C♯ minor	C♯ minor—4♯
5♯—G♯ minor	G♯ minor—5♯
6♯—D♯ minor	D♯ minor—6♯
7♯—A♯ minor	A♯ minor—7♯

Flats

1♭—D minor	D minor—1♭
2♭—G minor	G minor—2♭
3♭—C minor	C minor—3♭
4♭—F minor	F minor—4♭
5♭—B♭ minor	B♭ minor—5♭
6♭—E♭ minor	E♭ minor—6♭
7♭—A♭ minor	A♭ minor—7♭

THE CIRCLE OF FIFTHS

When the sharp major keys were first presented in an earlier lesson, we found that by going *up* to the fifth step of a major scale we obtained the keynote of a new major scale with a signature containing one additional sharp. There is a scientific reason for this (the "overtone series") which will not be presented in this book. However, the predominance of the fifth step of the scale, proven by the overtone series, accounts for the placement of scales in the Circle of Fifths, illustrated below. (For further reading on this subject, see any book on the science of music.)

Likewise, when the flat major scales were presented, we discovered that by going *down* five steps of a major scale we obtained the keynote of a new major scale with a signature containing one additional flat. This also is explained by the overtone series.

Placing the keys on the Circle of Fifths, we find that the sharp scales "go up five tones" for each new scale and they "go to the right" (clockwise) on the circle; whereas the flat scales "go down five tones" for each new scale and they "go to the left" (counter-clockwise) on the circle. The major scales are represented by capital letters on the outside of the circle.

The relative minor keys appear in small letters inside the circle line, just across from their relative majors. They are so placed because a minor and its relative major have the same key signature. Notice that the minor scales also "go up five tones" for the sharp scales and "go to the right" around the circle, whereas they "go down five tones" for the flat scales and "go to the left" around the circle.

We have learned that *enharmonic* means the same sound with a different name. Because C♯ major and D♭ major are enharmonic, they are put in the same position on the circle. Similarly, the relative minors of these major keys (A♯ minor and B♭ minor) are enharmonic, and they occupy the same position on the circle. Enharmonic major scales and their relative minors are boxed on the Circle of Fifths to show that they belong together.

The Circle of Fifths also indicates the key signature of a tonic minor. If you take the small letters to indicate tonic minors, you will find opposite each the major key that has the same signature as the tonic minor.Thus, for example, to find the key signature of the tonic minor scale of C major, locate C minor (small c) on the inside of the circle. By reading across the line, you will find that C minor has the same signature as E♭ major.

Note also, from their positions on the circle, that the key signature of the tonic minor of C major is three flats greater than the signature of C major.

The Circle of Fifths must be completely memorized by the student and should be retained in the memory like a picture, for he will constantly use this information throughout his entire musical experience.

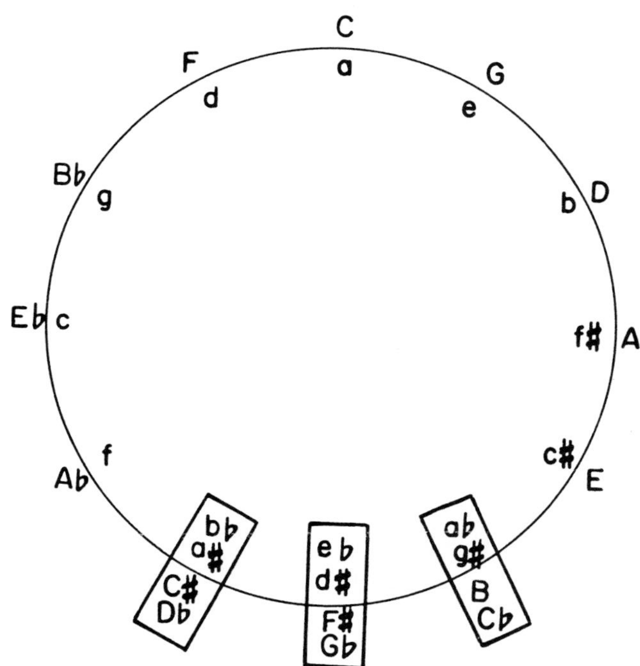

SUMMARY OF MINOR SCALE INFORMATION

Relative minor means the same key signature as the major scale.

Tonic minor means the same keynote as the major scale.

When the key signature is the same, then the keynote must be different.

When the keynote is the same, then the key signature must be different.

For every major scale there are two classifications of the minor scales: relative and tonic.

For every minor scale there are two classifications of the major scale: relative and tonic.

In the following chart the major-minor relationships are outlined, using C major as an example.

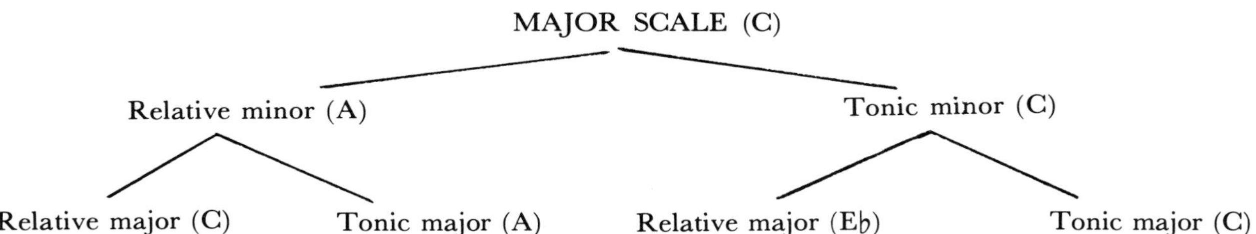

In the following pages the seven sharp scales and seven flat scales are shown, together with their relative and tonic minors, the tonic major of the relative minor, and the relative major of the tonic minor. For each major scale there are two versions of the natural form of the tonic minor. The first version shows how the signature contained in the second version is derived.

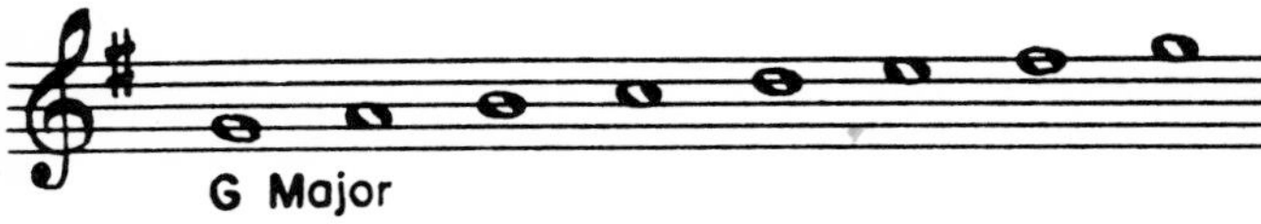

G Major

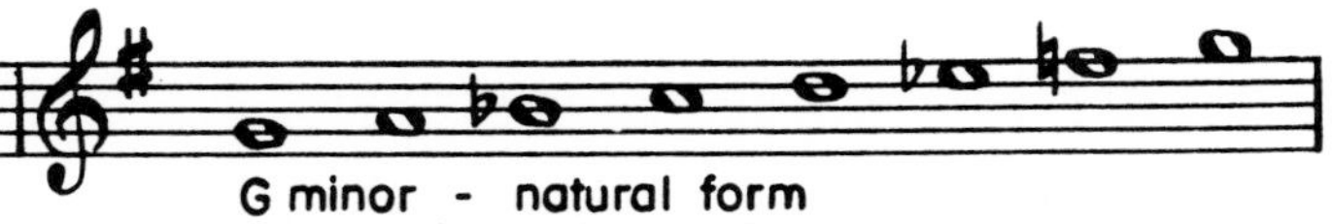

G minor - natural form
Tonic minor of G Major

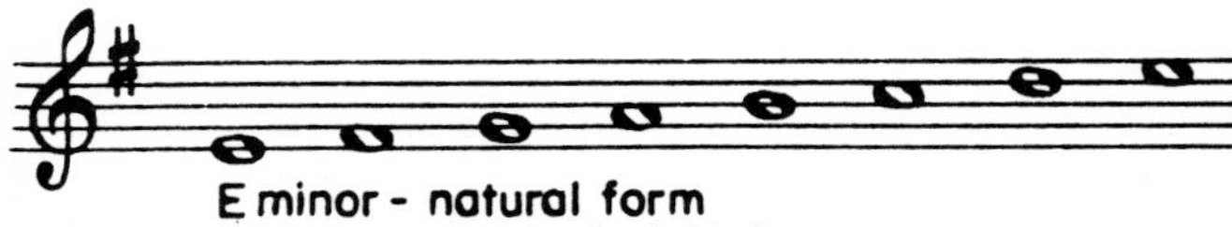

E minor - natural form
Relative minor of G Major

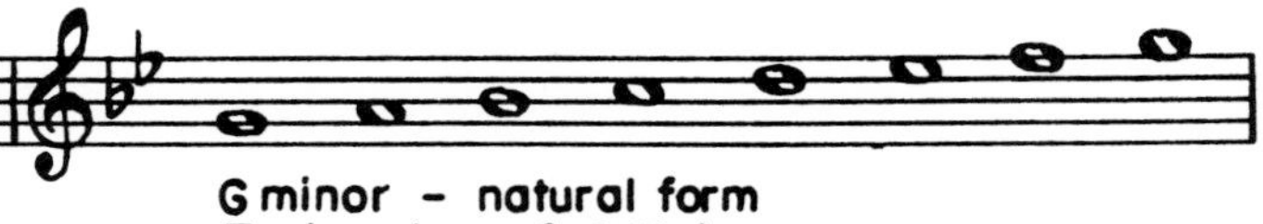

G minor - natural form
Tonic minor of G Major

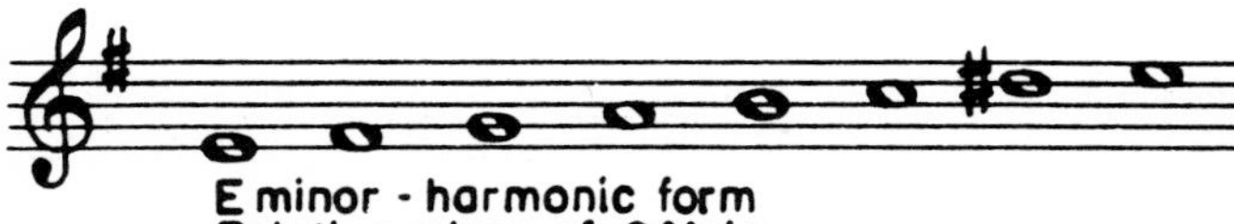

E minor - harmonic form
Relative minor of G Major

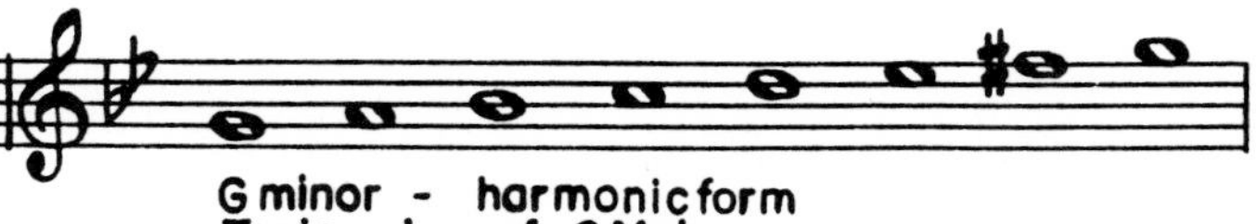

G minor - harmonic form
Tonic minor of G Major

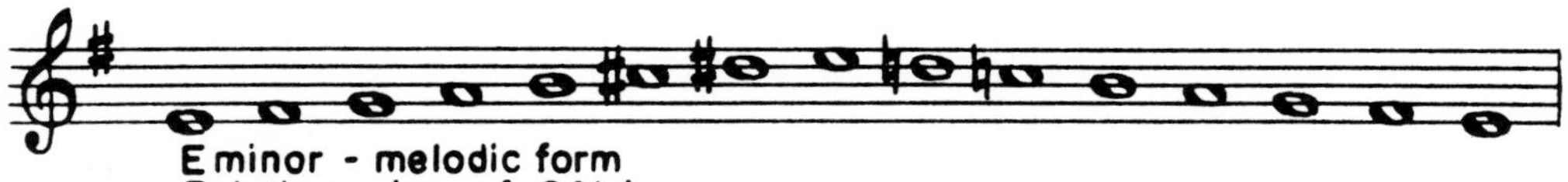

E minor - melodic form
Relative minor of G Major

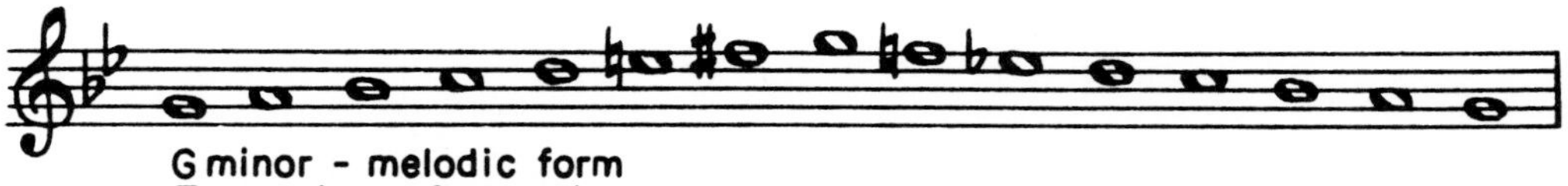

G minor - melodic form
Tonic minor of G Major

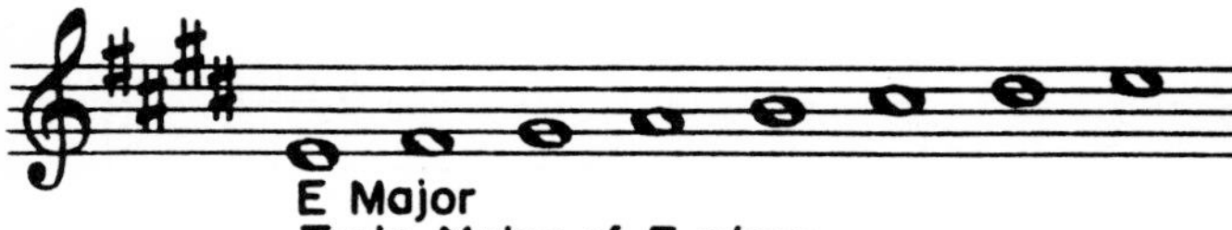

E Major
Tonic Major of E minor

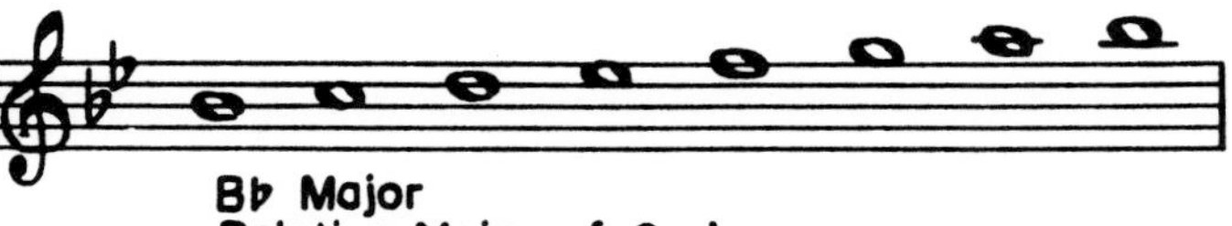

B♭ Major
Relative Major of G minor

Tonic minors of D Major
D Major
D minor - natural form
Relative minors of D Major
B minor - natural form
D minor - natural form
B minor - harmonic form
D minor - harmonic form
B minor - melodic form
D minor - melodic form
B Major
Tonic Major of B minor
F Major
Relative Major of D minor
Tonic minors
A Major
A minor - natural form
Relative minors
F♯ minor - natural form
A minor - natural form
F♯ minor - harmonic form
A minor - harmonic form

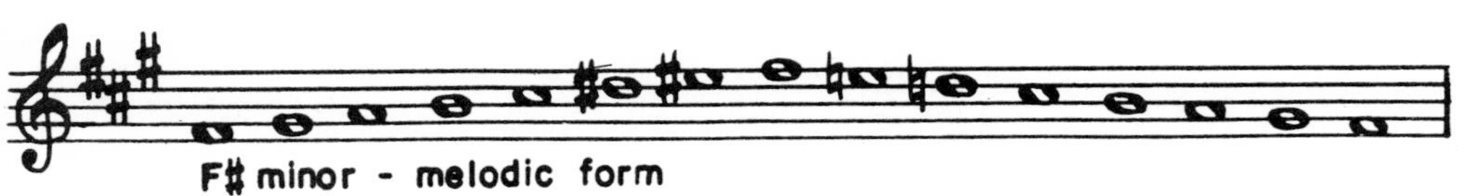
F# minor - melodic form

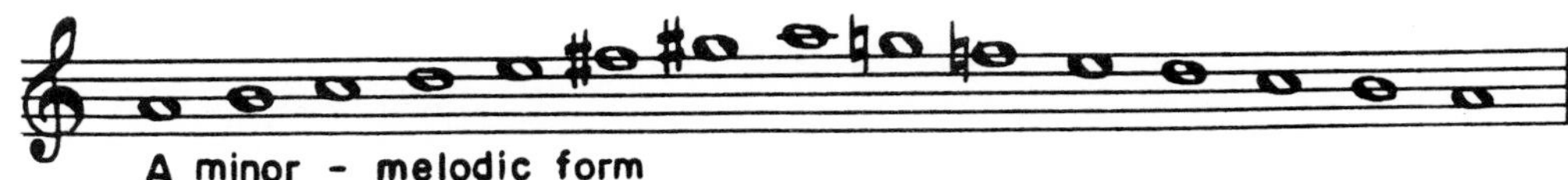
A minor - melodic form

F# Major
Tonic Major of F# minor
C Major
Relative Major of A minor

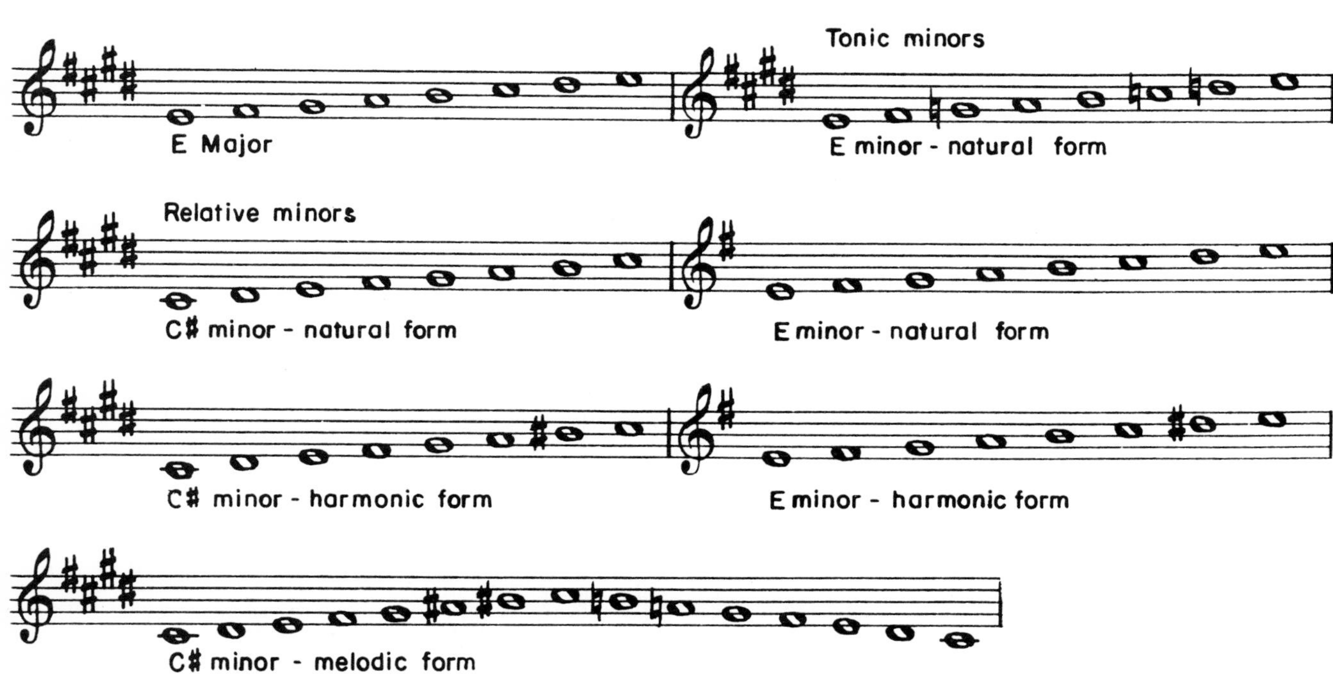
Tonic minors
E Major
E minor - natural form
Relative minors
C# minor - natural form
E minor - natural form
C# minor - harmonic form
E minor - harmonic form
C# minor - melodic form

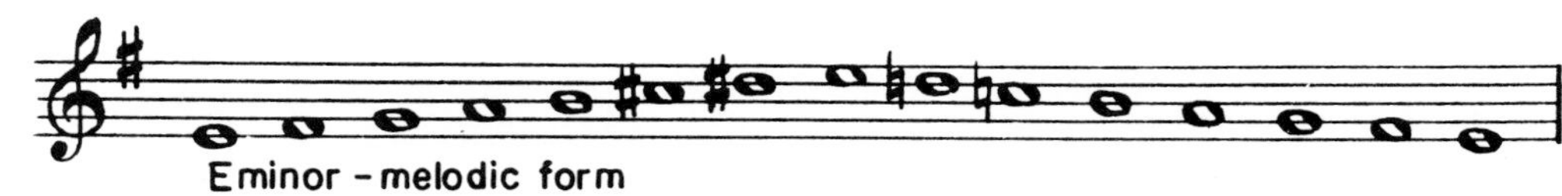
E minor - melodic form

C# Major
Tonic Major of C# minor
G Major
Relative Major of E minor

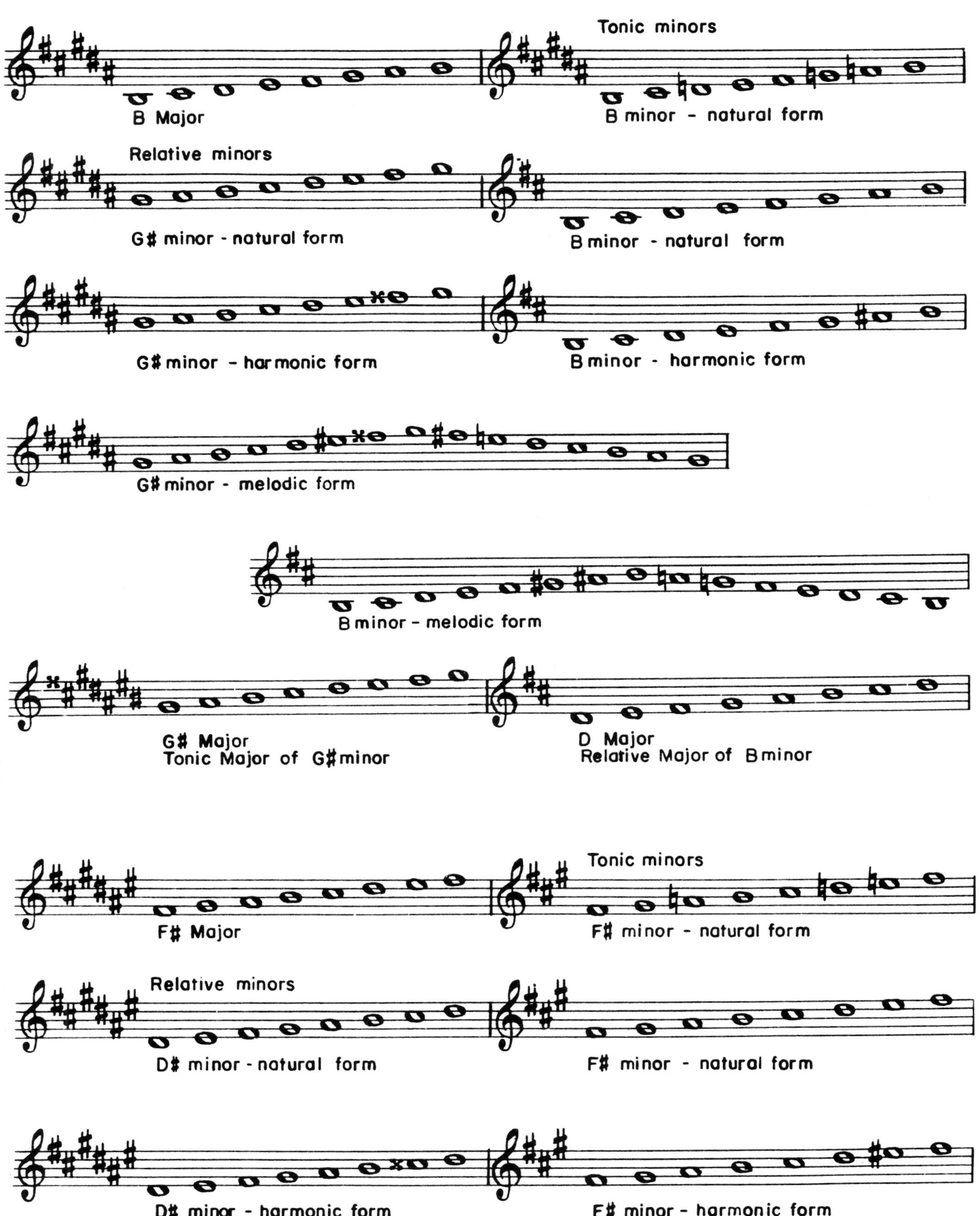
Tonic minors
B Major
B minor - natural form
Relative minors
G# minor - natural form
B minor - natural form
G# minor - harmonic form
B minor - harmonic form
G# minor - melodic form
B minor - melodic form
G# Major
Tonic Major of G# minor
D Major
Relative Major of B minor
Tonic minors
F# Major
F# minor - natural form
Relative minors
D# minor - natural form
F# minor - natural form
D# minor - harmonic form
F# minor - harmonic form

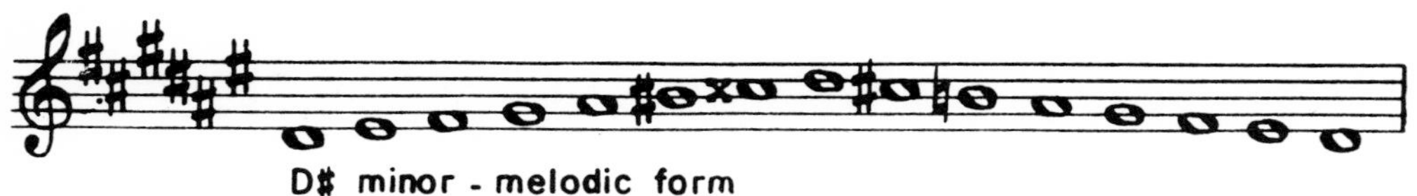

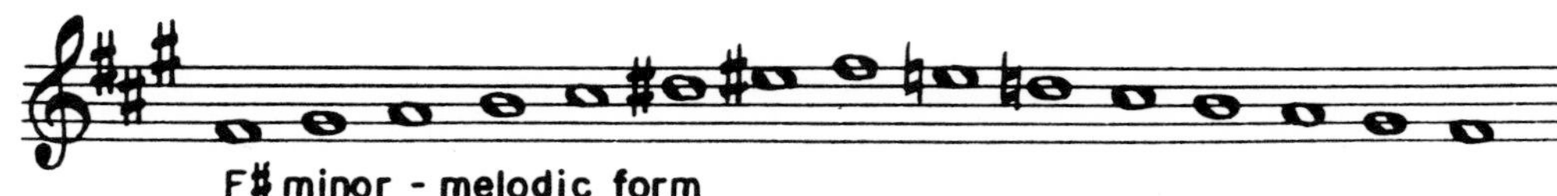

C♯ Major

Tonic minors

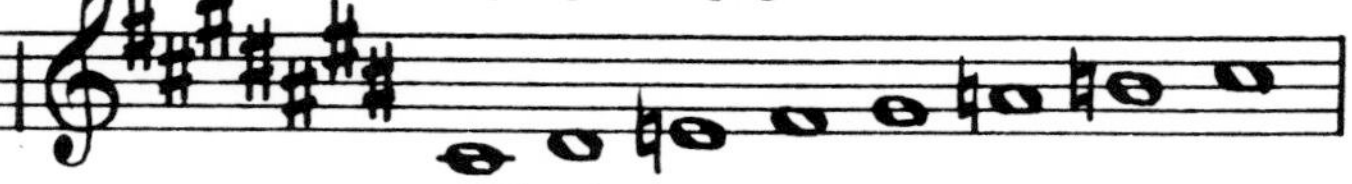

C♯ minor - natural form

Relative minors

A♯ minor - natural form

C♯ minor - natural form

A♯ minor - harmonic form

C♯ minor - harmonic form

A♯ minor - melodic form

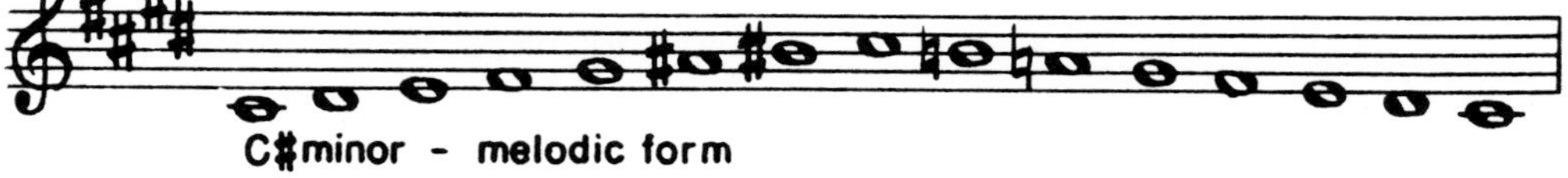

C♯ minor - melodic form

Tonic minors
F Major
F minor - natural form
Relative minors
D minor - natural form
F minor - natural form
D minor - harmonic form
F minor - harmonic form
D minor - melodic form
F minor - melodic form
D Major
Tonic Major of D minor
A♭ Major
Relative Major of F minor
Tonic minors
B♭ Major
B♭ minor - natural form
Relative minors
G minor - natural form
B♭ minor - natural form
G minor - harmonic form
B♭ minor - harmonic form

G minor - melodic form

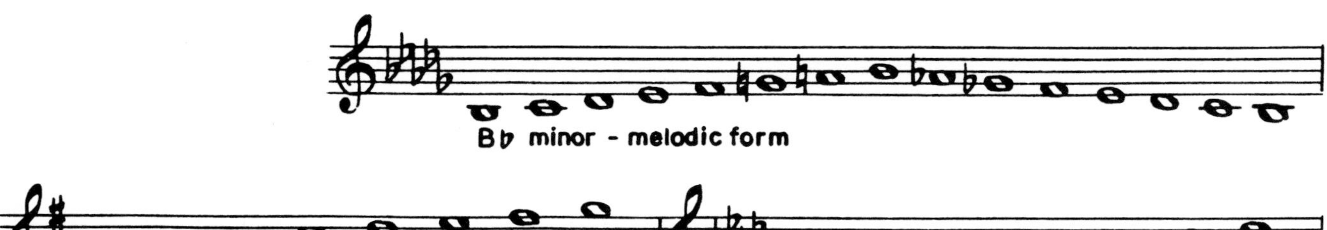

B♭ minor - melodic form

G Major
Tonic Major of G minor

D♭ Major
Relative Major of B♭ minor

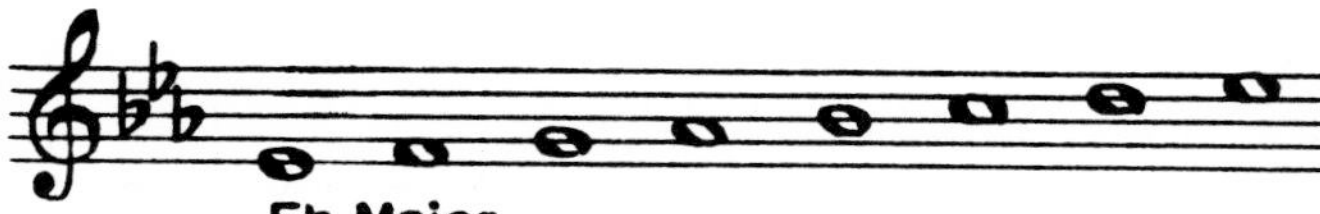

E♭ Major

Tonic minors

E♭ minor - natural form

Relative minors

C minor - natural form

E♭ minor - natural form

C minor - harmonic form

E♭ minor - harmonic form

C minor - melodic form

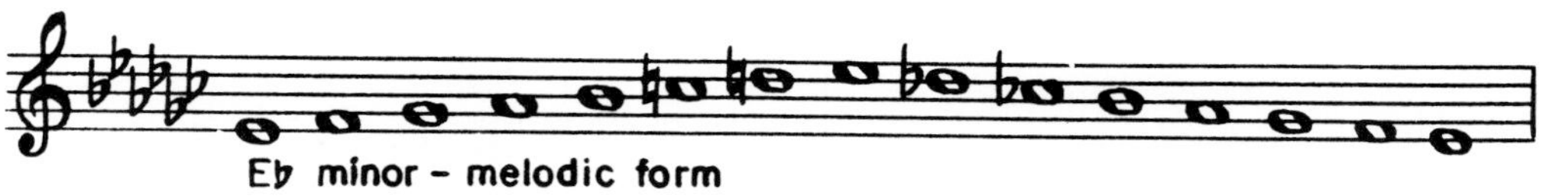

E♭ minor - melodic form

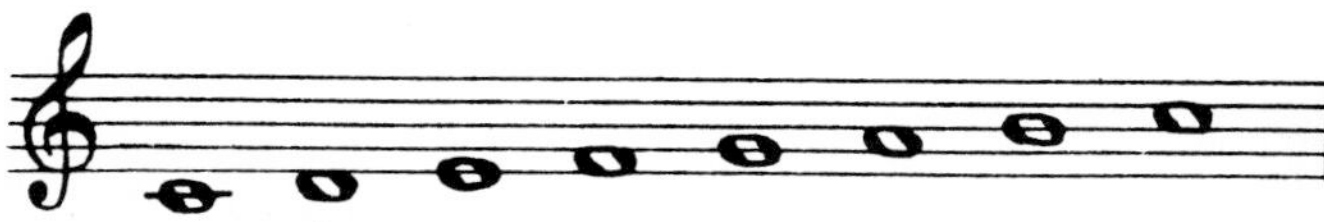

C Major
Tonic Major of C minor

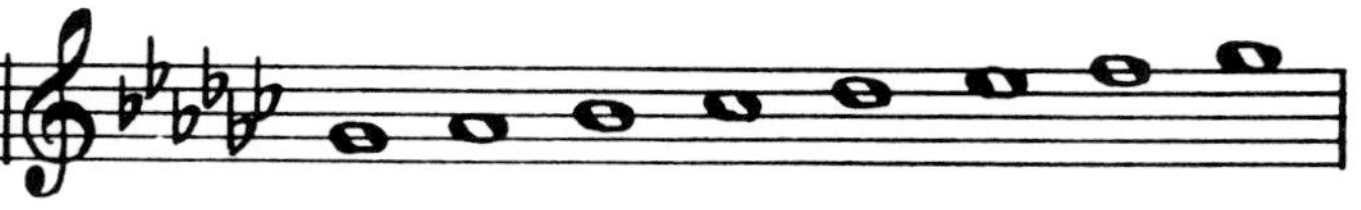

G♭ Major
Relative Major of E♭ minor

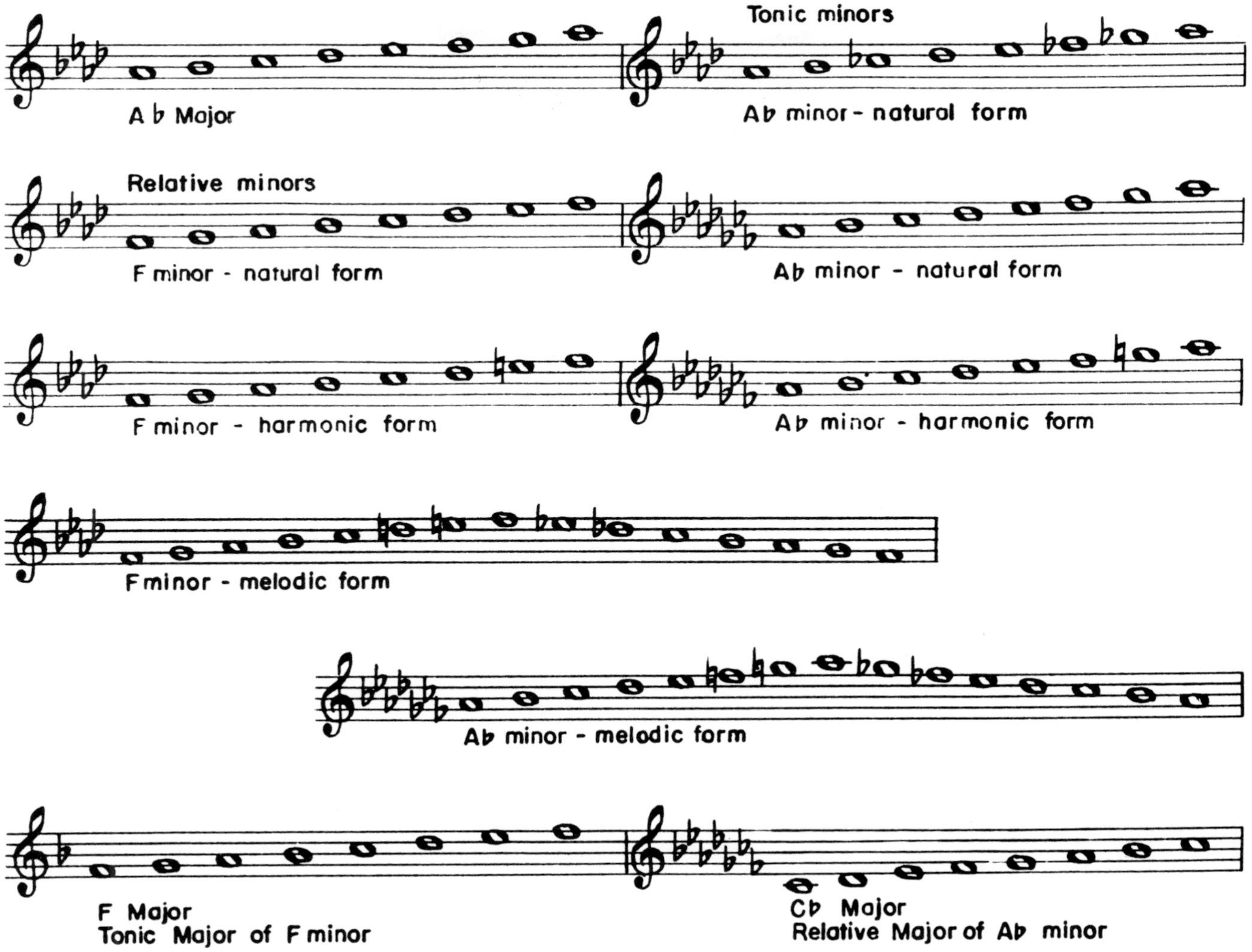

Tonic minors
A♭ Major
A♭ minor - natural form
Relative minors
F minor - natural form
A♭ minor - natural form
F minor - harmonic form
A♭ minor - harmonic form
F minor - melodic form
A♭ minor - melodic form
F Major
Tonic Major of F minor
C♭ Major
Relative Major of A♭ minor

Tonic minors
D♭ Major
D♭ minor - natural form
Relative minors
B♭ minor - natural form
D♭ minor - natural form
B♭ minor - harmonic form
D♭ minor - harmonic form

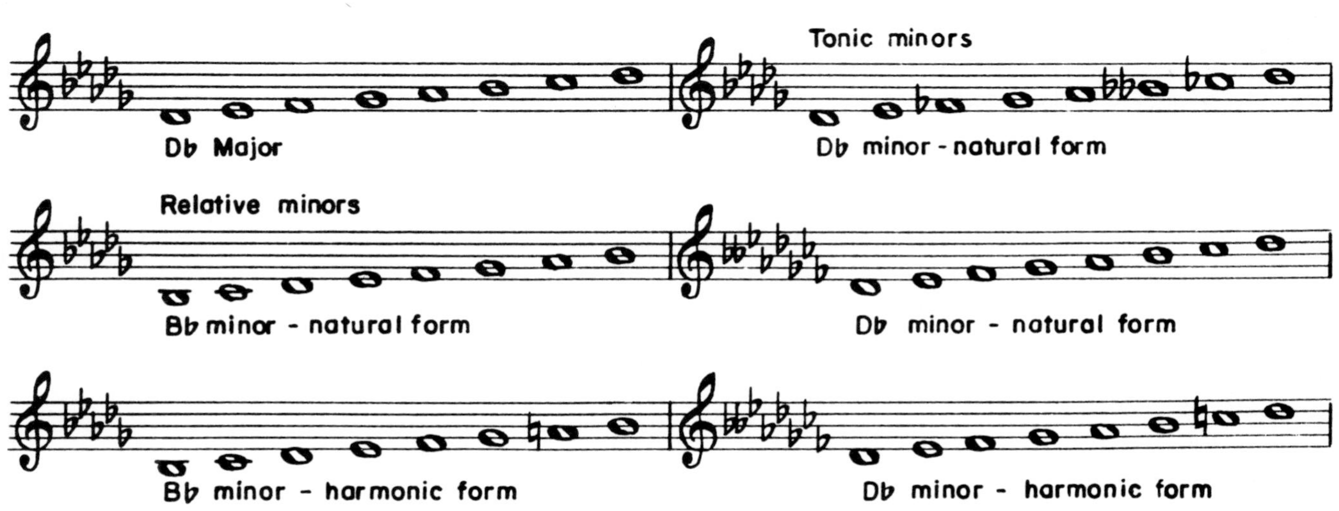

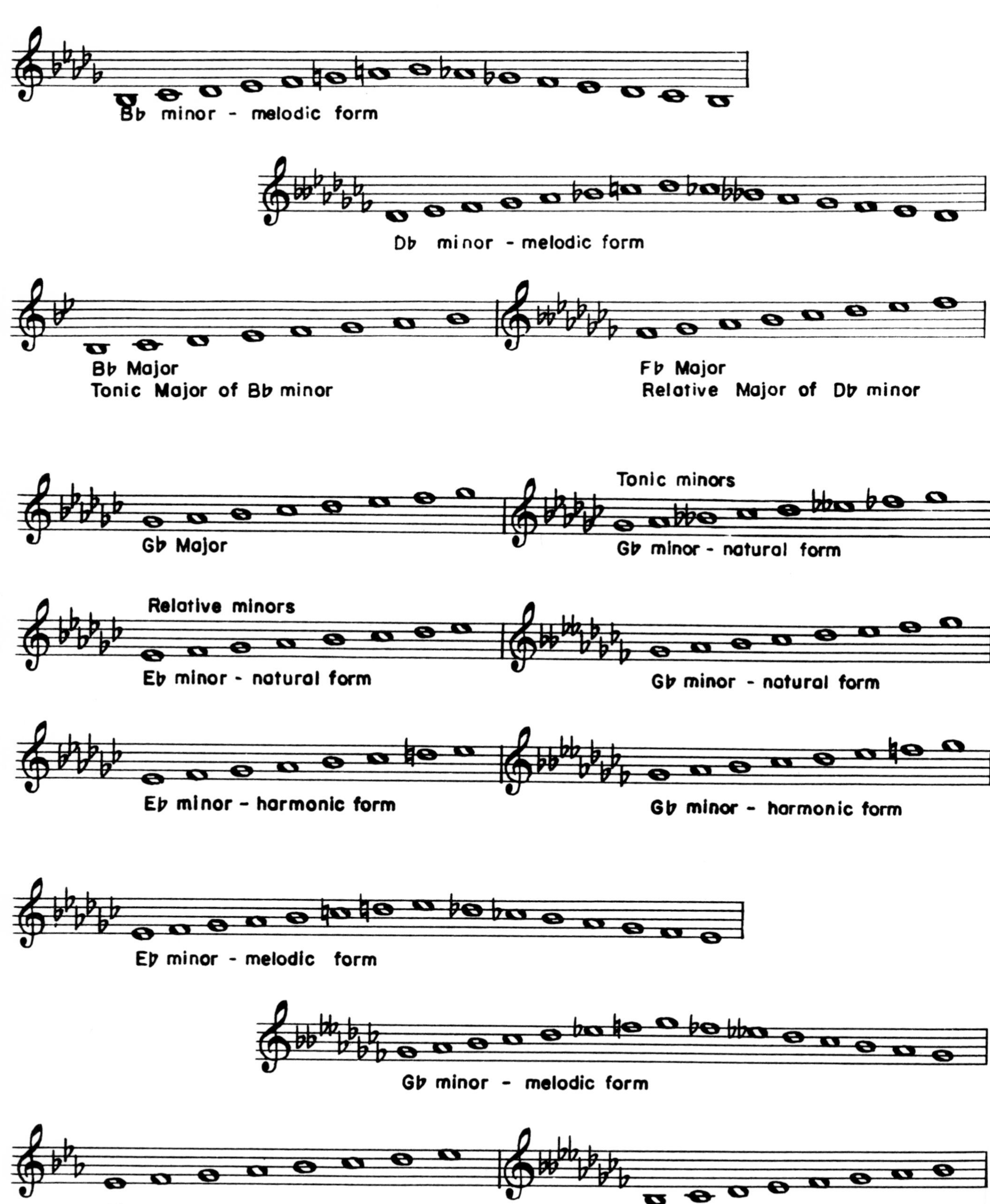
B♭ minor - melodic form
D♭ minor - melodic form
B♭ Major
Tonic Major of B♭ minor
F♭ Major
Relative Major of D♭ minor
G♭ Major
Tonic minors
G♭ minor - natural form
Relative minors
E♭ minor - natural form
G♭ minor - natural form
E♭ minor - harmonic form
G♭ minor - harmonic form
E♭ minor - melodic form
G♭ minor - melodic form
E♭ Major
Tonic Major of E♭ minor
B♭♭ Major
Relative Major of G♭ minor

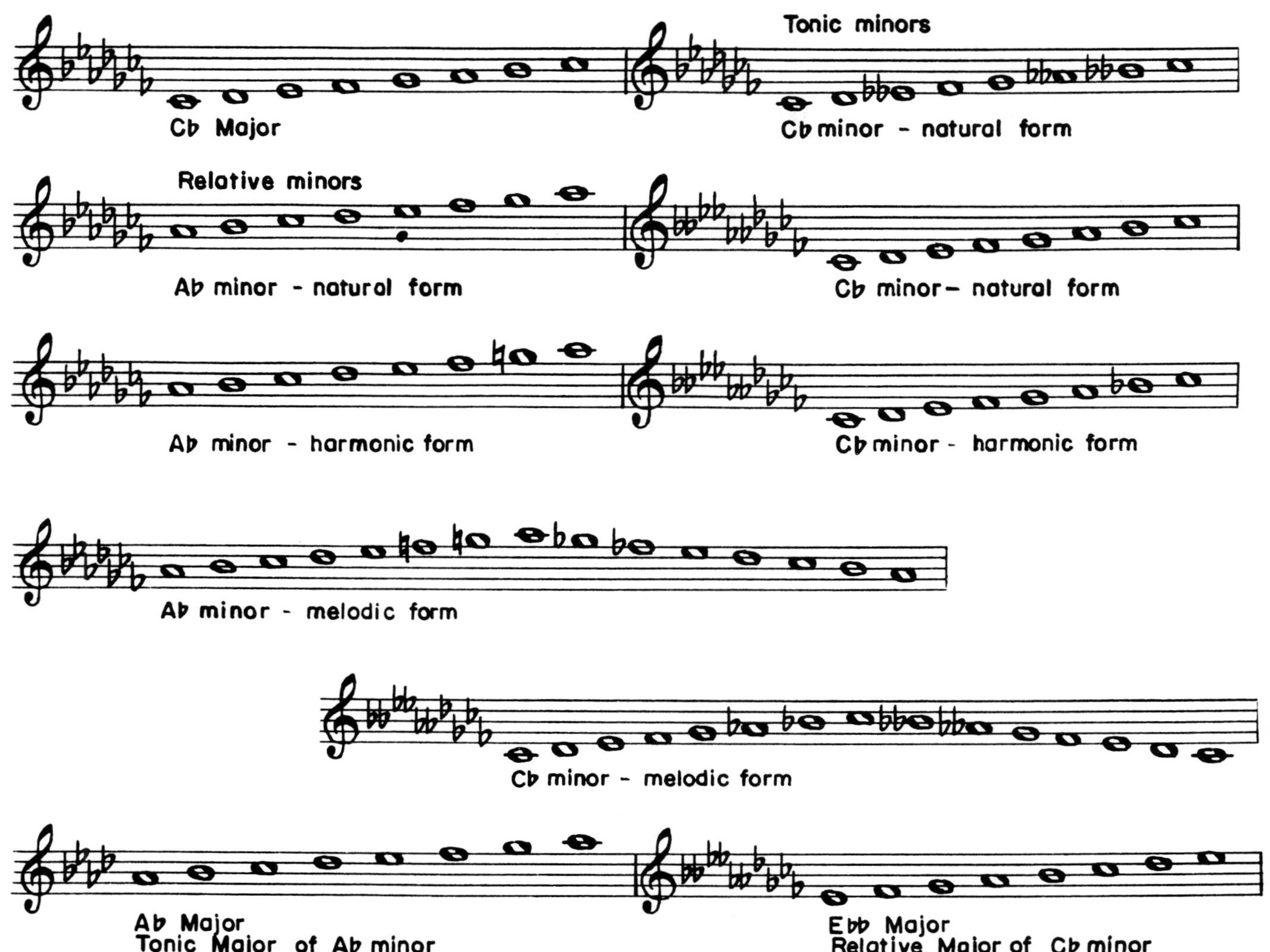
Tonic minors
C♭ Major
C♭ minor - natural form
Relative minors
A♭ minor - natural form
C♭ minor – natural form
A♭ minor - harmonic form
C♭ minor - harmonic form
A♭ minor - melodic form
C♭ minor - melodic form
A♭ Major
Tonic Major of A♭ minor
E♭♭ Major
Relative Major of C♭ minor

Name ....

Date ....

WORKSHEET NUMBER 1 FOR LESSON 6: Minor Scales

For each of the following, write the signature and scale:

1. Treble clef—relative minor of A major, melodic form

2. Bass clef—tonic minor of C major, melodic form

3. Treble clef—F minor, natural form

4. Treble clef—relative major of D minor

5. Bass clef—tonic minor of E♭ major, harmonic form

6. Bass clef—G minor, melodic form

7. Treble clef—relative minor of F♯ major, melodic form

8. Bass clef—tonic minor of B♭ major, harmonic form

9. Treble clef—tonic major of G minor

10. Bass clef—relative minor of A♭ major, melodic form.

Check your answers against the scales written on the previous pages.

Name ....

Date ....

WORKSHEET NUMBER 2 FOR LESSON 6: Minor Scales

For each of the following, write the signature and scale:

1. Bass clef—relative minor of A♭ major, natural form

2. Bass clef—relative minor of A major, harmonic form

3. Treble clef—relative minor of B♭ major, melodic form

4. Treble clef—tonic minor of B major, natural form

5. Bass clef—tonic minor of C major, harmonic form

6. Bass clef—tonic minor of C♯ major, melodic form

7. Treble clef—relative major of D minor

8. Treble clef—tonic major of E♭ minor

9. Bass clef—relative minor of E major, natural form

10. Bass clef—relative minor of F major, harmonic form

Check your answers against the scales written on the previous pages.

Name .... Date ....

SAMPLE TEST FOR LESSON 6: Minor Scales

For each of the following, write the signature and scale:

1. Treble clef—tonic minor of C major, melodic form

2. Bass clef—relative minor of D♭ major, harmonic form

3. Treble clef—relative minor of E major, natural form

4. Bass clef—tonic minor of F♯ major, melodic form

5. Bass clef—relative major of G minor

6. Treble clef—tonic major of A♭ minoı

7. Treble clef—relative minor of B major, harmonic form

8. Bass clef—tonic minor of C♯ major, melodic form

9. Bass clef—relative minor of D major, harmonic form

10. Treble clef—tonic minor of E♭ major, harmonic form

LESSON 7

Rest and Active Tones in Minor Scales

DRILL ON REST AND ACTIVE TONES

Sing from every minor scale keynote the rest tones 1-3-5-8-5-3-1. The following are the tonic chords in each of the minor scales through the seven sharp and the seven flat keys.

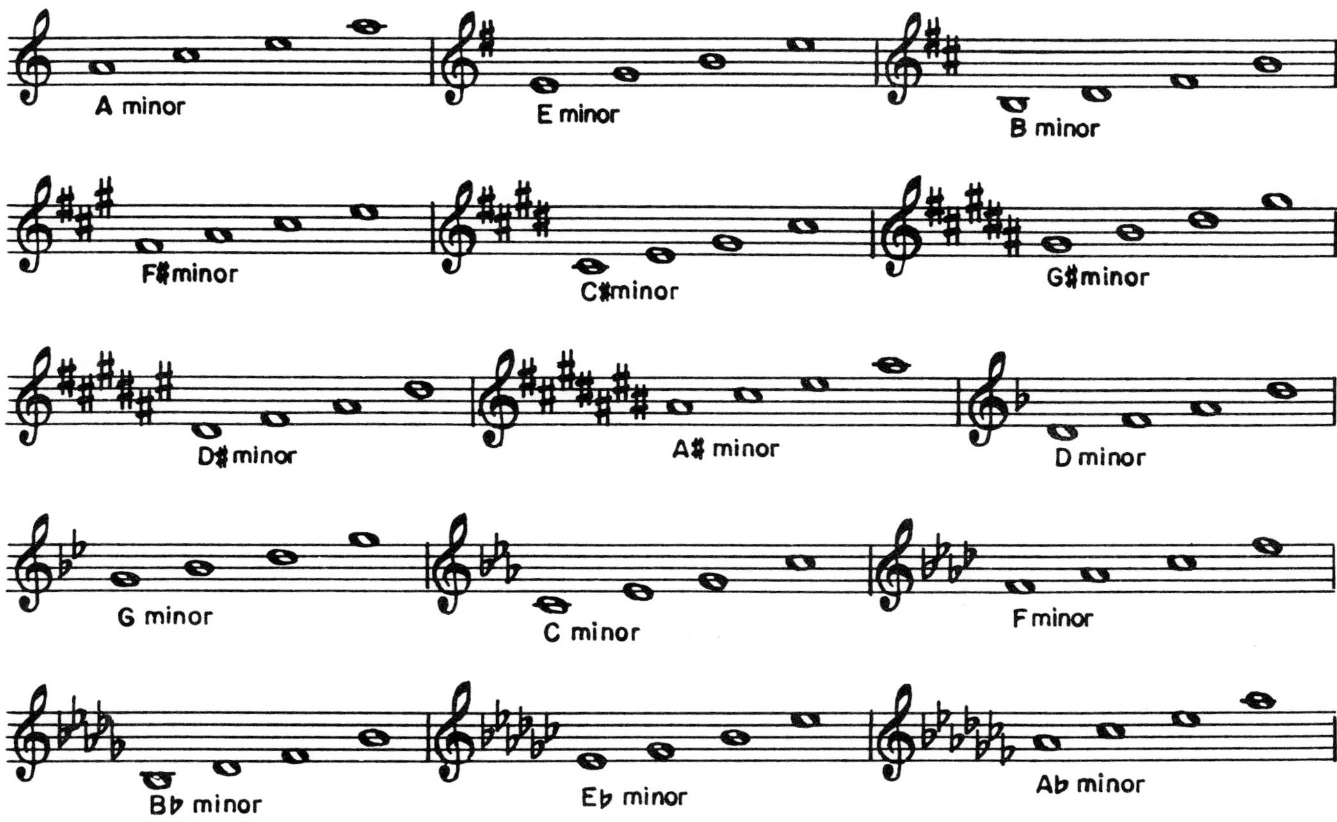

Sing the following numbers with their proper pitches in the key of C minor; and then substitute letter names for the numbers. Next, sing in the keys of A minor, E minor, B minor, F♯ minor, C♯ minor, G♯ minor, D♯ minor, and A♯ minor the letter names that correspond to the numbers. Use the harmonic minor form unless otherwise directed.

3-1-3-5-8-5-3-1
5-8-5-3-1-5-1
5-3-1-3-5-8-1
5-3-5-1-5-3-1
5-8-5-1-5-8-1
5-1-5-8-5-3-1-5
1-3-4-5-8-5-3-2-1

1-2-1-4-3-5-6-7-8 (melodic)
1-4-3-6-5-4-3-2-1
1-6-5-7-8-5-3-2-1
8-7-8-5-3-5-2-5-1
3-4-5-3-6-5-7-8
3-2-3-1-5-8-7-8-1

3-8-7-8-1-8-5-3-2-1
5-4-3-5-8-7-8-1
5-6-5-8-7-8-1-2-3-5-1
5-3-2-1-5-6-5-8-1
8-1-8-7-8-1-3-2-1
8-7-6-5-4-3-8-1 (natural)
8-1-8-5-3-4-3-5-6-5-1

8-7-8-1-3-4-5-3-2-1
1-3-5-8-3-4-3-2-1
5-3-2-1-5-8-7-8
8-3-8-5-8-1-2-1
8-5-6-5-7-5-6-7-8 (melodic)
1-3-5-1-8-5-6-7-8 (melodic)

Sing the following numbers with their proper pitches in the key of D minor; and then substitute letter names for the numbers. After this has been done, sing in the keys of G minor, B♭ minor, F minor, E♭ minor, and A♭ minor the letter names that correspond to the numbers. Sing the harmonic minor form unless otherwise directed.

1-2-1-3-5-8-7-8
1-2-3-5-6-7-8-1 (melodic)
1-3-4-3-5-6-5-8-7-8
1-5-4-3-5-8-1-2-1
1-6-5-4-3-5-8-7-8
8-7-8-1-2-3-2-5-1
3-2-1-3-4-5-1-6-5-8
3-5-6-5-1-2-3-4-5-5-1
3-4-5-1-8-7-8-1-2-1
5-1-1-3-3-5-6-5-8-7-8
5-6-5-8-7-8-1-2-3-2-1

5-3-1-3-5-6-5-5-3-3-2-2-1
8-7-6-5-3-2-3-1-2-1 (natural)
1-5-5-6-7-8-5-3-2-1 (melodic)
8-7-8-5-6-5-4-3-4-3-2-1
5-6-7-8-1-2-3-2-3-1 (melodic)
1-1-3-3-5-6-5-4-5-4-3-4-3-1
8-7-6-5-6-7-8-1-8-1 (melodic ascending; natural descending)
1-8-7-6-5-3-4-3-2-1 (natural)
1-3-4-3-5-6-7-8-5-8 (melodic)
1-2-1-3-1-4-3-1-5-6-5-3-1

DICTATION

The instructor plays these exercises, or similar ones, and the student places on the staff the notes heard. Dictation should be in all the minor keys through the seven sharps and the seven flats.

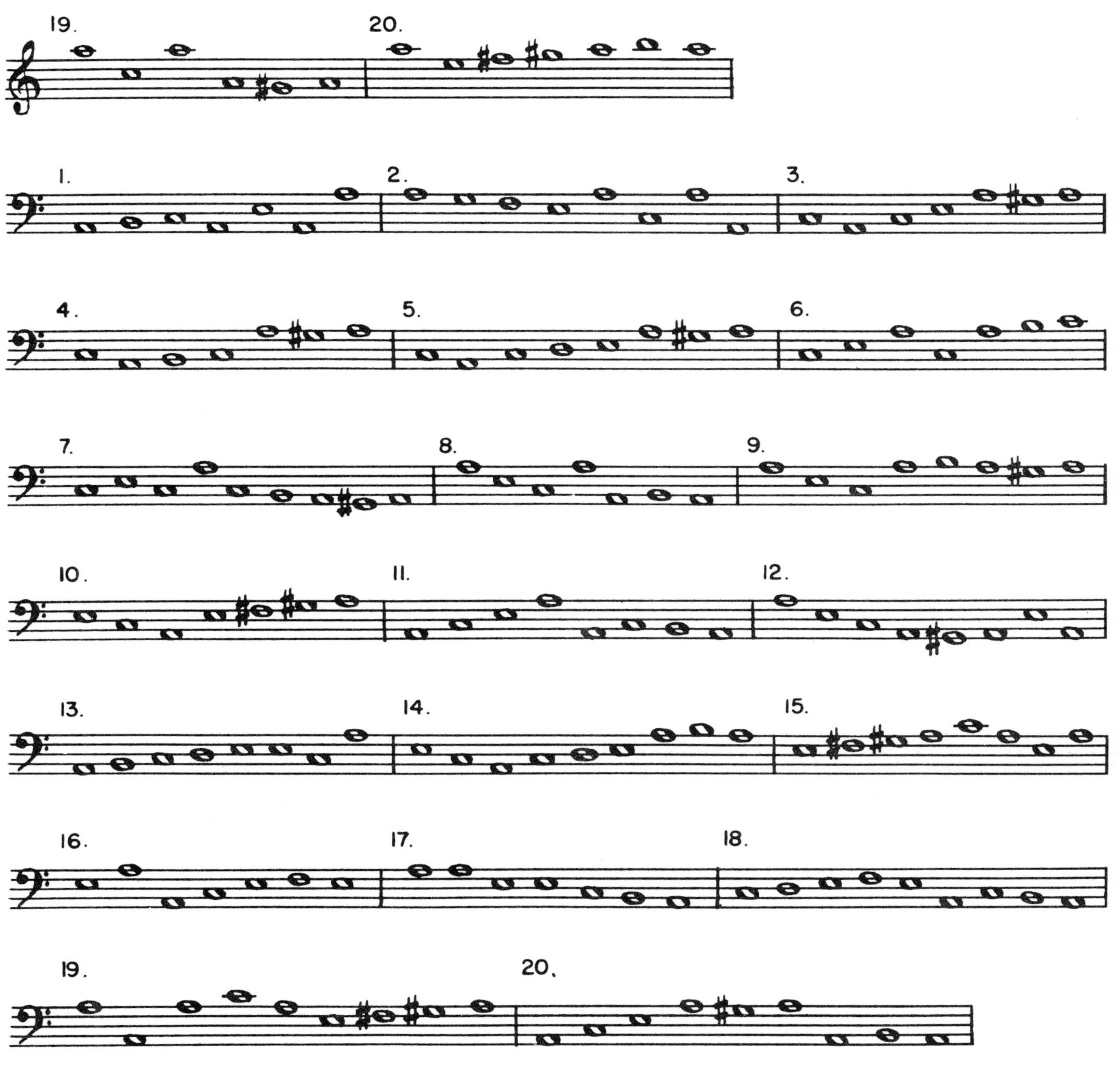

KEYBOARD DRILL FOR MINOR SCALES

Play the minor scales in all three forms from every keynote (right hand and left hand separately). The fingering for these scales is:

A, E, D, G, C minor—natural, harmonic, and melodic forms

R.H. ascending	1-2-3-1-2-3-4-5
descending	5-4-3-2-1-3-2-1
L.H. ascending	5-4-3-2-1-3-2-1
descending	1-2-3-1-2-3-4-5

B minor—all three forms

R.H.	ascending	1-2-3-1-2-3-4-5
	descending	5-4-3-2-1-3-2-1
L.H.	ascending	4-3-2-1-4-3-2-1
	descending	1-2-3-4-1-2-3-4

F♯ minor—natural and harmonic forms

R.H.	ascending	2-3-1-2-3-1-2-3
	descending	3-2-1-3-2-1-3-2
L.H.	ascending	4-3-2-1-3-2-1-2
	descending	2-1-2-3-1-2-3-4

F♯ minor—melodic form

R.H.	ascending	2-3-1-2-3-4-1-2
	descending	2-1-3-2-1-4-3-2
L.H.	ascending	4-3-2-1-3-2-1-2
	descending	2-1-2-3-1-2-3-4

C♯ minor—natural and harmonic forms

R.H.	ascending	2-3-1-2-3-1-2-3
	descending	3-2-1-3-2-1-3-2
L.H.	ascending	3-2-1-4-3-2-1-2
	descending	2-1-2-3-4-1-2-3

C♯ minor—melodic form

R.H.	ascending	2-3-1-2-3-4-1-2
	descending	2-1-4-3-2-1-3-2
L.H.	ascending	3-2-1-4-3-2-1-2
	descending	2-1-2-3-4-1-2-3

G♯ minor and A♭ minor—all three forms

R.H.	ascending	2-3-1-2-3-1-2-3
	descending	3-2-1-3-2-1-3-2
L.H.	ascending	3-2-1-3-2-1-3-2
	descending	2-3-1-2-3-1-2-3

D♯ minor and E♭ minor—all three forms

R.H.	ascending	2-1-2-3-4-1-2-3
	descending	3-2-1-4-3-2-1-2
L.H.	ascending	2-1-4-3-2-1-3-2
	descending	2-3-1-2-3-4-1-2

A♯ minor and B♭ minor—all three forms

R.H.	ascending	2-1-2-3-1-2-3-4
	descending	4-3-2-1-3-2-1-2
L.H.	ascending	2-1-3-2-1-4-3-2
	descending	2-3-4-1-2-3-1-2

F minor—all three forms

R.H.	ascending	1-2-3-4-1-2-3-4
	descending	4-3-2-1-4-3-2-1
L.H.	ascending	5-4-3-2-1-3-2-1
	descending	1-2-3-1-2-3-4-5

KEYBOARD DRILL FOR REST AND ACTIVE TONES

1. Play the rest tones (the tonic triad), in each of the minor keys (right hand only).
2. Play and resolve each note, making it the second degree of the minor scale, and name the key to which it belongs (right hand only): B, F♯, C♯, G♯, D♯, A♯, E♯, B♯, E, A, D, G, C, F, B♭,
3. Play and resolve each note, making it the fourth degree of the minor scale, and name the key to which it belongs (right hand only): D, A, E, B, F♯, C♯, G♯, D♯, G, C, F, B♭, E♭, A♭, D♭.
4. Play and resolve each note, making it the sixth degree of the minor scale, and name the key to which it belongs (right hand only): F, C, G, D, A, E, B, F♯, B♭, E♭, A♭, D♭, G♭, C♭, F♭.
5. Play and resolve each note, making it the seventh degree of the minor scale, and name the key to which it belongs (right hand only):G♯, D♯, A♯, E♯, B♯, F𝄪, C𝄪, G𝄪, C♯, F♯, B, E, A, D, G.

Name ....   Date ....

WORKSHEET FOR LESSON 7: Rest and Active Tones in Minor Scales

1. Write the rest tones (tonic chord) on the staff in each of these keys:

1. 2. 3. 4. 5. 6. 7. 8. 9. 10. 11. 12. 13. 14. 15. 16. 17. 18. 19. 20.

2. Resolve the following active tones and state the minor key to which each belongs. Identify the rest and active tones by number (for example, 2 to 1, 4 to 3, and so on).

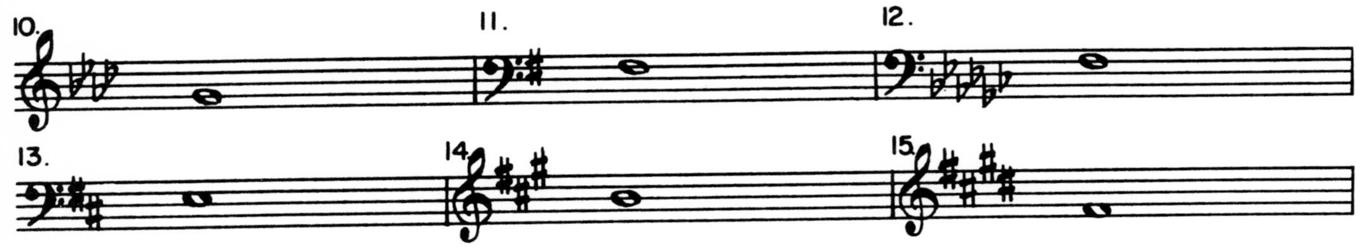
10.
11.
12.
13.
14.
15.

MUSIC PAPER for Dictation

Name .... Date ....

SAMPLE TEST FOR LESSON 7: Rest and Active Tones in Minor Scales

I. (1) In the treble clef, write the signature and the tonic chord of E minor, C♯ minor, A♭ minor, F♯ minor, C minor, D♯ minor, and B♭ minor.

(2) In the bass clef, write the signature and the tonic chord of A minor, B minor, G minor, G♯ minor, A♯ minor, D minor, and F minor.

II. (1) Write the following on the staff in G minor (treble clef) as the teacher dictates the actual notes on the piano. Use the key signature and whole notes to indicate the pitches heard.

(a) 1-5-3-4-5-3-1
(b) 3-5-8-7-8-5-3-2-1
(c) 5-6-5-8-7-8-1-8-1
(d) 8-5-3-2-1-5-1
(e) 3-5-1-5-6-5-8
(f) 5-6-7-8-1-2-1

(2) Write the following on the staff in F♯ minor (bass clef) as the teacher dictates the actual notes on the piano. Use key signature and whole notes to indicate the pitches heard.

(a) 1-2-3-5-8-3-2-1
(b) 3-1-5-6-7-8-1-2-1
(c) 5-4-3-2-1-5-8
(d) 8-7-6-5-6-7-8-1-8
(e) 1-3-5-6-5-8-7-8-1
(f) 3-3-4-4-5-5-3-2-1

III. (1) Write the active tones with their resolutions, in the following keys (treble clef):
(2 stands for second step of scale, 4 stands for fourth step of scale, etc.)

(a) 2—A♭ minor
(b) 4—B minor
(c) 6—C♯ minor
(d) 7—D minor
(e) 2—E♭ minor
(f) 4—F♯ minor

(2) Write the active tones with their resolutions in the following keys (bass clef)

(a) 6—G minor
(b) 6—A minor
(c) 7—B♭ minor
(d) 2—C minor
(e) 4—D♯ minor
(f) 6—E minor

IV. (1) Write the following on the staff in A♭ minor (treble clef) as the teacher dictates the actual pitches on the keyboard.

(a) 1-2-3-5-8-7-8-1-8
(b) 3-2-1-5-6-7-8-1
(c) 1-3-2-1-5-6-7-5-8
(d) 8-7-6-5-3-2-1-8-1
(e) 1-5-6-5-3-4-3-8-7-8-1
(f) 3-4-5-3-2-3-1-7-1

(2) Write the following on the staff in B minor (bass clef) as the teacher dictates the actual pitches on the keyboard.

(a) 8-7-8-1-2-1-3-5-3-1
(b) 1-3-5-6-5-6-7-8-1
(c) 8-7-8-7-6-5-3-2-1
(d) 3-5-4-3-5-6-5-6-7-8
(e) 5-6-5-6-7-8-1-2-3-1
(f) 3-5-4-3-5-6-7-8-1-2-1

There are 50 points on this test. Each point, therefore, equals 2 per cent.

Name ....

Date ....

MUSIC PAPER for Test

Name .... Date ....

MUSIC PAPER for Test

LESSON 8

Intervals

An interval is the distance between any two tones.

PRIMES

The closest interval is, of course, the note itself repeated. This interval is called the *perfect prime,* and the abbreviation for it is P.P.

When the second note is raised a half-step, the interval becomes larger. To increase something, you augment it. Therefore this interval is called an *augmented prime* (A.P.).

SECONDS

From the first to the second step of a major scale is a whole step. This interval is called a *major second* (M2).

Raising the second note of a major second a half-step enlarges the interval to an *augmented second* (A2).

Lowering the second note of a major second a half-step decreases the interval to a *minor second* (m2).

Lowering the second note of a major second another half-step decreases the interval to a *diminished second* (D2).

THIRDS

The interval from the first step to the third step of a major scale is called a *major third* (M3) (2 whole steps).

Raising the top note of a major third a half-step enlarges the interval to an *augmented third* (A3).

Lowering the top note of a major third a half-step decreases the interval to a *minor third* (m3).

Lowering the top note of a major third another half-step decreases the interval to a *diminished third* (D3).

FOURTHS

The interval from the first step to the fourth step of a major scale is called a *perfect fourth* (P4) (2½ steps).

Raising the top note of the perfect fourth a half-step enlarges the interval to an *augmented fourth* (A4).

Lowering the top note of a perfect fourth a half-step decreases the interval to a *diminished fourth* (D4).

FIFTHS

The interval from the first step to the fifth step of a major scale is called a *perfect fifth* (P5) (3½ steps).

Raising the top note of a perfect fifth a half-step enlarges the interval to an *augmented fifth* (A5).

Lowering the top note of a perfect fifth a half-step decreases the interval to a *diminished fifth* (D5).

SIXTHS

The interval from the first step to the sixth step of a major scale is called a *major sixth* (M6) (4½ steps).

Raising the top note of a major sixth a half-step enlarges the interval to an *augmented sixth* (A6).

Lowering the top note of a major sixth a half-step decreases the interval to a *minor sixth* (m6).

Lowering the top note of a major sixth another half-step decreases the interval to a *diminished sixth (D6)*.

SEVENTHS

The interval from the first step to the seventh step of a major scale is called a *major seventh* (M7) (5½ steps).

Raising the top note of a major seventh a half-step increases the interval to an *augmented seventh* (A7).

Lowering the top note of a major seventh a half-step decreases the interval to a *minor seventh* (m7).

Lowering the top note of a major seventh another half-step decreases the interval to a *diminished seventh (D7).*

OCTAVES

The interval from the first step to the eighth step of a major scale is called a *perfect octave* (P8) (6 steps).

Raising the top note of a perfect octave a half-step increases the interval to an *augmented octave* (A8).

Lowering the top note of a perfect octave a half-step decreases the interval to a *diminished octave* (D8).

When the notes are farther than an octave apart, the interval is determined as if the octave were not there. For example, an interval of a ninth consists of an octave and a second; and an interval of a tenth consists of an octave and a third.

PERFECT AND MAJOR INTERVALS

From what we have said above, the following can be deduced:

1. The *perfect* intervals are the primes, fourths, fifths, and octaves. These intervals have three dimensions: perfect, augmented, and diminished. (The diminished prime, not shown above, is an impractical interval that actually sounds larger than the perfect prime.)
2. The *major* intervals are seconds, thirds, sixths, and sevenths. These intervals have four dimensions: major, augmented, minor, and diminished.
3. The lowest note of any interval may be considered the keynote of a major scale and the interval is named accordingly, even though the composition in which the interval is found may be in a different key. Consider this example:

The scale of B♭ major may contain the A to E♭ interval shown above. To name this interval, think of A as the keynote of the scale. A perfect fifth from A is E. However, the interval illustrated is from A to E♭; hence the interval is a diminished fifth.

CHART FOR THE STUDY OF INTERVALS

Intervals may be classified in two main groups.

Perfect	*Major*
primes	seconds
fourths	thirds
fifths	sixths
octaves	sevenths

These groups are never interchangeable. There is no such interval, for example, as a perfect second or a major fourth.

Perfect intervals occur in three dimensions:

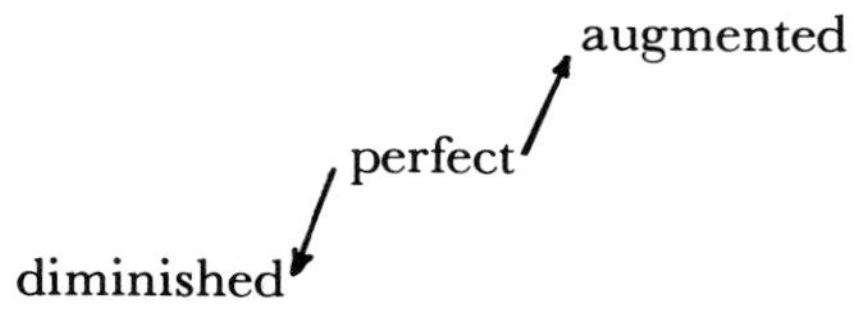

Major intervals occur in four dimensions:

augmented
major
minor
diminished

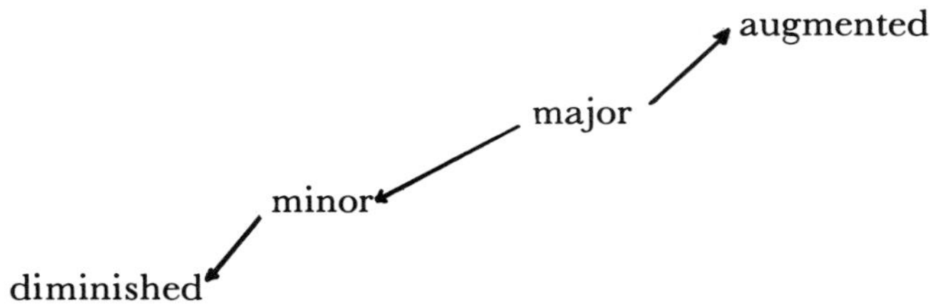

The student must be sure to memorize this summary of information before he attempts to write the intervals called for on the worksheet.

EXAMPLES OF THE 27 INTERVALS

The 27 different intervals may be built from any note of the scale. Those below have been built from G, F♯, and D♭. They may be referred to when you are building intervals from any other note.

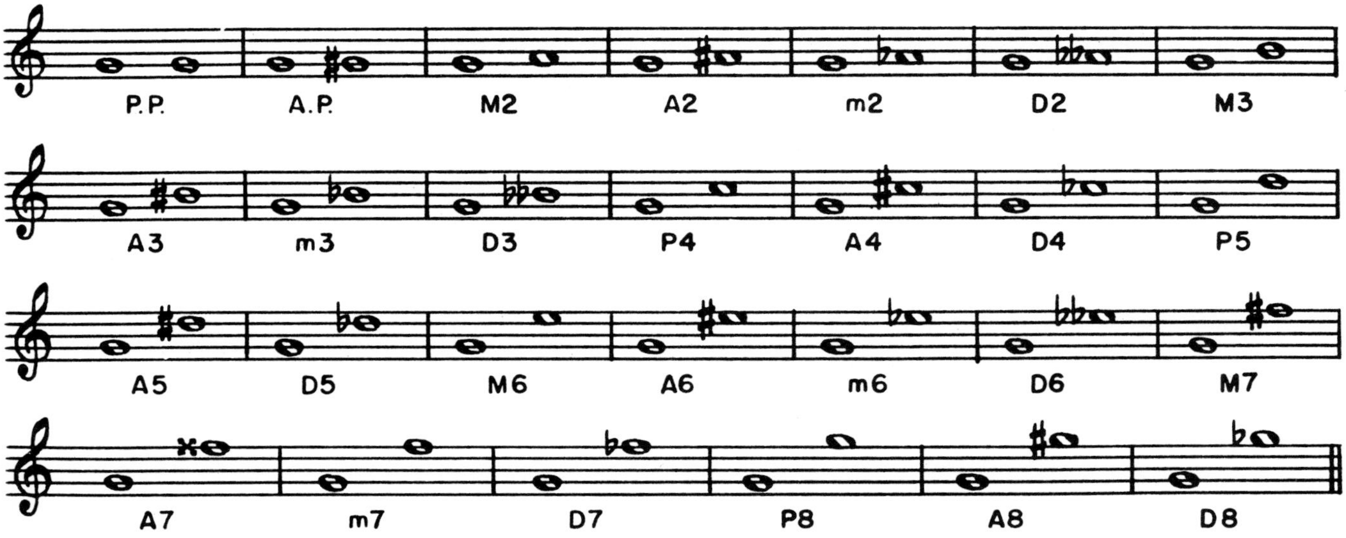

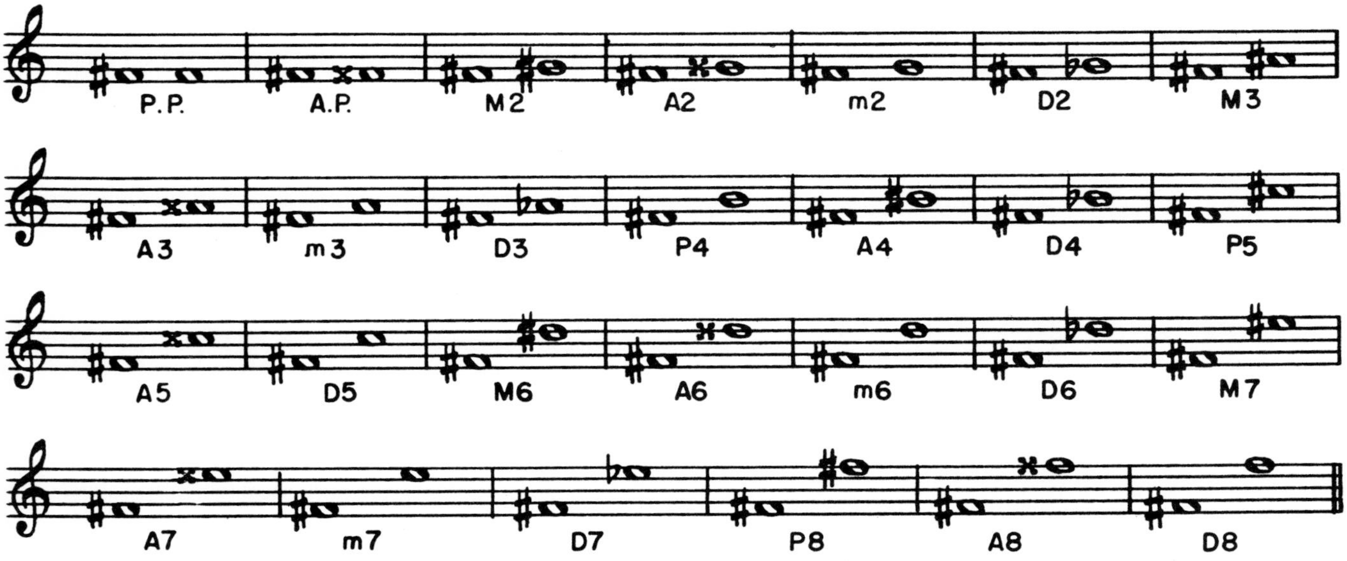

P.P. A.P. M2 A2 m2 D2 M3
A3 m3 D3 P4 A4 D4 P5
A5 D5 M6 A6 m6 D6 M7
A7 m7 D7 P8 A8 D8

P.P. A.P. M2 A2 m2 D2 M3
A3 m3 D3 P4 A4 D4 P5
A5 D5 M6 A6 m6 D6 M7
A7 m7 D7 P8 A8 D8

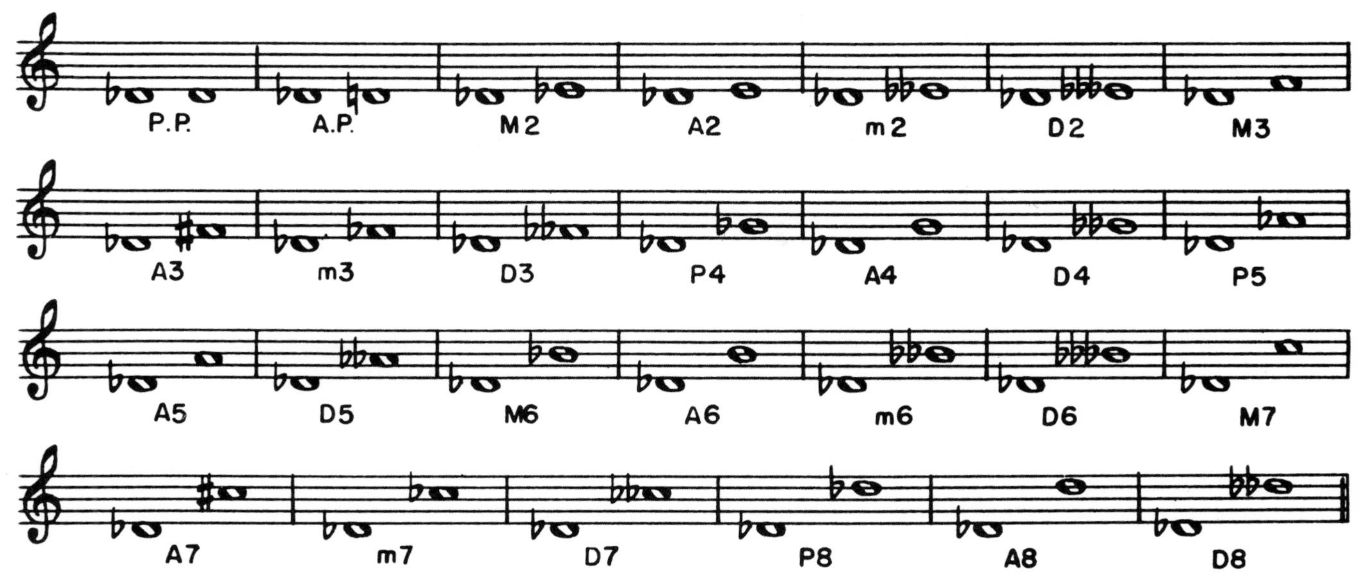
P.P.
A.P.
M2
A2
m2
D2
M3
A3
m3
D3
P4
A4
D4
P5
A5
D5
M6
A6
m6
D6
M7
A7
m7
D7
P8
A8
D8

Name ....   Date ....

WORKSHEET NUMBER 1 FOR LESSON 8: Intervals

In writing the intervals called for on these worksheets, write the intervals *up* from the given notes.

1. Write a perfect octave from each of the following notes on the staff.

2. Write a perfect fifth from each of these notes:

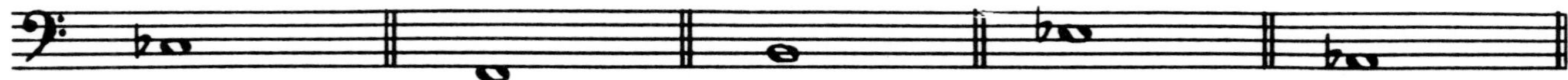

3. Write the perfect fourths:

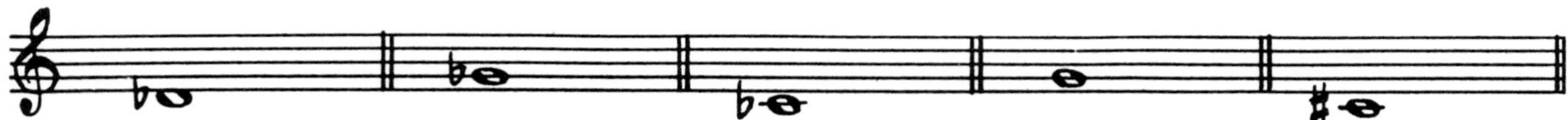

4. Write the perfect primes:

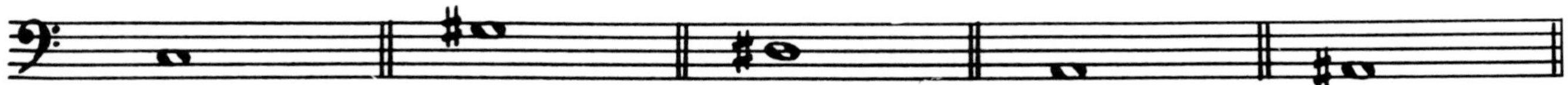

5. Write the major seconds:

6. Write the major thirds:

7. Write the major sixths:

8. Write the major sevenths:

9. Write the minor seconds:

10. Write the minor thirds:

11. Write the minor sixths:

12. Write the minor sevenths:

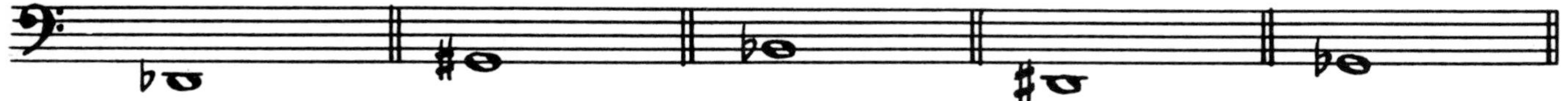

13. Write the intervals called for on the following staves:

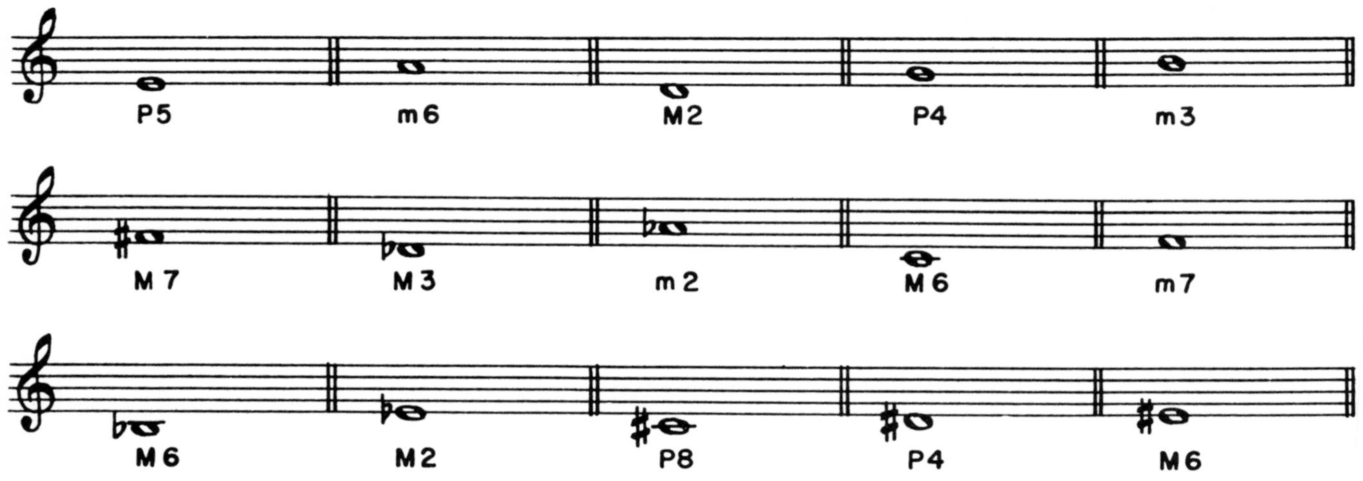

Name .... Date ....

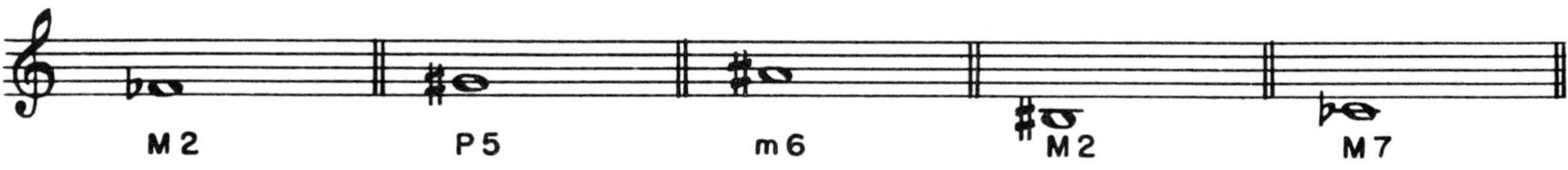

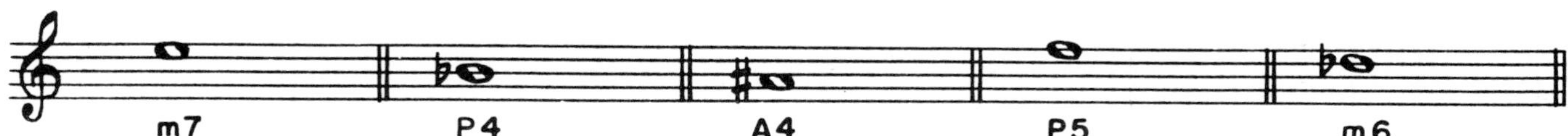

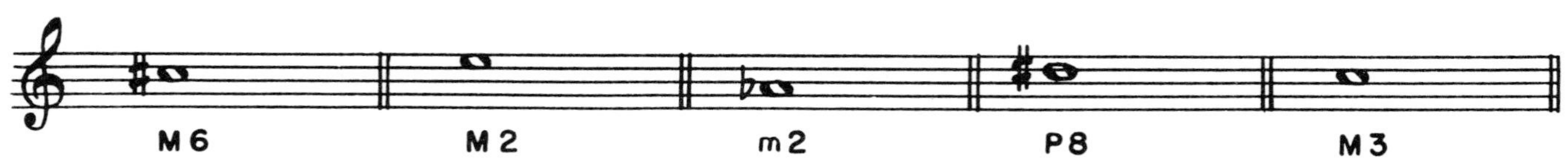

14. Name the following intervals:

15. Write the diminished seconds:

16. Write the diminished thirds:

17. Write the diminished fourths:

18. Write the diminished fifths:

19. Write the diminished sixths:

20. Write the diminished sevenths:

21. Write the diminished octaves:

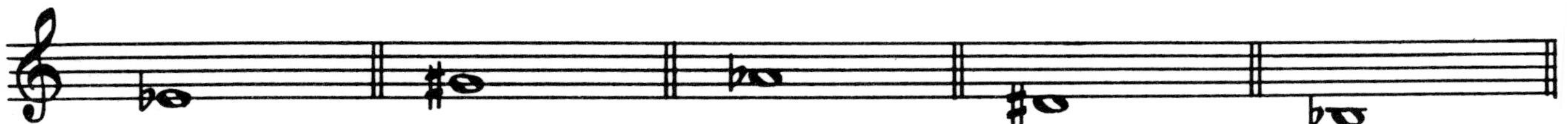

22. Write the augmented primes:

23. Write the augmented seconds:

Name .... Date ....

24. Write the augmented thirds:

25. Write the augmented fourths:

26. Write the augmented fifths:

27. Write the augmented sixths:

28. Write the augmented sevenths:

29. Write the augmented octaves:

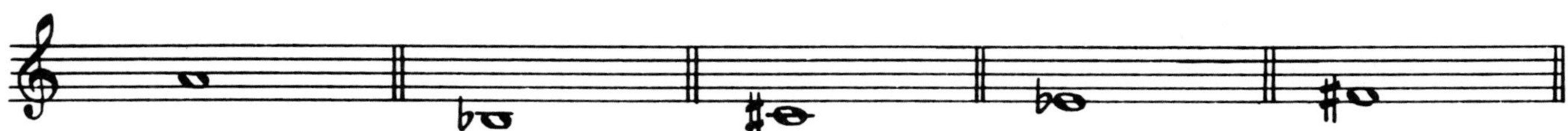

30. Write the intervals called for on the following staves:

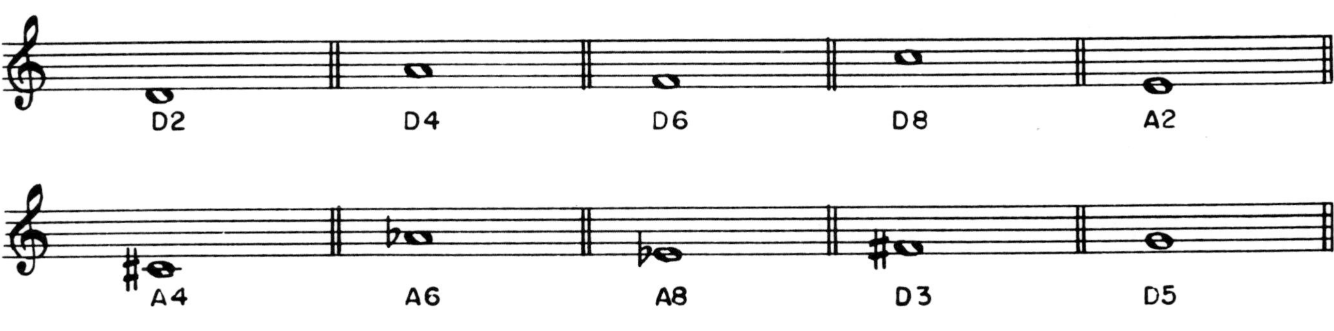

31. Name the following intervals in the bass clef:

CONSTRUCTING INTERVALS DOWN FROM A GIVEN NOTE

Intervals may also be constructed *down* from any note, following this method:

1. Take the given note as the top note of the interval to be constructed.
2. Select the major scale in which the given note will have a scale step number that is the same as the numerical value of the desired interval. For example, if you wish to construct some form of a sixth, regard the given note as the sixth step of the scale.
3. Place on the staff the keynote of the scale selected.
4. If the interval desired is a major or perfect interval, the lower tone does not require alteration. (Measured from the keynote, the steps of a major scale are either major or perfect.)
5. If the interval sought is an augmented interval, lower the keynote a half-step.
6. If the interval sought is a minor interval, raise the keynote a half-step.
7. If the interval sought is a diminished second, third, sixth, or seventh, raise the keynote a whole step.
8. If the interval sought is a diminished fourth, fifth, or octave, raise the keynote a half-step.

Example: To construct a major second down from C.

1. C will be the second degree of the scale of the lower note.
2. C is the second degree of the scale of B♭ major.
3. Therefore a major second down from C is B♭.

Example: To construct a minor third down from F♯.

1. F♯ is the third degree of the scale of D major.
2. From D to F♯ is a major third.
3. Alter the major third to a minor third by raising the D a half-step.
4. A minor third down from F♯ is therefore D♯.

Example: To construct an augmented fifth down from B.

1. B is the fifth degree of the scale of E major.
2. From E to B is a perfect fifth.
3. Alter the perfect fifth to an augmented fifth by lowering E a half-step.
4. An augmented fifth down from B is therefore E♭.

Summary:
1. Given the lower tone:
   (a) To enlarge the size of the interval, *raise* the top tone.
   (b) To decrease the size of the interval, *lower* the top tone.
2. Given the top tone:
   (a) To enlarge the size of the interval, *lower* the bottom tone.
   (b) To decrease the size of the interval, *raise* the bottom tone.

Name .... Date ....

WORKSHEET NUMBER 2 FOR LESSON 8: Intervals

Place on the staff, using the *treble clef,* the following intervals.
Construct the intervals *down* from the given note.

1. M3—A	6. A4—C	11. A5—G♯	16. PP—F
2. P4—G	7. M7—E♯	12. M7—B♯	17. A2—G♯
3. M3—A♯	8. m7—B♭	13. AP—A♯	18. A4—A♭
4. P5—F	9. m2—G♭	14. D3—C	19. A3—E♯
5. M2—E	10. AP—B	15. D4—D♭	20. D2—B♭

Place on the staff, using the *bass clef,* the following intervals.
Construct the intervals *down* from the given note.

1. P4—E♭	6. M6—C	11. M2—F	16. D7—G
2. m3—C♭	7. M3—G	12. M3—B♭	17. A8—B
3. m2—F♯	8. M3—C♯	13. m3—D	18. A7—A♯
4. m6—A♭	9. M6—D♯	14. D5—C	19. D6—F
5. m2—F♭	10. m7—D♭	15. A6—E	20. A5—D

SINGING OF INTERVALS

Sing the intervals indicated below first with numbers and then with letters. Next, transpose these same intervals to all of the major keys through seven sharps and seven flats.

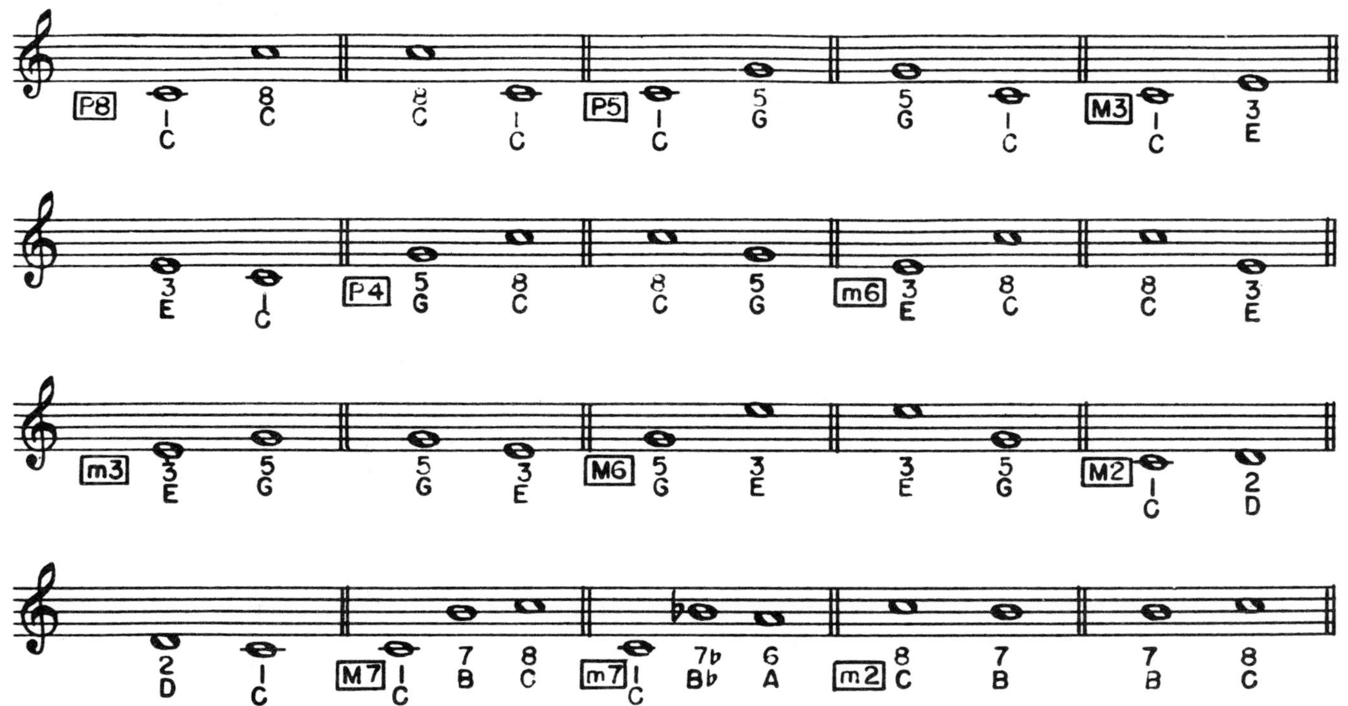

DICTATION OF INTERVALS

Directions for distinguishing intervals heard:

P8 is 1 to 8 of any scale
P5 is 1 to 5 of any scale
M2 is 1 to 2 of any scale
M3 is 1 to 3 of the major scale
m2 is the note heard and the closest note above it
m3 is 1 to 3 of the minor scale
P4 is 5 to 8 of any scale (or the first two notes of the melody of "When Day Is Done")
M6 is the first two notes of "My Bonnie Lies Over the Ocean." For a descending major sixth think of the first two notes of "Over There."
m6 is 3 to 8 of the major scale.

The instructor plays many intervals and the student records the intervals heard by writing M2, M6, and so on.

The following is a group of intervals that may be used for this sort of drill. The instructor may wish to substitute intervals of his own choice. Drills of this kind should be done every day until the student can distinguish very quickly any interval he hears at any time.

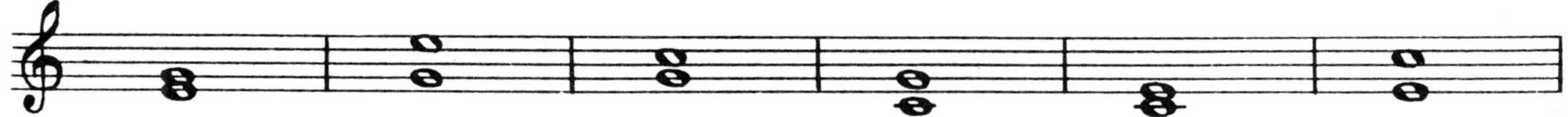

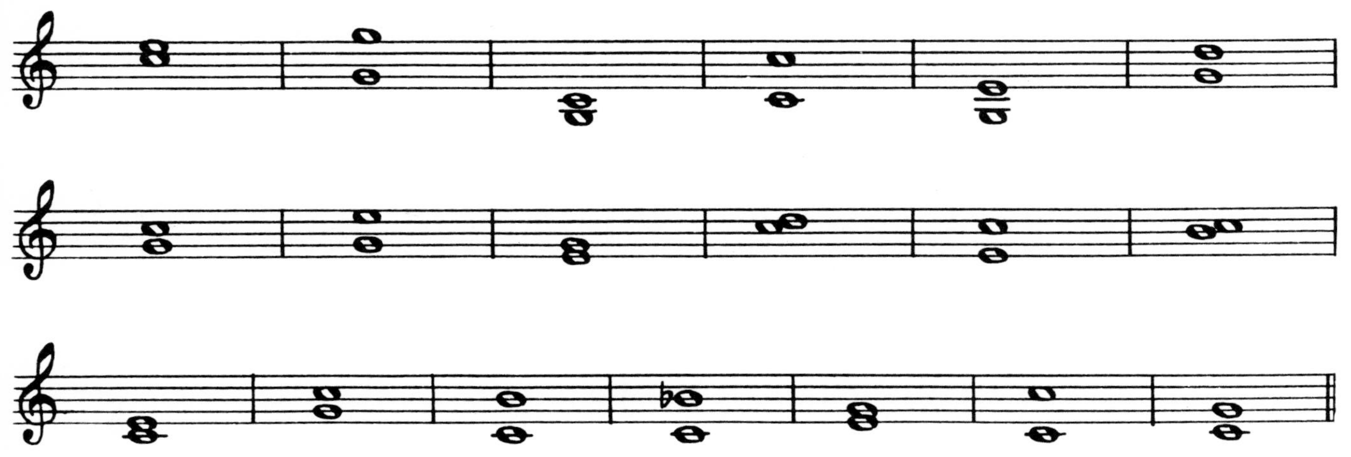

INVERSION OF INTERVALS

If the lower note of an interval is raised an octave, we say that the interval has been *inverted.* Here are all of the intervals inverted:

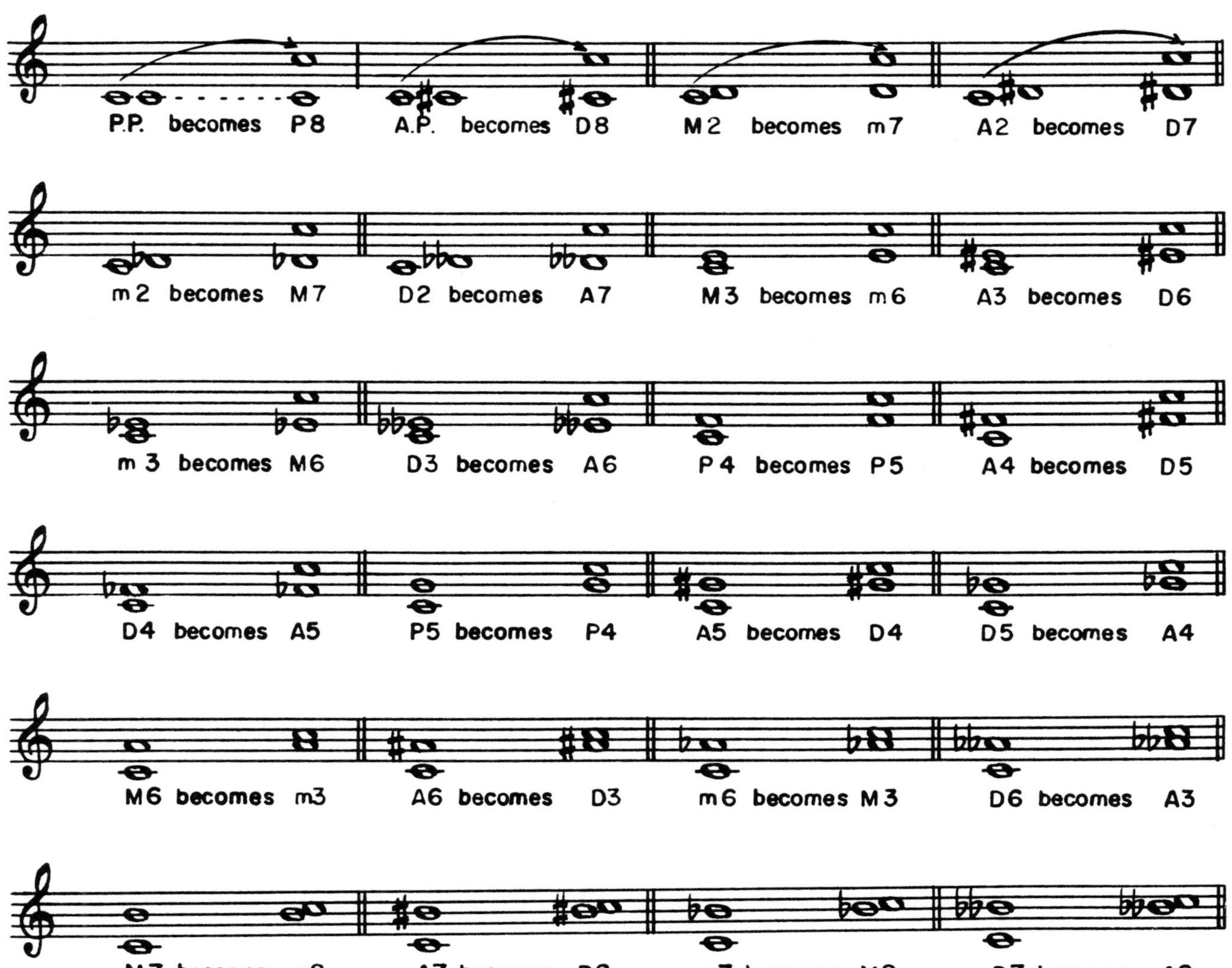

From the above, we see that when inverted,

Perfect intervals remain perfect
Augmented intervals become diminished
Diminished intervals become augmented.
Major intervals become minor
Minor intervals become major

It is also true that when inverted:

Primes become octaves (1-8)
Seconds become sevenths (2-7)
Thirds become sixths (3-6)

Fourths become fifths (4-5)
Fifths become fourths (5-4)
Sixths become thirds (6-3)
Sevenths become seconds (7-2)
Octaves become primes (8-1)

Note that the numerical value of an interval plus the numerical value of its inversion always totals nine.

ILLUSTRATION OF INTERVALS FOUND IN STANDARD COMPOSITIONS

On the succeeding pages are examples of intervals as they are found in the compositions of well-known composers.

The first interval shown is the perfect prime. It appears in Beethoven's Sonata for the Piano No. 23 in F minor, Op. 57 *(Appassionata),* first movement, and is used for special emphasis on the D♭ against the right-hand diminished chord of E-G-B♭.

Another example of the perfect prime appears in Chopin's Prelude in D♭ major *(Raindrop Prelude).* Here the interval of the perfect prime on G♯ is repeated for twelve measures before another perfect prime is introduced on B. The G♯ perfect prime continues for a total of 48 measures, which creates the effect of constantly falling rain.

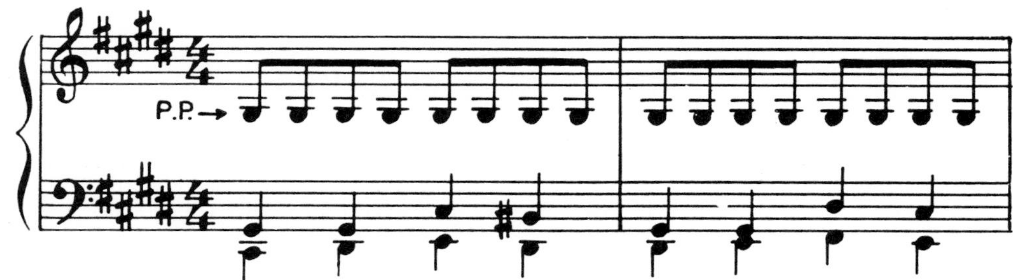

Many composers use major and minor seconds as intervals on which to build their themes. In the third movement of Symphony No. 3 in E♭ major, Op. 55, Beethoven used these two intervals for an opening theme in the first violin part.

In Mozart's Symphony No. 40 in G minor, K. 550, the first theme of the first movement is made up mainly of major and minor seconds.

For the choral theme of his great Symphony No. 9 in D minor, Op. 125 *(Choral Symphony)*, Beethoven used a theme based on major and minor seconds. The theme is first introduced in the cello and double bass parts.

The interval of a third is possibly the favorite interval of the composers. There are many examples of its use. Beethoven's Symphony No. 5 in C minor, Op. 67, begins with two emphatic thirds: a major third from G down to E♭, followed by a minor third from F down to D. Almost an entire movement is built around these two thirds.

In Schubert's Symphony No. 8 in B minor *(Unfinished Symphony)*, the clarinets play a beautiful theme based on thirds. This is found in the second movement, measures 66 through 83.

In Mozart's Symphony No. 40 in G minor, K. 550, the violins introduce a theme based on thirds in the trio of the third movement. The oboe follows with an accompanying figure that also is based on thirds.

Chopin must have been delighted with the interval of a third, for he used it as the theme for an entire etude, called "A Study in Thirds." The right hand plays nothing but an interval of a third for 61 measures.

The second theme of the last movement of Beethoven's *Third Symphony* is based on the interval of a third. This is played by the first violins.

In Beethoven's Symphony No. 4 in B♭ major, Op. 60, the second violin part in the second movement begins an accompaniment figure using the interval of a fourth for a complete measure before the first violin starts the theme. Another perfect fourth, used as an accompaniment in the double bass part, continues for five measures.

In Beethoven's Symphony No. 6 in F major, Op. 68 *(Pastorale Symphony)*, first movement, measures 125 through 131, the interval of a perfect fourth is repeated many times in the first violin part and then it is repeated several times an octave lower in the second violin part.

In Beethoven's *Ninth Symphony*, first movement, theme 3, the clarinet, oboe, and bassoon use a theme based mainly on the interval of a fourth.

In the third movement of the *Ninth Symphony*, Beethoven wrote the first theme using two perfect fourths as basic intervals. They are played by the first violins.

Beethoven opens his *Ninth Symphony* with the interval of the fifth, constantly repeated for fourteen measures in the second violin and cello parts. The first violin then plays the interval of the fifth, answered by the same interval in the viola and double bass parts. The French horns also play the interval of a perfect fifth and hold it for fourteen measures.

Horns in D

Vln. I

Vln. II

Viola

Vcl.

Double Bass

In his Symphony No. 3 in F major, Op. 90, Brahms uses the interval of a perfect fifth in the first movement, measures 36 through 39, in the cello and viola parts as an accompaniment to the melody played by the woodwinds. In the next four measures the interval is played in the second violin, cello, and French horn parts.

The interval of a sixth, like that of the third, is a very popular interval with composers. In Mendelssohn's *A Midsummer Night's Dream,* overture, measures 197 through 203, the first and second violins play in sixths and the clarinets play in sixths with an accompanying figure.

In Beethoven's Sonata for Piano No. 22 in F major, Op. 54, first movement, measures 30 through 33, the right hand plays a continuing group of intervals of a sixth. These are repeated in measures 44 through 49.

Chopin wrote an etude using the interval of a sixth in the right hand throughout the entire composition (34 measures).

In his *Valse Brilliante,* Op. 34, No. 1, Chopin uses the interval of a sixth in the main theme of the composition.

In a short piano composition called "Für Elise," Beethoven uses the interval of a seventh very effectively in the second theme.

Beethoven also uses the seventh in the trio of the menuetto movement of his Sonata for Piano No. 18 in E♭ major, Op. 31, No. 3.

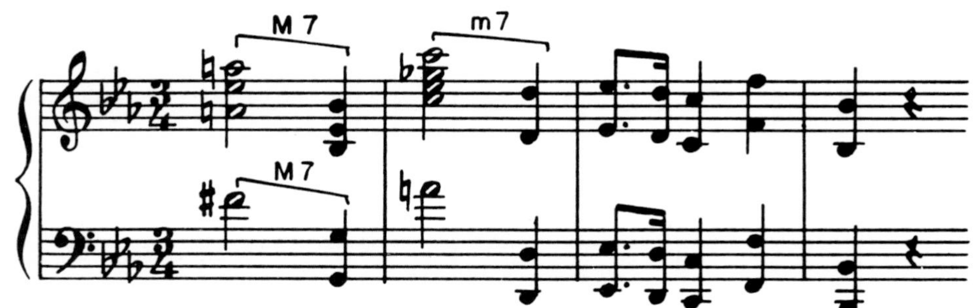

In his Sonata for Piano No. 23 in F minor, Op. 57 *(Appassionata),* Beethoven in the allegro ma non troppo uses the interval of the seventh for five consecutive measures in the right hand.

Chopin, in the *Valse,* Op. 42, makes use of the interval of a seventh in the accompaniment to the melodic line.

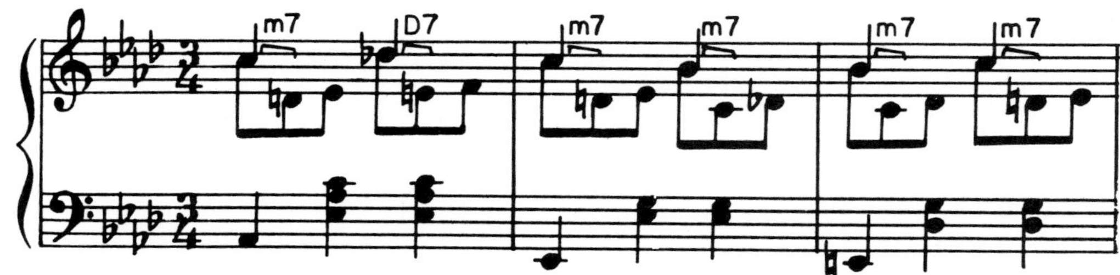

Brahms, in his Symphony No. 1 in C minor, Op. 68, uses one interval of the seventh very effectively in the first violin part of the first movement. A few measures later he also uses this interval in the cello part.

In the second movement of his *Unfinished Symphony,* Schubert uses the interval of an octave in a very interesting manner to introduce the third theme. It is played by the first violins. The theme itself is written for the clarinet.

In the *Ninth Symphony* of Beethoven, second movement, the second theme is built completely on the interval of an octave.

Chopin used the interval of an octave for a complete composition. One hundred and nine measures contain this interval, and most of the time the octave is used simultaneously in the right and left hands.

In Brahms's Symphony No. 2 in D major, Op. 73, at the end of the statement of the first theme, the first violins have a figure based almost entirely on the interval of the octave.

KEYBOARD DRILL ON INTERVALS

1. Play from all pitches (right hand only) the perfect intervals P.P., P4, P5, P8. (All pitches means from C, G, D, A, E, B, F♯, C♯, F, B♭, E♭, A♭, D♭, G♭, C♭, D♯, E♯, F♭, G♯, A♯, and B♯.)
2. Play from all pitches (left hand only) the major intervals M2, M3, M6, M7.
3. Play from all pitches (right hand only) the minor intervals m2, m3, m6, m7.
4. With the right hand only, play these intervals:

   a. perfect 5 from G♯
   b. major 2 from B♭
   c. minor 6 from C♯
   d. perfect 4 from B♭
   e. major 7 from G♭
   f. perfect 8 from B
   g. minor 3 from F♯
   h. minor 7 from D
   i. major 6 from E♭
   j. major 3 from A♭

Name .... Date ....

WORKSHEET NUMBER 3 FOR LESSON 8: Intervals

Name the following intervals, then invert and rename them:

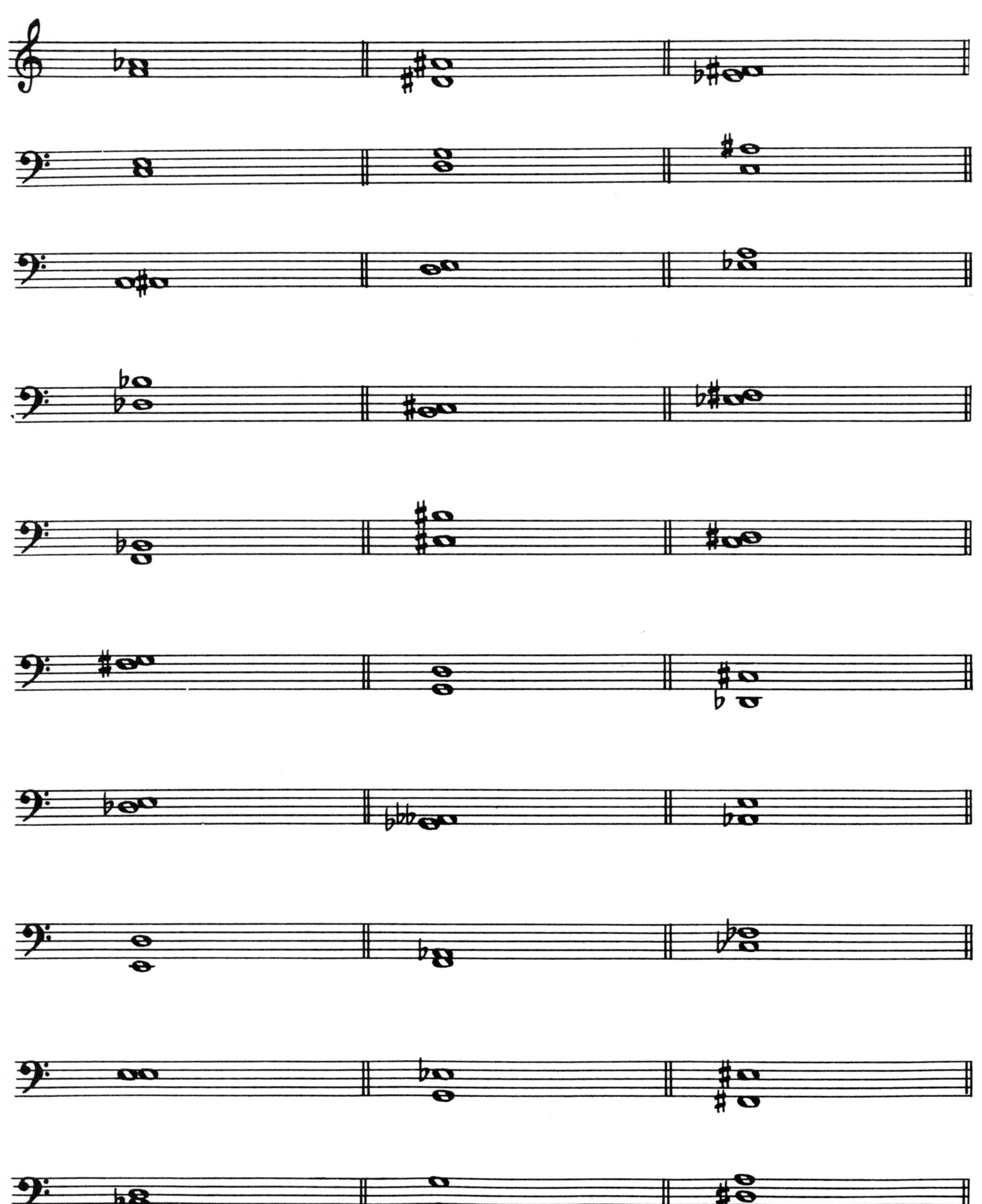

MUSIC PAPER for Dictation

Name ....   Date ....

SAMPLE TEST FOR LESSON 8: Intervals

1. Write on the staff the intervals called for (up from the given note):

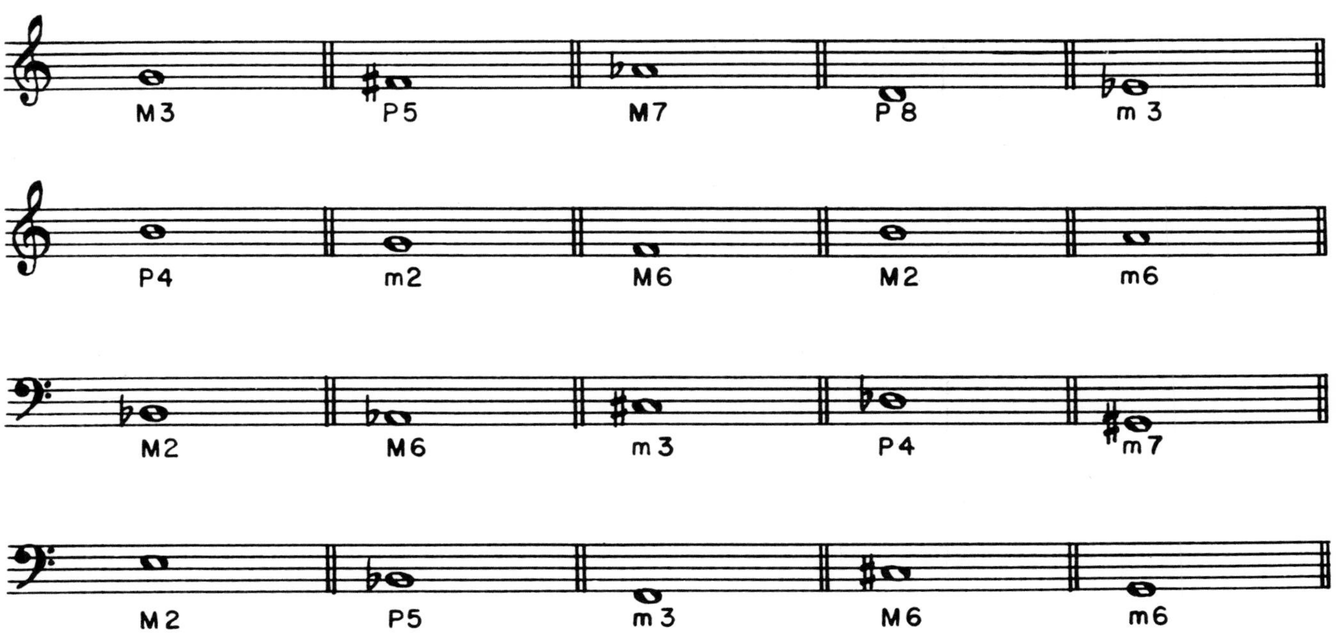

2. Name these intervals:

3. Name the following intervals, then invert and rename them:

4. Write the name of the intervals that the instructor dictates to you. (The instructor selects his own intervals for dictation.)

LESSON 9

The Identification of Melodic Intervals

In Lesson 8, the *harmonic* intervals were presented. A harmonic interval is the distance between two tones that are sounded simultaneously. This is the kind of interval found in chord construction.

In this lesson, the *melodic* interval will be studied. A melodic interval is the distance between two consecutive tones in a melody.

To identify a melodic interval, arrange the two tones in the form of a harmonic interval. In so doing, two things must be considered.

1. You must take into account the key signature of the melody, for the key signature designates that certain notes which may be contained in the interval are to be sharped or flatted. For example, if the two adjacent notes on the staff are A and C, you must be sure to look at the key signature before naming the interval to see if the notes are A and C, A and C♯, A♭ and C, or any other combination established by the key signature.
2. Place the lowest note on the staff, whether it is the first or second note of the melodic interval, as the bottom note of the harmonic interval. This note will then be the keynote of a major scale, from which you measure the interval to the higher note just as you did in the preceding lesson.

Using this method of rearrangement into harmonic form, we can name the intervals in the following melody:

The arrangement of the first three melodic intervals in harmonic form would be as follows:

1. In A♭ major there is an E♭; therefore this interval is a perfect fifth.
2. In E♭ major there is an F♮; this interval is a major second.
3. The lowest of these two notes on the staff is the D♭. Therefore it is placed on the bottom of the interval even though it appears as the second note of the interval in the melody. In D♭ major there is an F♮; this interval is a major third.

We can now proceed to name the remaining intervals in the melody:

4. For the next interval the lowest note on the staff is B♭. Therefore this interval reads from B♭ to D♭. In B♭ there is a D♮. The note given in the melody is D♭. B♭ to D♮ is a major third; therefore B♭ to D♭ is a minor third.
5. The lowest note on the staff of the next interval is G. Therefore the interval reads from G to B♭. In G major there is a B♮ which makes a major third. The note given in the melody is B♭; therefore the interval is a minor third.
6. In G major, G to A♮ is a major second; therefore this G to A♭ is a minor second.
7. In A♭ major there is a C♮; this interval is a major third.
8. In B♭ major there is a C♮; this interval is a major second.
9. In B♭ major there is an E♭; this interval is a perfect fourth.
10. In G major, G to E♮ is a major sixth; therefore this G to E♭ is a minor sixth.
11. In G major, G to A♮ is a major second; therefore this G to A♭ is a minor second.
12. In A♭ major there is a C♮; this interval is a major third.
13. In B♭ major there is a C♮; this interval is a major second.
14. Same as 13.
15. In C major there is a D♮ which makes a major second; therefore this C to D♭ is a minor second.
16. In G major there is a D♮ which makes a perfect fifth; therefore this G to D♭ is a diminished fifth.
17. In G major there is an A♮ which makes a major second; therefore this G to A♭ is a minor second.

The following exercises may be worked out in the same manner for further drill in naming intervals. Write the answers on the worksheet.

Name ....   Date ....

WORKSHEET FOR LESSON 9: Melodic Intervals

Write the answers to the four exercises in melodic intervals found on the previous page:

I. In E major, treble clef

1
2.
3.
4.
5.
6.
7.
8.
9.
10.
11.
12.
13.

II. In B♭ major, treble clef

1.
2.
3.
4.
5.
6.
7.
8.
9.
10.
11.
12.
13.

III. In D major, bass clef

1.
2.
3.
4.
5.
6.
7.
8.
9.
10.
11.
12.

IV. In G♭ major, bass clef

1.
2.
3.
4.
5.
6.
7.
8.
9.
10.
11.
12.
13.
14.
15.
16.
17.
18.
19.
20.
21.
22.

Name .... Date ....

SAMPLE TEST FOR LESSON 9: Melodic Intervals

1. Name the following melodic intervals:

2. Name these melodic intervals:

LESSON 10

Note Values and Rhythms

The next item of importance on the staff, after the clef sign and the key signature, is the *time signature* A time signature has two numbers, one placed above the other on the staff. (It is never written as a fraction.) The upper figure always tells how many beats there are in a measure, and the lower figure always tells what kind of note receives one beat.

NOTE VALUES

The *note values* are as follows:

𝅝 is a whole note. 𝅗𝅥 is a half note.

If the note is placed above the third line of the staff, the stem goes down on the left-hand side of the note head:

If the note is below the third line of the staff, the stem goes up on the right-hand side of the note head:

If the note is placed on the third line, the stem may go in either direction:

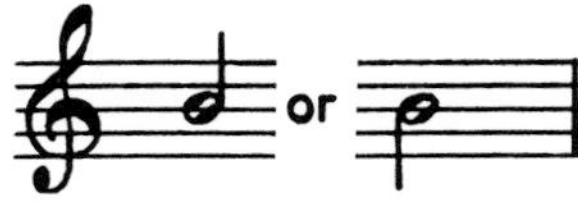

♩ is a quarter note.

♪ is an eighth note.

𝅘𝅥𝅯 is a sixteenth note.

𝅘𝅥𝅰 is a thirty-second note.

𝅘𝅥𝅱 is a sixty-fourth note.

REST VALUES

Each note value has a corresponding rest value.

𝄻 is a whole rest.

𝄼 is a half rest.

A homely illustration for differentiating between these two rests is: A gentleman always takes off his hat when meeting a lady (the whole rest represents the whole gentleman, since the top of the hat hangs down from the fourth line, like a hat tipped to a lady). A half a gentleman, on the other hand, leaves his hat on his head when he meets a lady (the half rest sits on top of the third line).

Examples:

whole rest

half rest

𝄽 is a quarter rest.

𝄾 is an eighth rest.

𝄿 is a sixteenth rest.

𝅀 is a thirty-second rest.

𝅁 is a sixty-fourth rest.

METER

Meter in music is a regular pulsation which creates a sensation of stress or accent followed by a period of relaxation or non-accent. There are three fundamental meters in music:

Duple:	accent 1	non-accent 2		
Triple:	accent 1	non-accent 2	non-accent 3	
Quadruple:	accent 1	non-accent 2	secondary 3	non-accent 4

How a conductor generally expresses these meters when conducting a composition is shown by the following diagrams:

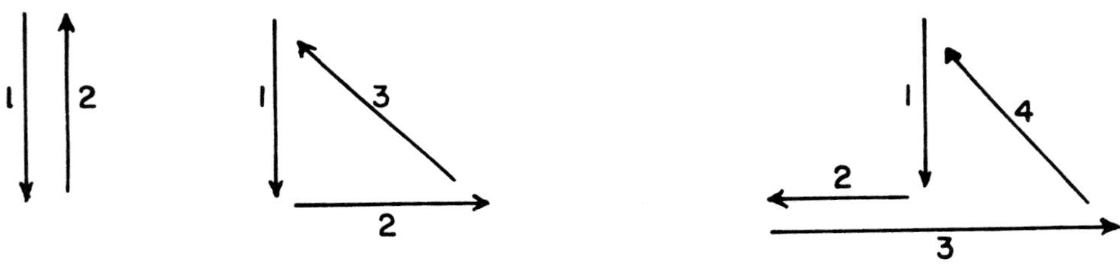

RHYTHM

Rhythm in music results from the arrangement of different note values within the meter. A bar is drawn across the staff to show the accented pulse of the meter. The distance between two bar lines is called a *measure*.

$\frac{2}{4}$ means $\frac{\text{two beats in a measure}}{\text{a quarter note receives one beat}}$

$\frac{3}{4}$ means $\frac{\text{three beats in a measure}}{\text{a quarter note receives one beat}}$

$\frac{4}{4}$ means $\frac{\text{four beats in a measure}}{\text{a quarter note receives one beat}}$

$\frac{2}{2}$ means $\frac{\text{two beats in a measure}}{\text{a half note receives one beat}}$

$\frac{3}{2}$ means $\frac{\text{three beats in a measure}}{\text{a half note receives one beat}}$

$\frac{5}{4}$ means $\frac{\text{five beats in a measure}}{\text{a quarter note receives one beat}}$

$\frac{3}{8}$ means $\frac{\text{three beats in a measure}}{\text{an eighth note receives one beat}}$

$\frac{6}{8}$ means $\frac{\text{six beats in a measure}}{\text{an eighth note receives one beat}}$

When the value of a note is greater than one beat, it is known as an *added beat:*

When the value of a note is less than one beat, it is known as a *divided beat:*

A *triplet* is a group of three equal-value notes sounded in the same amount of time as two would regularly be sounded.

Example:

without the triplet — with the triplet

Note that the numeral 3 is written between the note heads and the slur.

A *quintuplet* is a group of five equal-value notes sounded in the same amount of time as four would regularly be sounded.

Example:

without the quintuplet — with the quintuplet

A *dot* after a note receives one-half the value of the note it follows.

Example:

$\frac{4}{4}$ ♩. The quarter note equals 1 beat; the dot equals one-half the quarter note, or ½ beat; note plus dot equals 1½ beats.

$\frac{3}{4}$ 𝅗𝅥. The half note equals 2 beats; the dot equals one-half of two, or 1 beat; note plus dot equals 3 beats.

$\frac{6}{8}$ ♩. The quarter note equals 2 beats; the dot equals one-half of two, or 1 beat; note plus dot equals 3 beats.

Sometimes a *double dot* is used. The second dot equals one-half the value of the first dot.

Example:

$\frac{2}{4}$ ♩.. 𝅘𝅥𝅯 The quarter note equals 1 beat; the first dot equals ½ beat; the second dot equals half of the ½ beat, or ¼ beat.

The note plus dots then equals 1¾ beats.

Therefore a sixteenth note is needed to fill out the measure in $\frac{2}{4}$ time.

The $\frac{6}{8}$ time signature has its own special problem. In $\frac{6}{8}$ there are two accents which make the $\frac{6}{8}$ a duple meter and not a triple meter.

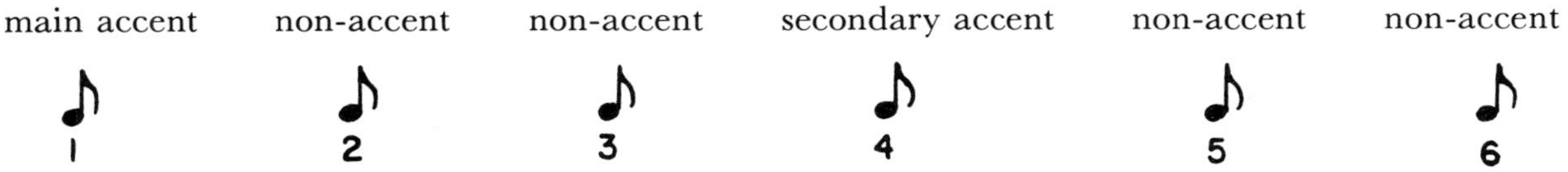

main accent	non-accent	non-accent	secondary accent	non-accent	non-accent
♪	♪	♪	♪	♪	♪
1	2	3	4	5	6

Therefore, $\frac{6}{8}$ ♩ ♩ ♩ is impossible, because the secondary accent on the fourth beat cannot be seen or heard in this rhythm. To obtain the same sound, but to give the appearance of $\frac{6}{8}$ this rhythm would be written:

♩ ♪⌣♪ ♩

The signatures $\frac{6}{8}$, $\frac{9}{8}$, and $\frac{12}{8}$ are considered compound time signatures; that is, they are simply enlargements of $\frac{2}{4}$, $\frac{3}{4}$, and $\frac{4}{4}$

The signature $\frac{9}{8}$ becomes a triple meter because of the accents:

main accent	non-accent	non-accent	secondary accent	non-accent	non-accent	secondary accent	non-accent	non-accent
♪	♪	♪	♪	♪	♪	♪	♪	♪
1	2	3	4	5	6	7	8	9

These are some possible $\frac{9}{8}$ rhythms:

The signature $\frac{12}{8}$ becomes a quadruple meter because of the accents:

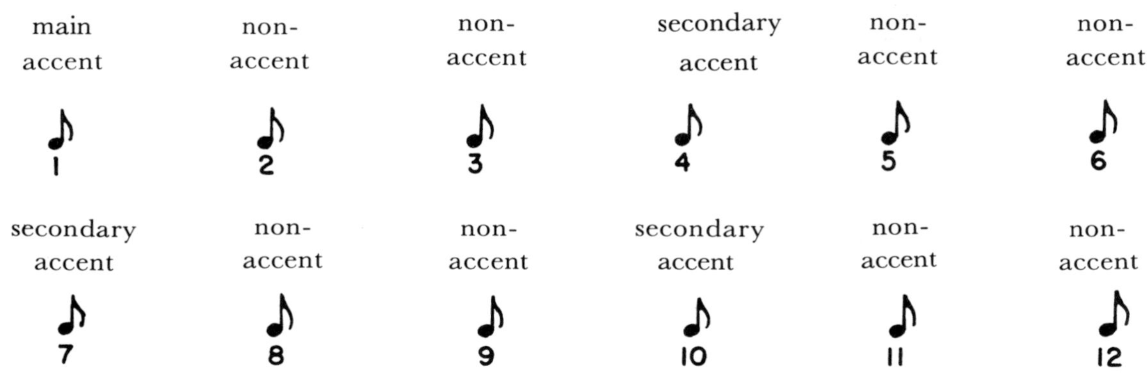

These are some possible $\frac{12}{8}$ rhythms:

DRILL ON RHYTHMIC PATTERNS

1. Clap the following rhythms, observing the accents by clapping more softly for the non-accented notes than for the accented notes.

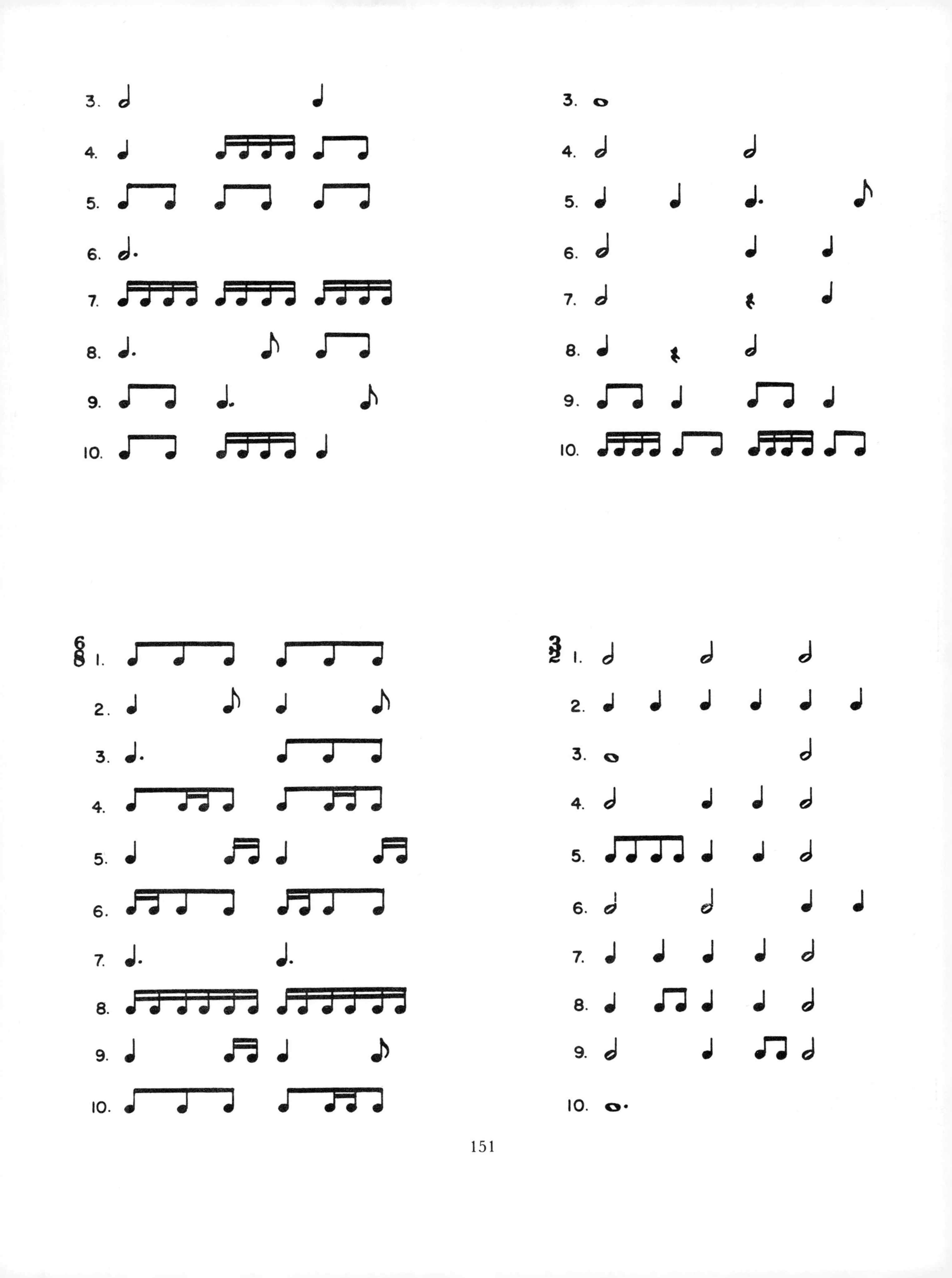

3.

4.

5.

6.

7.

8.

9.

10.

3.

4.

5.

6.

7.

8.

9.

10.

6/8

1.

2.

3.

4.

5.

6.

7.

8.

9.

10.

3/2

1.

2.

3.

4.

5.

6.

7.

8.

9.

10.

Four-measure phrases to be clapped:

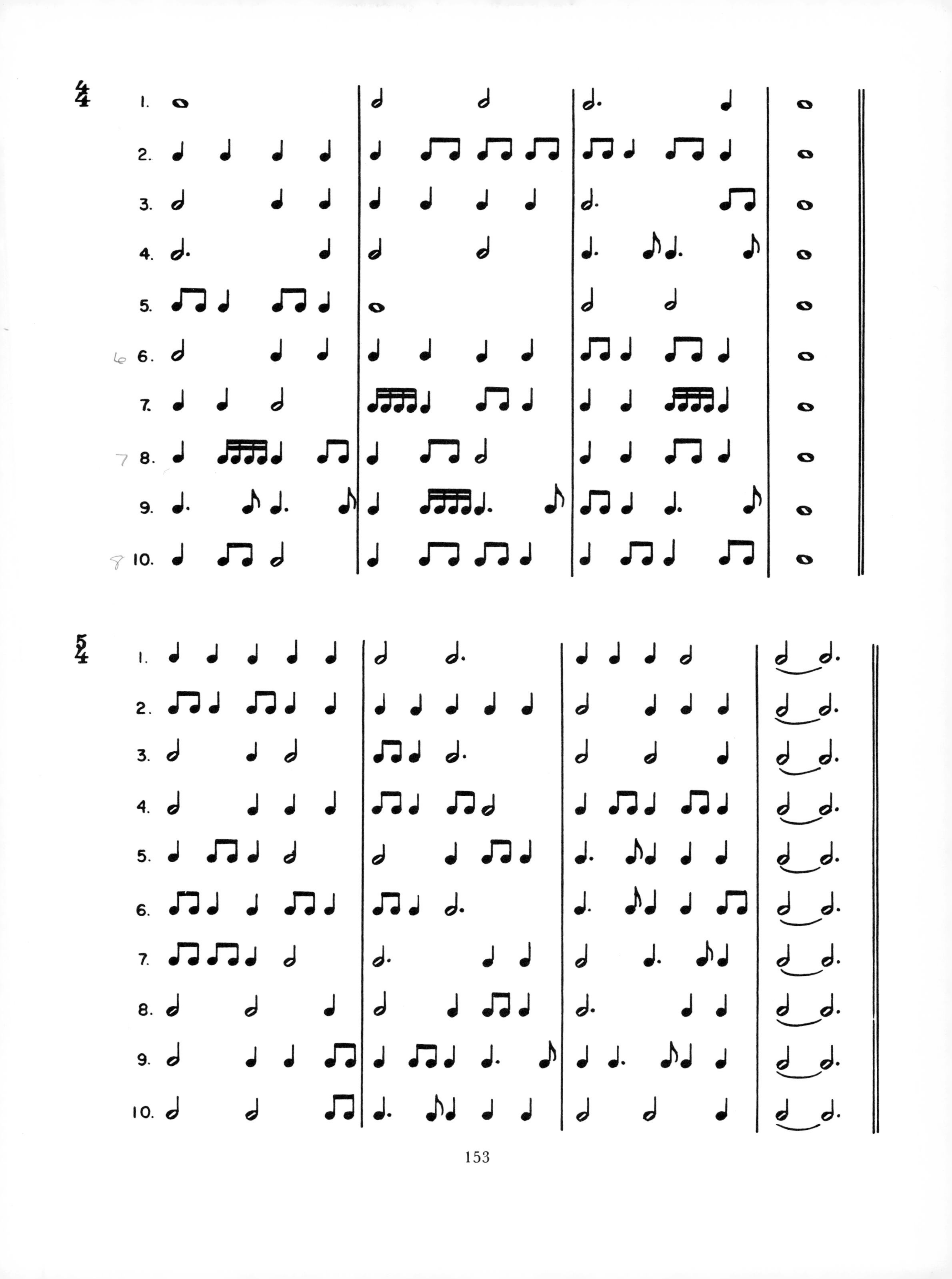

4/4

1.

2.

3.

4.

5.

6.

7.

8.

9.

10.

5/4

1.

2.

3.

4.

5.

6.

7.

8.

9.

10.

$\frac{2}{2}$

1.

2.

3.

4.

5.

6.

7.

8.

9.

10.

$\frac{3}{2}$

1.

2.

3.

4.

5.

6.

7.

8.

9.

10.

6/8

1.

2.

3.

4.

5.

6.

7.

8.

9.

10.

9/8

1.

2.

3.

4.

5.

6.

7.

8.

9.

10.

2. The instructor claps one of the rhythmic patterns shown above and the student writes out the pattern in note values (all on the same pitch).
3. The instructor claps a rhythm and the student writes the pattern in various time signatures.

   Example (original exercises clapped by the instructor):

Student rewrites as:

or as:

3. Sing the rhythmic patterns on pages 150 to 155 with syllables (if you are familiar with syllables) or with letters. Use one syllable or one letter for each pattern. Sing these in any key desired.

   Example:

3/4			
	do	or	C
	re	or	D
	mi	or	E
	fa	or	F
	so	or	G
	la	or	A
	ti	or	B
	do	or	C

These patterns can be sung up and down the scale, or the instructor may put them on the blackboard and, with the aid of a pointer, skip from one pattern to another as the class or individual student sings.

Name .... Date ....

WORKSHEET FOR LESSON 10: Note Values and Rhythms

1. In $\frac{2}{4}$ meter, write four measures, each with a different rhythm. Use A as the pitch.

2. In $\frac{3}{4}$ meter, write four measures, using a divided beat in each measure.

3. In $\frac{4}{4}$ meter, write four measures, using an added beat in each measure.

4. In $\frac{6}{8}$ meter, write four measures, each with a different rhythm.

5. Write a measure of $\frac{5}{4}$, using a triplet figure.

6. Write a measure of $\frac{2}{2}$, using a dot after a note.

7. Write two measures of $\frac{9}{8}$ meter, making each measure different.

8. Write two measures of $\frac{12}{8}$ meter, making each measure different.

9. What is the time signature of the following measure if a quarter note receives one beat?

10. Rewrite this measure in $\frac{3}{8}$ time and in $\frac{3}{2}$ time:

Name .... Date ....

SAMPLE TEST FOR LESSON 10: Note Values and Rhythms

1. Name the following rests:

2. Draw diagrams for the conductor's beat in $\frac{2}{4}$, $\frac{3}{4}$, and $\frac{4}{4}$ time.

3 Put in the *one* missing note in each of the following measures:

4. Write a measure of $\frac{4}{4}$, using both the triplet figure and the quintuplet.

5. Write one measure of $\frac{6}{8}$, using a dotted eighth note.

6. The instructor claps several rhythmic patterns and the student writes them below, with the proper note values. The instructor will announce the time signature, and will count one measure aloud to set the tempo, before clapping the pattern for dictation.

(a)

(b)

(c)

(d)

(e)

(f)

There are 20 points on this test; therefore each point equals 5 per cent.

LESSON 11

Sight-Singing Exercises

The following are sight-singing exercises with rhythmic patterns employing rest and active tones and scale passages previously studied. They are to be sung with numbers, letter names, and then with the neutral syllable *loo,* so that no prop will be necessary in order to read music.

GLOSSARY OF COMMON MUSICAL TERMS

(These are for use in musically interpreting the following melodies which have been chosen from standard musical literature.)

piano (***p***) —soft

forte (***f***) —loud

mezzo (***m***) —medium or half

mezzo piano (***mp***) —medium soft

mezzo forte (***mf***) —medium loud

fortissimo (***ff***) —very loud

pianissimo (***pp***) —very soft

sforzando (***sf***) —forced; one particular chord or note is to be played with force and emphasis

crescendo (cresc.) —to increase the amount of tone. This is often indicated by the following sign:

<

decrescendo (decresc.) —to decrease the amount of tone. This is often indicated by the following sign:

>

These two signs are often used together as follows:

< >

Moderato—in moderate time
Andante—easily moving in moderate time
Cantabile—in a singing expressive style
Allegro—quick and lively
Vivace—quite fast and animated
Presto—quickly and rapidly
Sempre—always
Con Brio—with brilliance

Con Spirito—with spirit and animation
Staccato—detached
Menuetto—in the style of a minuet, which is a slow dance in ¾ time.
, —a breath mark indicating the end of a phrase
⁀ —a phrase mark (generally meaning these notes are to be sung on one breath)
Largo—slowly
Adagio—slowly

MAJOR KEYS

Treble Clef

1. This song is known as "Twinkle, Twinkle, Little Star."

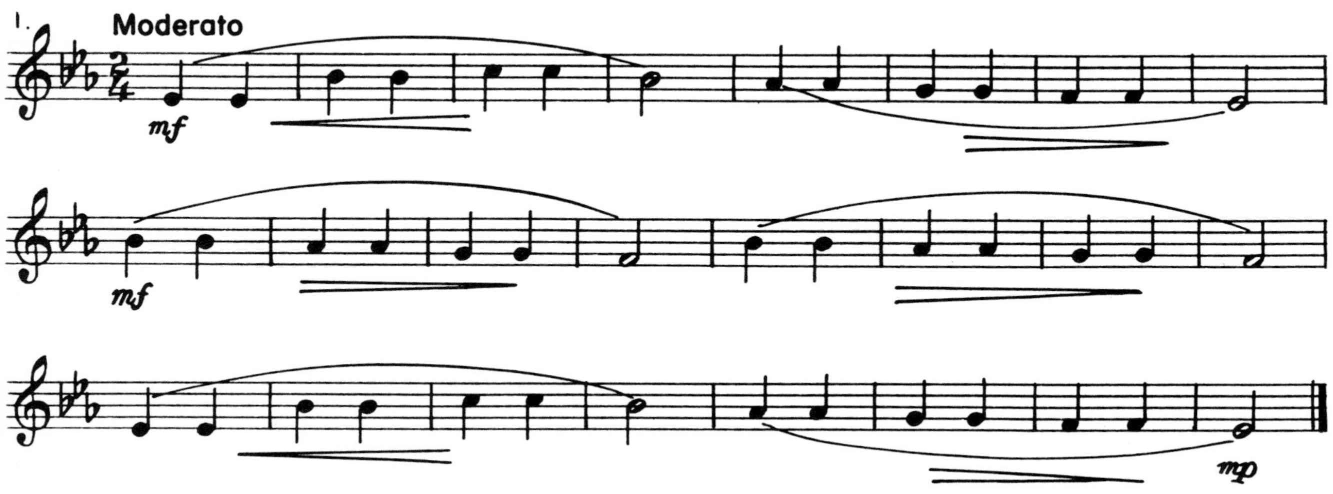

2. This melody is found in the second violin part of the second movement of Beethoven's Symphony No. 1 in C major, Op. 21. Ludwig van Beethoven was born in Bonn-on-the-Rhine in 1770 and died in Vienna in 1827. The symphony was composed in 1799-1800.

3. In the last movement of Beethoven's *First Symphony*, the first violins play this theme after the first five measures of introduction. The theme has been transposed from C major to A major for ease in singing.

4. In the trio of the third movement of Beethoven's Symphony No. 2 in D major, Op. 36, the violins play this melody (last 14 measures). It is first played by the oboe, at the beginning of the trio. The symphony was completed in 1802.

5. In his Symphony No. 3 in E♭ major, Op. 55, Beethoven uses this melody for the first violins (first 14 measures). The symphony, known as the *Eroica,* was composed in 1804, and originally was dedicated to Napoleon Bonaparte. Beethoven tore up the title page when he heard that Napoleon had proclaimed himself emperor.

6. This is theme 1 in the first movement of Beethoven's *First Symphony*. It is played by the fiirst violins.

7. In the last movement of Brahms's Symphony No. 1 in C minor, Op. 68, is found this lovely C major theme. The symphony was written in 1876. Johannes Brahms was born in Hamburg in 1833 and died in Vienna in 1897.

8. This is theme 1 of the first movement of Haydn's Symphony No. 103 in E♭ major. Here some of the notes have been lowered by an octave for easier singing. Theme is played by the first violins. Franz Joseph Haydn was born in Lower Austria in 1732 and died in Vienna in 1809. This symphony, often referred to as the *Drum-Roll Symphony,* was composed in 1795.

8. **Allegro con spirito**

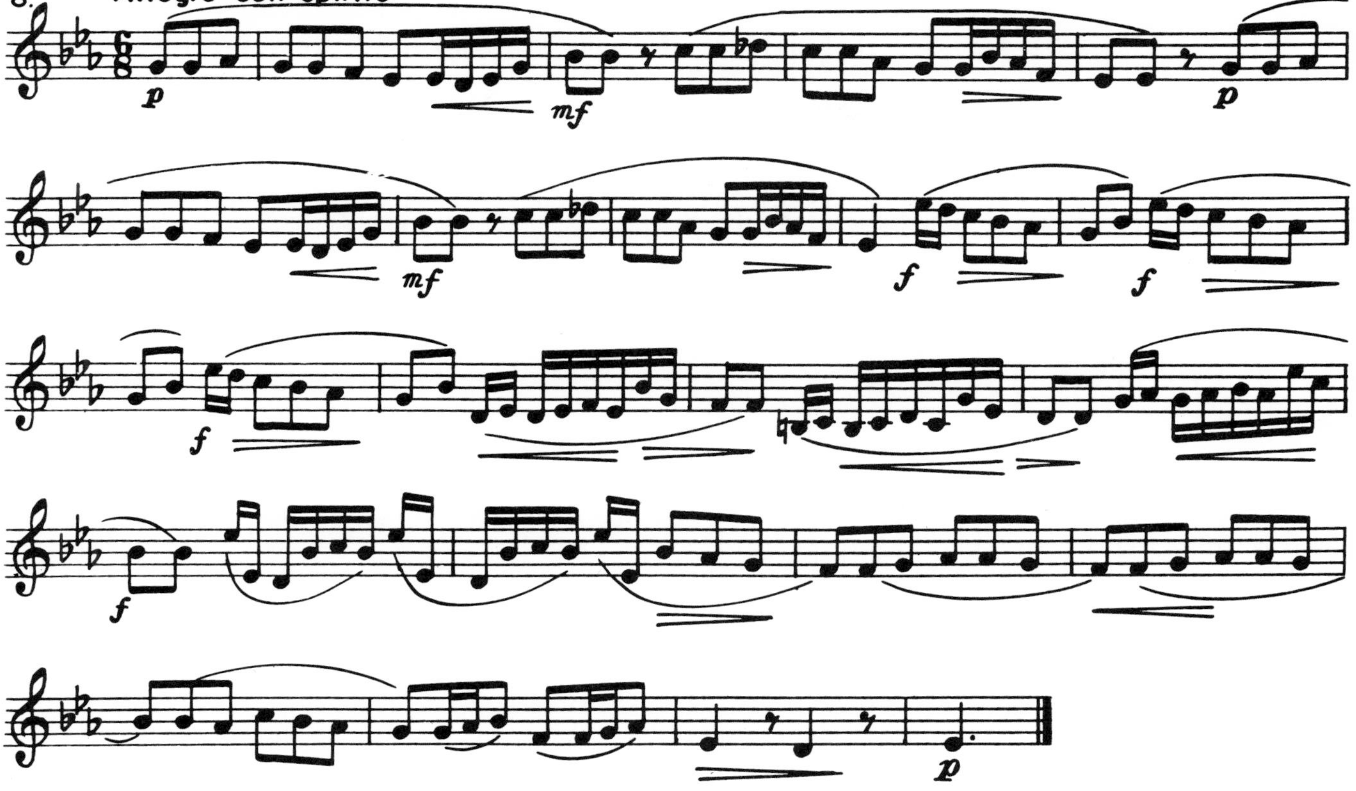

9. This melody is adapted from the first and second violin parts in the second movement of the same symphony. The first theme of this movement is in C minor; in contrast, in measure 28, this major section appears.

9. **Andante**

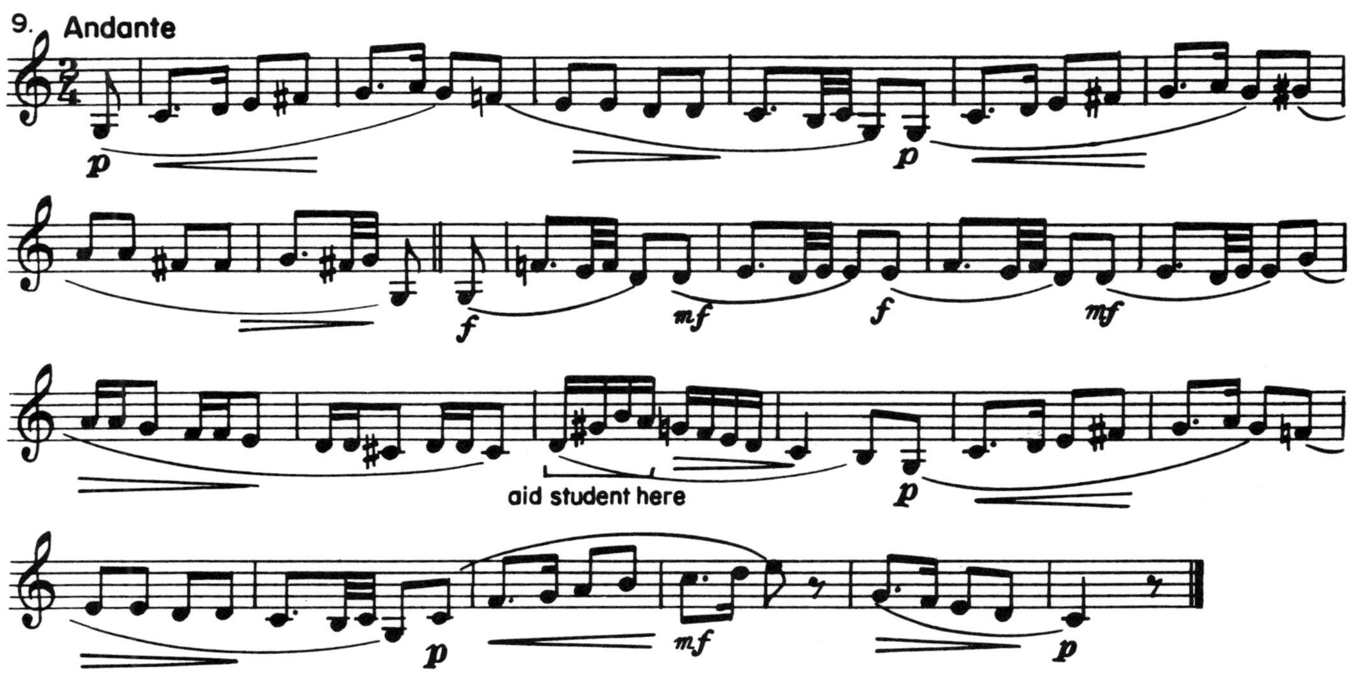

10. This melody is adapted from the first violin part of the menuetto movement (third) of the *Drum Roll Symphony*. The theme is introduced in the flute and first violin parts. Some of the theme has been changed here to suit it to the range of singing voices.

11. This is the theme of the trio in the third movement of Mozart's Symphony No. 35 in D major, K. 385, known as the *Haffner Symphony*. This is the first violin part of the trio. Wolfgang Amadeus Mozart was born in Salzburg in 1756 and died in Vienna in 1791.

12. Here is the second theme of the last movement of Mozart's *Haffner Symphony*. It is played by violins. Although the movement is in D major, this particular theme is in A major.

13. This is the first theme of the first movement of Schubert's Symphony No. 5 in B♭ major. Here the original score of the first violin part has been altered for ease in singing. Franz Schubert was born near Vienna in 1797 and died in Vienna in 1828. The symphony was written in 1816.

13. Allegro

7 5 R R

diminished 7th

14. This is the second theme of the first movement of the same symphony. The passage is taken from the end of the first movement, inasmuch as this key suits the singing voice better than when the theme is first introduced.

15. Also from the same symphony, this melody occurs in the first violin part of the trio in the third movement.

16. In the same Schubert symphony we find this opening theme in the last movement, played by the first violins. The last part of the melody has here been lowered an octave.

17. This melody is from the fourth number in a collection of piano pieces by Felix Mendelssohn-Bartholdy. This collection of pieces is best known as *Songs Without Words:* this particular number is called "Confidence." Felix Mendelssohn was born in Hamburg in 1809 and died in Leipzig in 1847.

18. This is the opening theme from a loure by J. S. Bach. A loure is a stately French dance of the early days. Johann Sebastian Bach, one of the very greatest of all composers, was born in Eisenach in 1685 and died in Leipzig in 1750.

19. This is the opening theme from a minuet by Boccherini. A minuet is a stately French dance, always in triple meter and slow in tempo. Boccherini, noted Italian composer and cellist, was born in Lucca in 1743 and died in Madrid in 1805.

20. This is a caprice (a fanciful and free style of composition) from the opera *Alceste*. Its composer, Christoph W. von Gluck, was born in Weidenwang, Austria, in 1714 and died in Vienna in 1787.

Bass Clef

1. Here is the first theme of the first movement of Beethoven's Symphony No. 2 in D major, Op. 36, which is first introduced in the cello and viola parts.

1. Allegro con brio

2. This is the third theme of the first movement of Beethoven's *Second Symphony*. It has been adapted from the bassoon part that first introduces the theme. Although the symphony is written in D major, this particular theme is in A major, modulating to the key of E major at the close of this melody.

2. Allegro

3. The following melody is made up of the first and second themes of the second movement of Beethoven's *Second Symphony*. The themes are first played by the first violins and then answered by the woodwinds.

3. Slowly

4. The first clarinet part of Brahms's Symphony No. 3 in F major, Op. 90, contains this first theme of the second movement.

5. The first violins play this first theme of the first movement of Haydn's Symphony No. 104 in D major *(London Symphony)*. The symphony was written about 1795.

6. This is the first theme from the last movement of Haydn's *London Symphony*. The first violins play this theme.

7. This is "Gavotte No. 2" from the English Suite No. 3 in G minor by Bach. A gavotte is a French dance in duple meter.

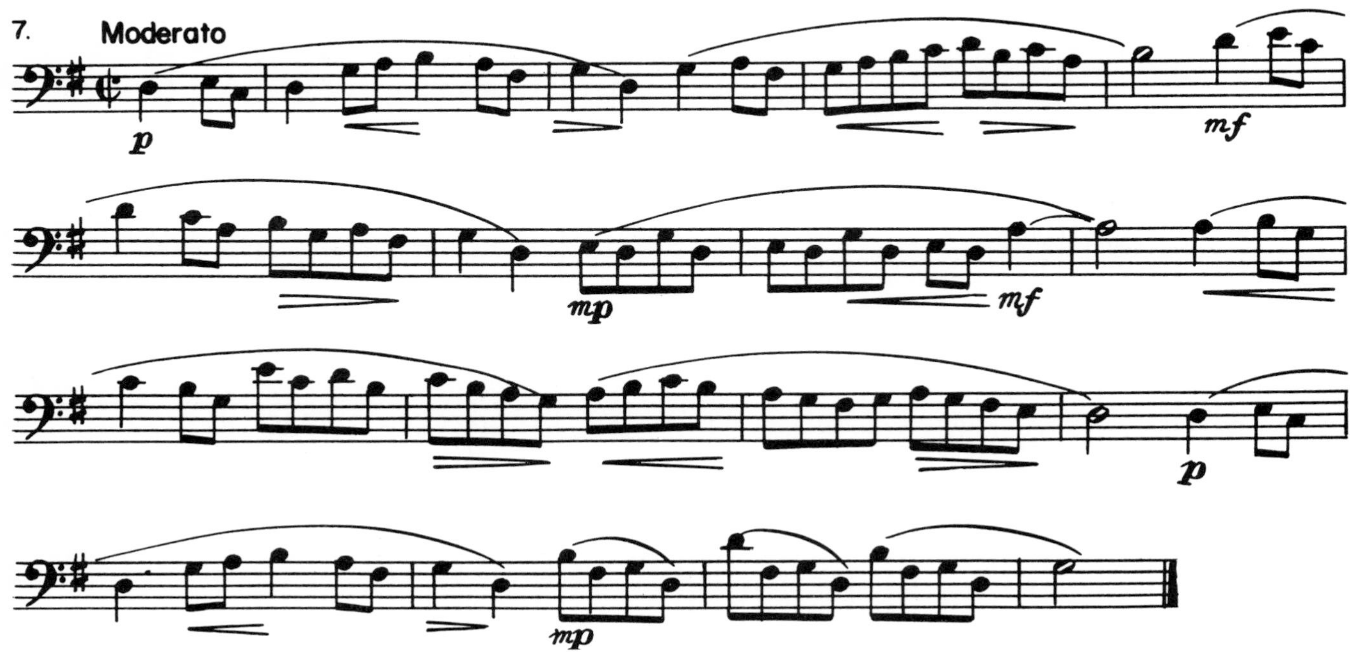

8. The oboe and the first violin introduce this second theme from the first movement of Mozart's Symphony No. 36 in C major, K. 425.

9. In the same symphony, the first violins play this first theme of the second movement. Some of the note values have been changed for singing.

10. Cellos play this second theme from the first movement of Schubert's Symphony No. 8 in B minor *(Unfinished Symphony)*. This particular theme is in G major.

11. This is No. 9 in Mendelssohn's *Songs Without Words*.

12. Here is the main theme of the last movement of Beethoven's *Third Symphony (Eroica)*. The theme has been adapted from the first violin and oboe parts.

13. Haydn's Symphony No. 101 in D major *(Clock Symphony)* has this first theme in the first movement. It is found in the first violin part.

14. This is the theme of the second movement of Haydn's *Clock Symphony*, adapted from the first violin part.

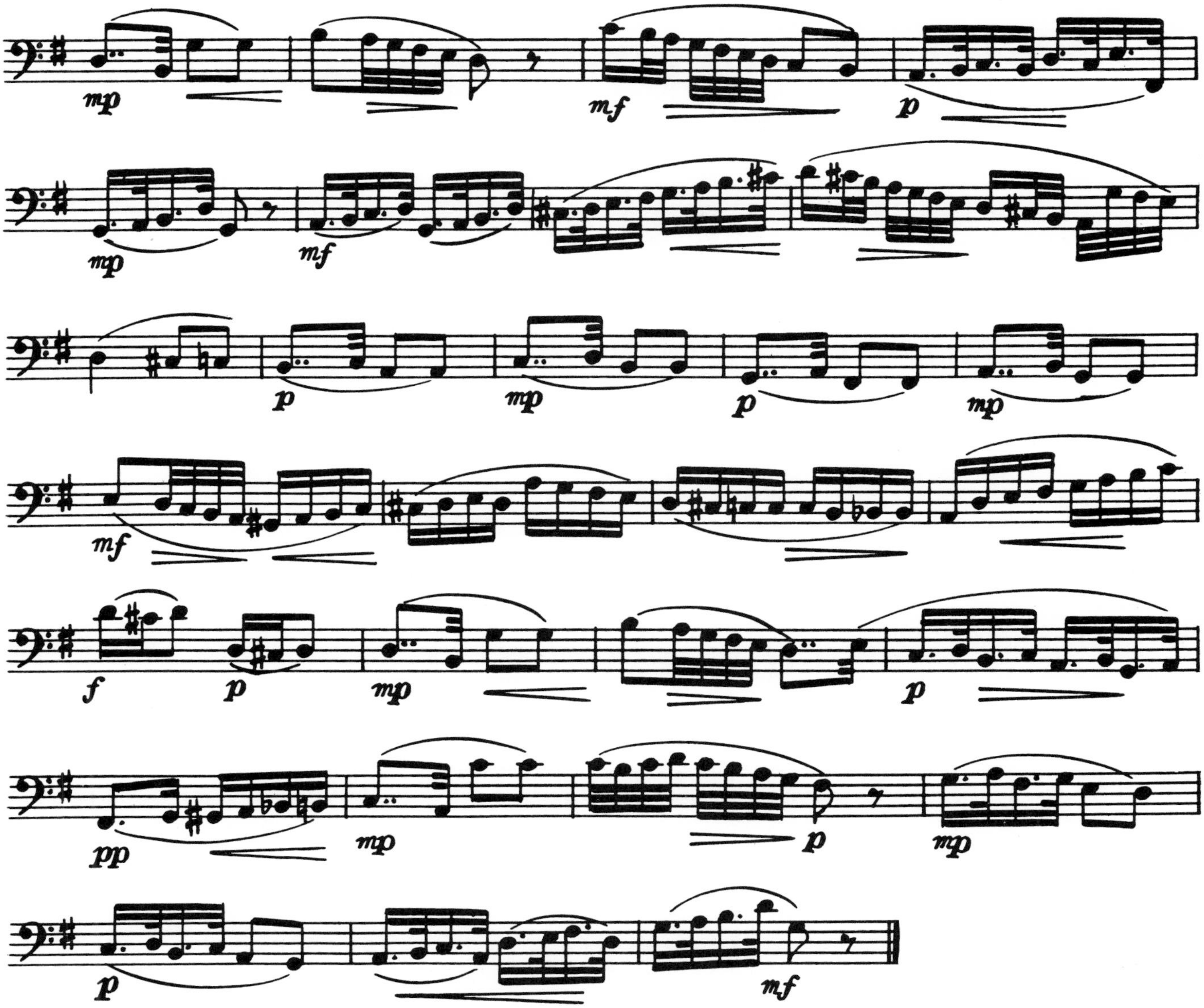

15. Here is the first theme, third movement, of the *Clock Symphony,* adapted from the first violin part. Starting in D major, the theme modulates to the key of A major.

15. **Moderato**

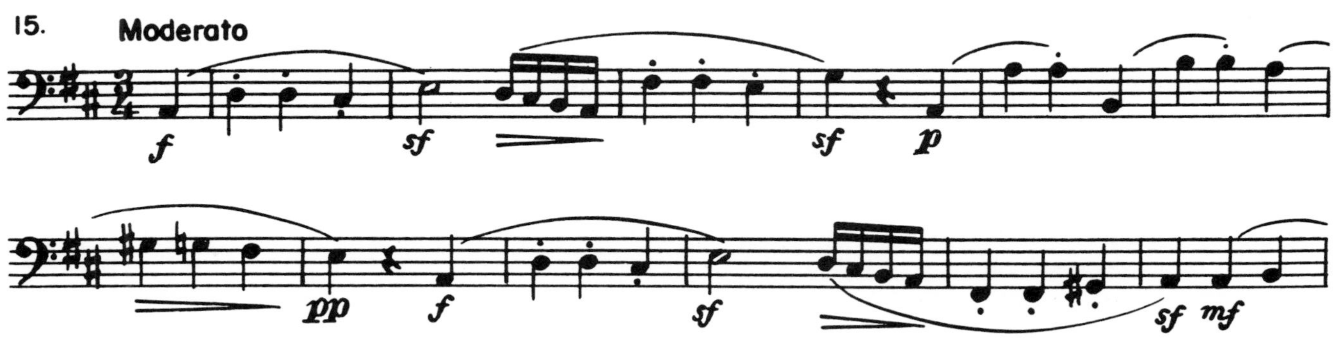

16. The slow movement of Haydn's Symphony No. 88 in G major contains this theme in the oboe and first violin parts. The tempo is largo in the score, but for singing, a moderato tempo is better.

16. **Moderato**

17. This is the theme of the rondo (last movement) of Haydn's Symphony No. 94 in G major *(Surprise Symphony)*. A rondo is any piece of music in which the first theme regularly reappears after the introduction of each new theme. This is the first violin part.

17.

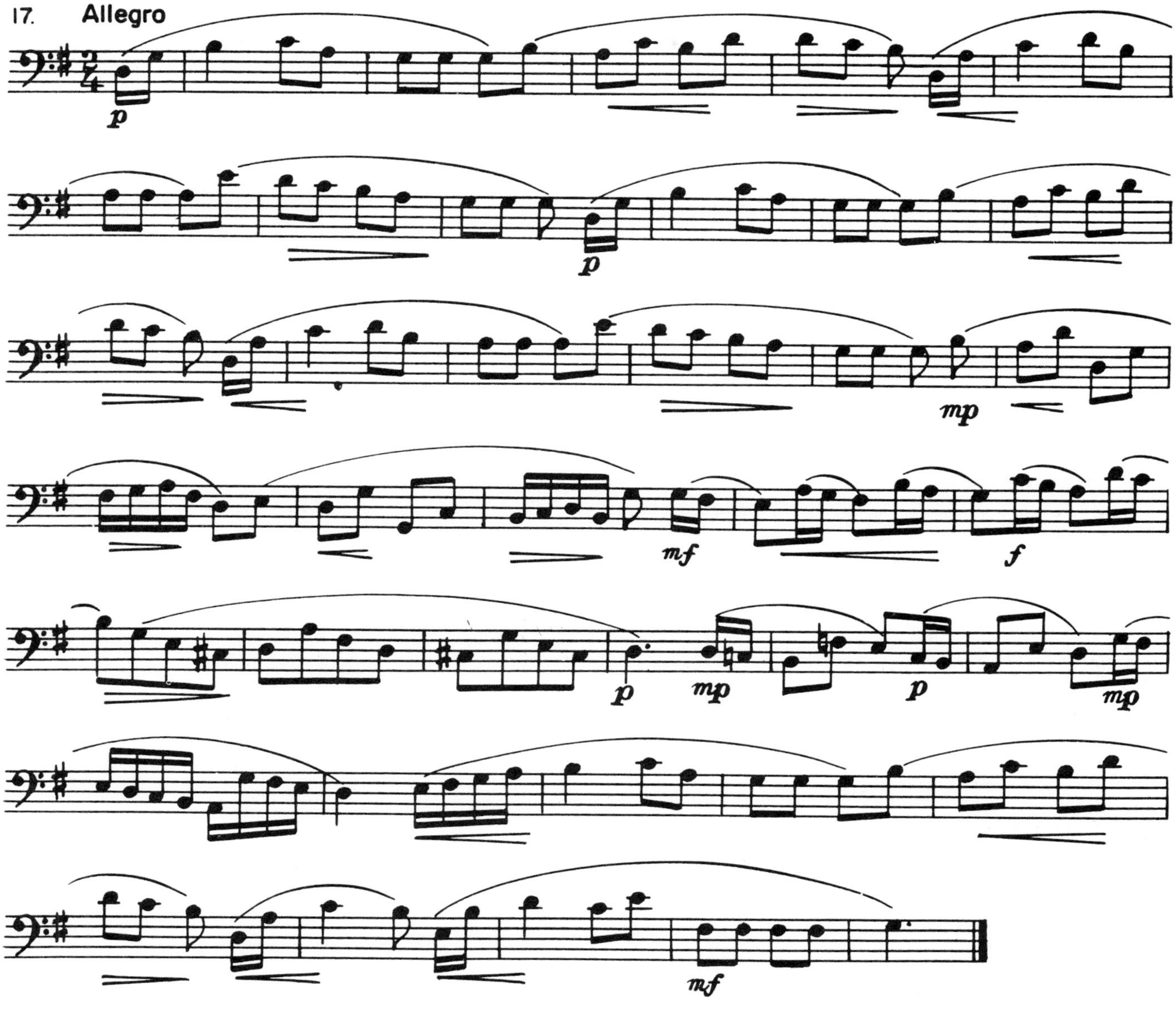
Allegro
p
p
mp
mf
f
p
mp
p
mp
mf

18. The Belgian composer F. J. Gossec (1734-1829) wrote this gavotte.

18.

Allegro
p
mp

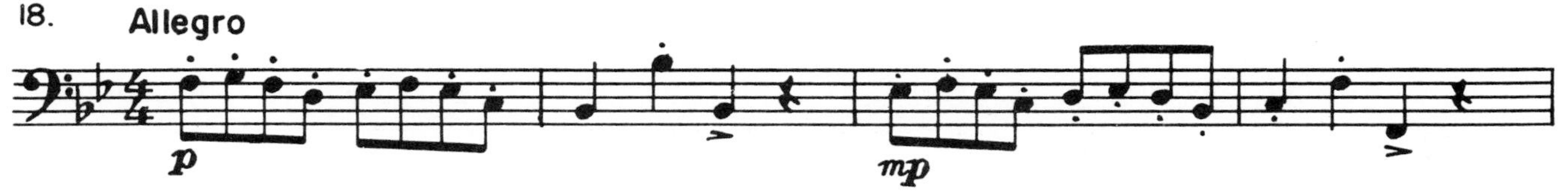

19. This is a bourrée by George Frederick Handel. A bourrée is an old French dance of very rapid and hearty character, usually in duple time. Handel was born at Halle in 1685 and died in London in 1759.

19. **Allegro**

20. This is a melody taken from the opera *Orpheus* by Christoph W. von Gluck. On the music, notice the *D.C. al Fine.* D. stands for the Italian word *da*, meaning "to"; the C stands for *capa*, "the head"; *Fine* means "finish." Therefore *D.C. al Fine* means go to the beginning and repeat to the end.

Baritone Clef

For best results in gaining facility in reading the lesser-known clefs, the student is advised to sing the letter names of the pitches.

1. This is a sarabande by George Frederick Handel. A sarabande is an old dance in triple measure. The lengthened second note of the measure lends majesty to the dance.

2. This is a gavotte by the French composer Lully (1639-1687), who was especially noted for his operas. Although considered a French composer, Lully was born in Italy.

3. Mozart wrote a number of minuets, a dance always in triple meter. One of his best-known minuets is this one from a divertimento (a series of airs and dances introduced between the acts or at the conclusion of an opera).

3. Moderato

Fine

D.C. al Fine

4. This charming serenade by Haydn is taken from the String Quartet Op. 3, No. 5

4. Andante

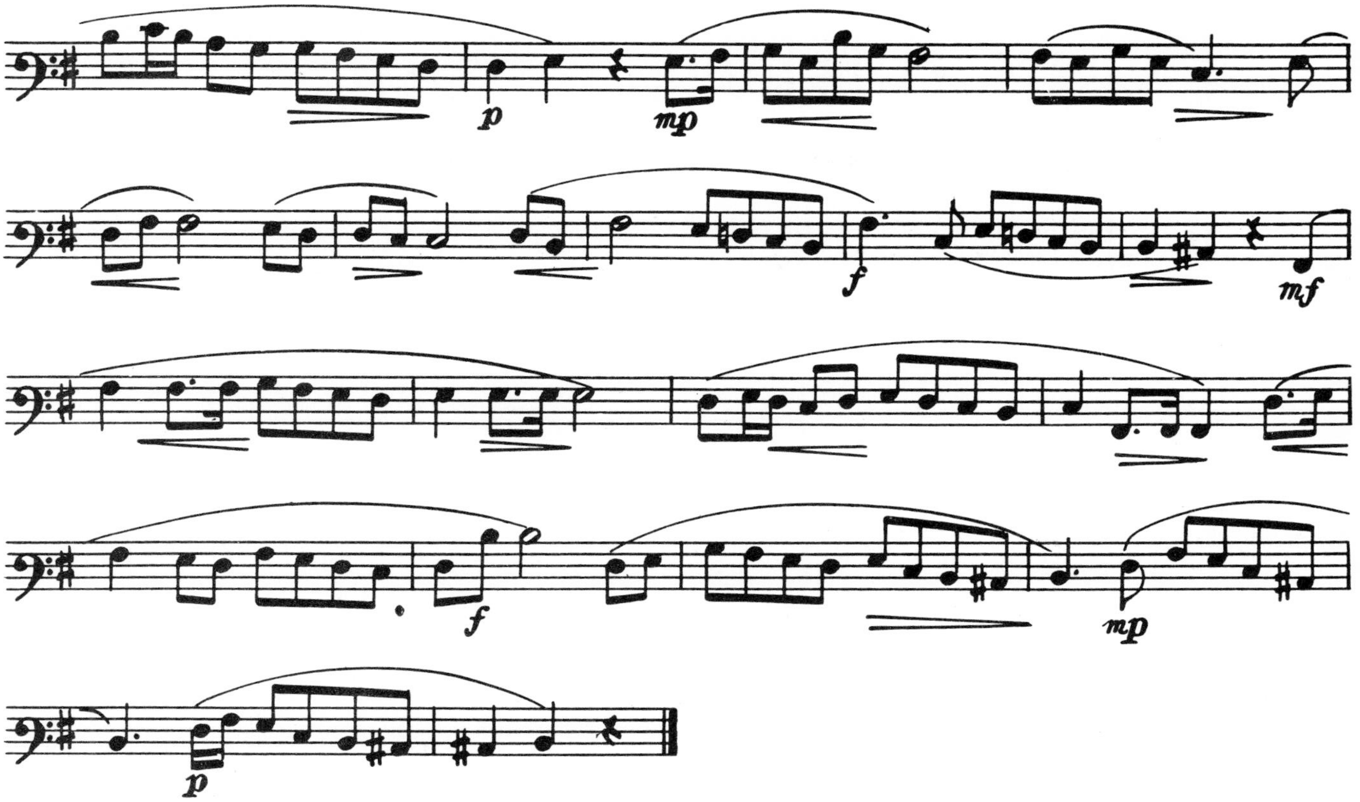

5. Here is Beethoven's famous Minuet in G. The range of Beethoven's genius was not confined to monumental works such as his Ninth Symphony.

5. **Menuetto**

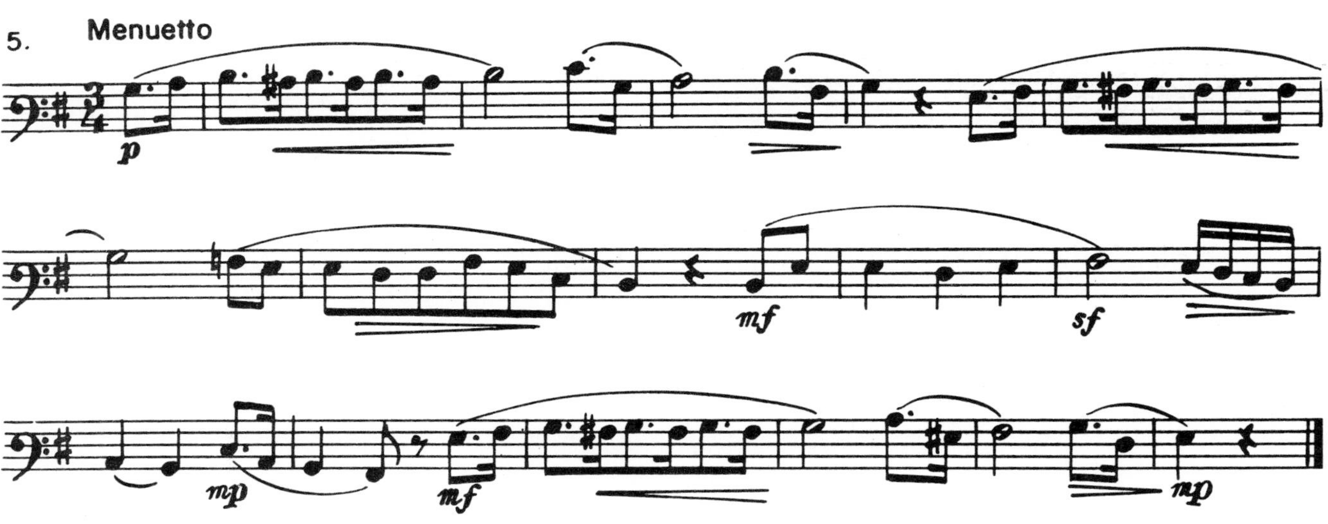

6. This is the trio (a contrasting movement) from the "Marche Militaire" by Franz Schubert. Originally written as a piano duet, this composition was later transcribed for the full orchestra. The march was dedicated to the Imperial Grenadiers, the emperor's bodyguard.

7. Robert Schumann's *Album for the Young,* Op. 68, contains this melody. It is No. 28, sometimes called "Remembrance." Schumann's wife, Clara, was a very well-known pianist.

8. The "Spinning Song," from Mendelssohn's *Songs Without Words,* reproduces in music the characteristic whirr of a spinning wheel.

9. From the *Midsummer Night's Dream* by Mendelssohn comes this wedding march, frequently played as the recessional at church weddings today.

9. Allegro

10. One of the loveliest melodies Robert Schumann ever wrote is this charming "Evening Song" (Op. 124).

Soprano Clef

1. The dignified "War March of the Priests" was composed by Mendelssohn for the play *Athalia.* It depicts the rejoicing of the Jews when their high priest overcame the wicked Queen Athalia after seven long years of terror.

2. This "Evening Song" is No. 4 in Robert Schumann's *Night Pieces,* Op. 23.

3. This is the first of a series of fifteen waltzes (Op. 39) written by Brahms. The dots above the notes indicate that they are to be sung staccato. A waltz is in triple meter. It has a swinging rhythm, with the accent on the first beat.

4. This is the second waltz in Brahms's Op. 39.

5. This is the eighth waltz in Brahms's Op. 39.

6. Here is the famous A♭ major waltz by Brahms, No. 15 in Op. 39.

6. Adagio

7. This is one of Handel's best-known compositions. Its name, "Largo," indicates the tempo of the work. Although Handel wrote forty operas, none is performed today. "Largo" was sung at the beginning of the first act of *Xerxes,* in praise of the sycamore tree whose branches shaded the hero of the opera. The music is so majestic and inspirational that it is now used as religious music, and sacred words have been added to the melody.

7. Largo

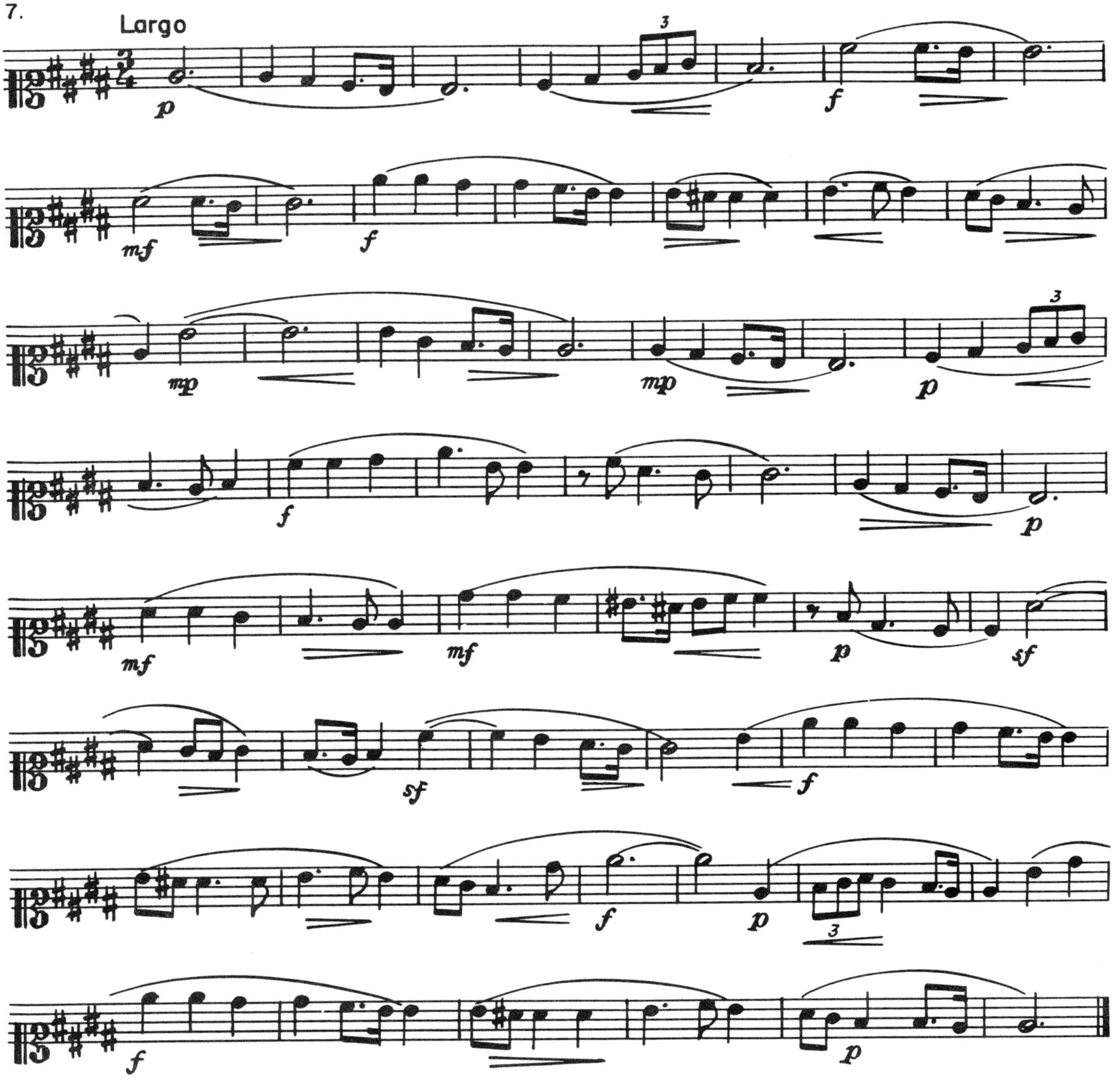

8. One of the most famous melodies ever written is Franz Schubert's "Ave Maria," inspired by the "Hymn to the Virgin" in Canto III of Scott's *The Lady of the Lake*.

8. Adagio

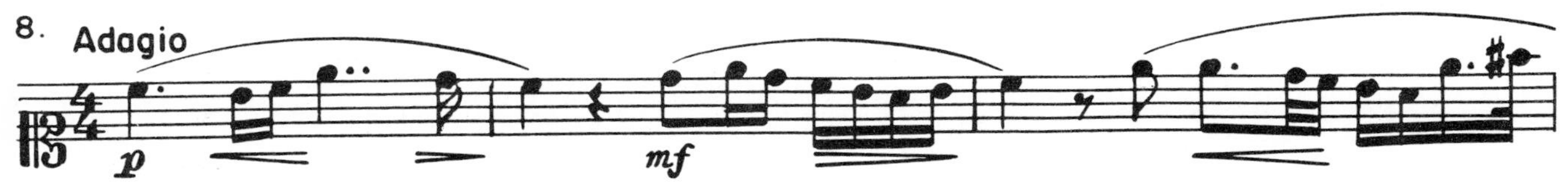

9. This is the "Dead March" from Handel's first oratorio, *Saul.* Although a funeral march, this is not excessively sombre, for it is written in a major key. An oratorio is a musical drama based on scriptural narrative. Unlike opera, it is performed without the aid of scenery or action.

9.

Largo

10. Felix Mendelssohn wrote a beautiful contralto solo in his oratorio *St. Paul.* The aria is called "But the Lord Is Mindful of His Own."

10. Andante

Mezzo-Soprano Clef

1. Chopin's "Funeral March," the second movement of his Sonata No. 2 in B♭ minor, Op. 35, reflects the composer's grief over the oppression of the people of his native Poland. In the middle of the composition there is inserted this very tender melody—the trio—in the major key which contrasts to the sadness of the minor key used elsewhere in the march. Frederic Chopin was born near Warsaw in 1810 and died in Paris in 1849.

2. "The Heavens Declare the Glory of God" is one of Beethoven's outstanding songs. Today it is generally performed by a large chorus.

2. **Broadly**

3. In the oratorio *The Creation,* by Franz Joseph Haydn, is found this inspiring chorus, "The Heavens Are Telling the Glory of God."

3. Allegro

4. This is a charming minuet from Mozart's opera *Don Juan*. It occurs at the end of the first act, where the scene is a ballroom.

5. This is music played between the acts (entr'acte) of Schubert's opera *Rosamunde*. Although the opera was a failure, this music has remained popular throughout the years.

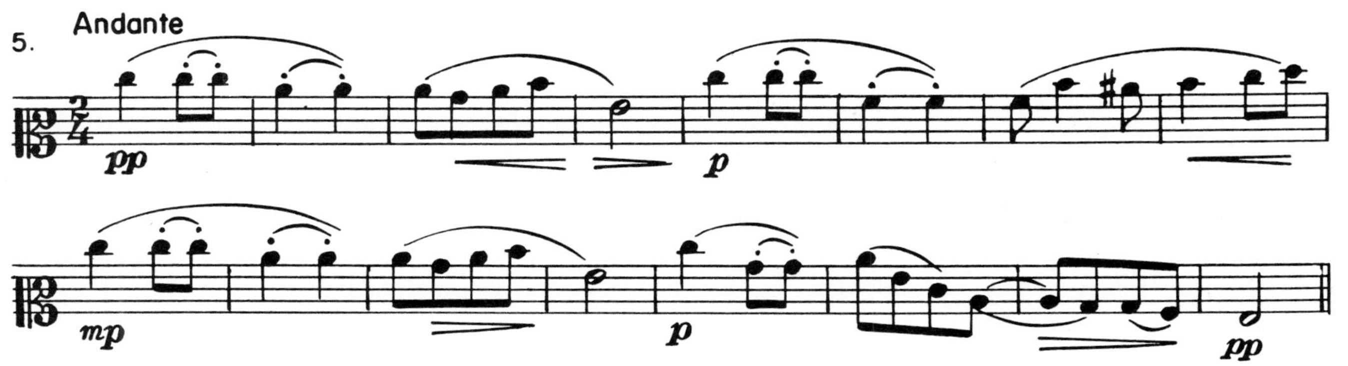

6. This composition by Carl Maria von Weber is called "The Hunter." Von Weber (1786-1826) was a German composer best known for his opera *Der Freischutz* (The Free Shooter).

6. Adagio

7. The French composer Edouard Batiste (1820-1876) used this theme, called "The Pilgrim's Song of Hope," for a set of variations.

7. Andante

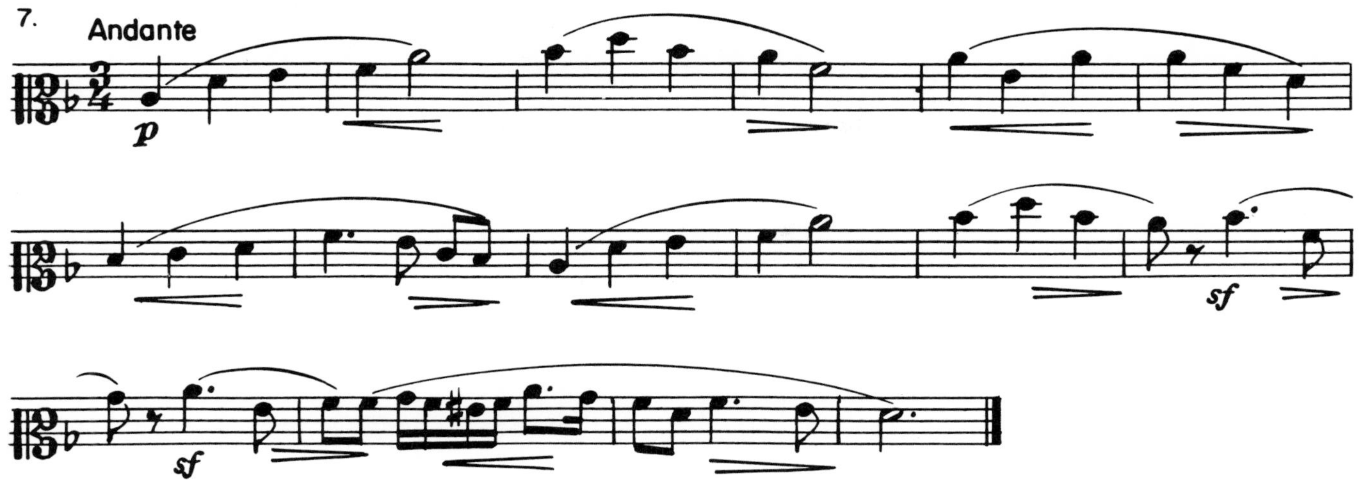

8. Here is the theme of the "Grand March" from the opera *Norma* by the noted Italian opera composer Vincenzo Bellini (1801-1835).

8. March Time

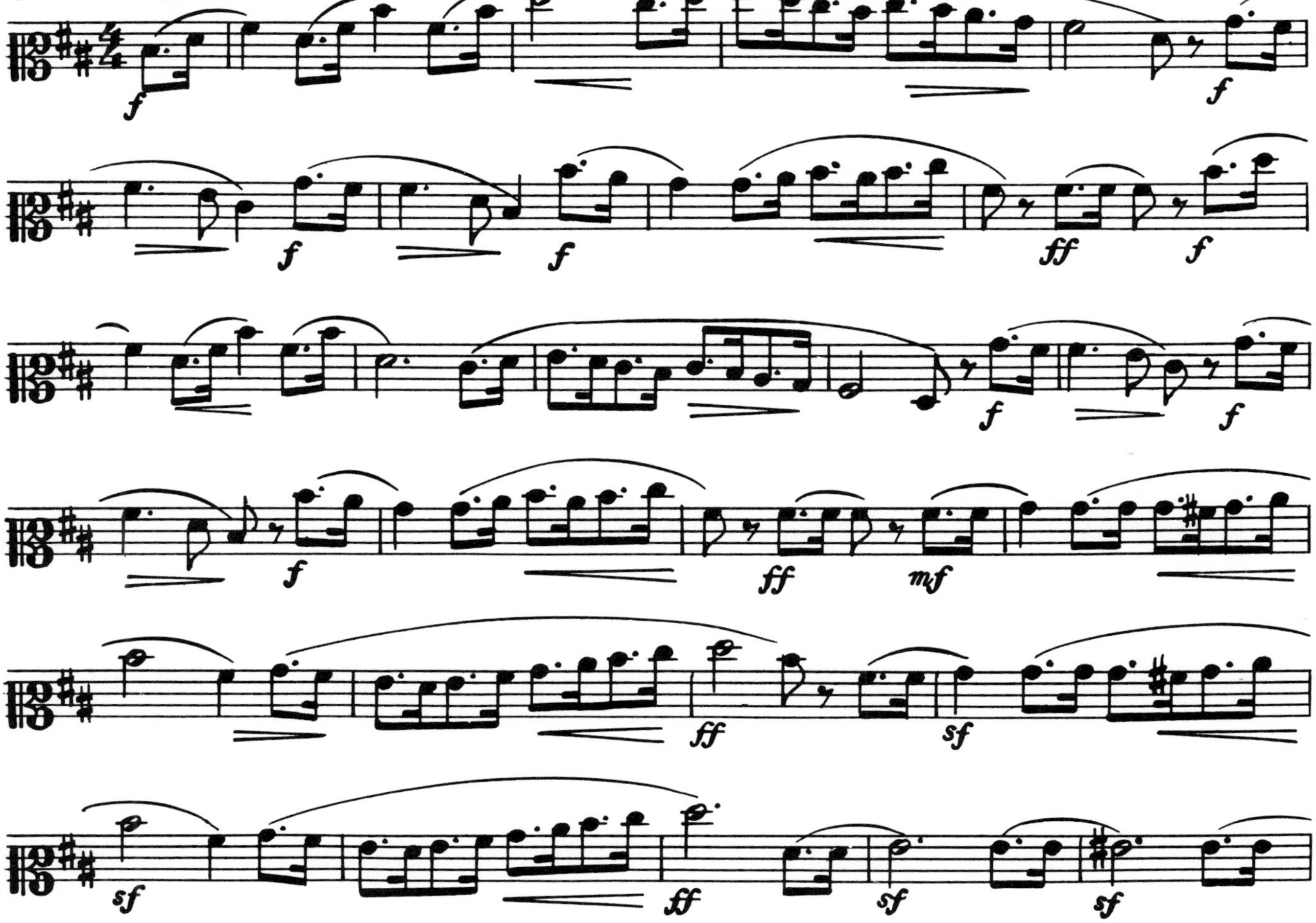

9. This is the last part of the nocturne (a night piece) from *Petite Suite* by the Russian composer Alexander Borodin (1834-1887).

10. Chopin was very fond of the mazurka, a lively Polish dance in triple meter, and he wrote many sets of these dances. This is from Op. 7, No. 1. Written in B♭ major, it has here been transposed to E♭ major for easier singing.

Alto Clef

1. This is the "Minute Waltz" by Frederic Chopin. It probably received its name because it can be played in about one minute. It reportedly was composed after Chopin had watched his dog whirling madly around in an effort to catch his own tail. Chopin was as fond of the waltz as he was of the mazurka, and he wrote many sets of waltzes.

1.

Presto

2. Chopin, sometimes called the "Poet of the Piano," shows his great capacity for writing a beautiful melody in this nocturne, originally written in E♭ major. Chopin wrote nineteen compositions in this form.

2.

Andante

3. One of the best-known sextettes (compostions for six performers) is this one from the opera *Lucia di Lammermoor.* Its composer, Gaetano Donizetti, was born in Bergamo in 1797 and died there in 1848. The sextette is one of the finest concerted numbers to be found in any opera.

4. John Field is probably remembered only for this one composition, *Nocturne*, a form of music he created. Chopin owes much to the composer who paved the way for writing in a lyric style. Field was born in Dublin in 1782 and died in Moscow in 1837.

5. This is the "Coronation March" from Giacomo Meyerbeer's opera *Le Prophete*. The music is so stately and dignified that it is often used for commencement exercises in our schools. Meyerbeer was born in Berlin in 1791 and died in Paris in 1864.

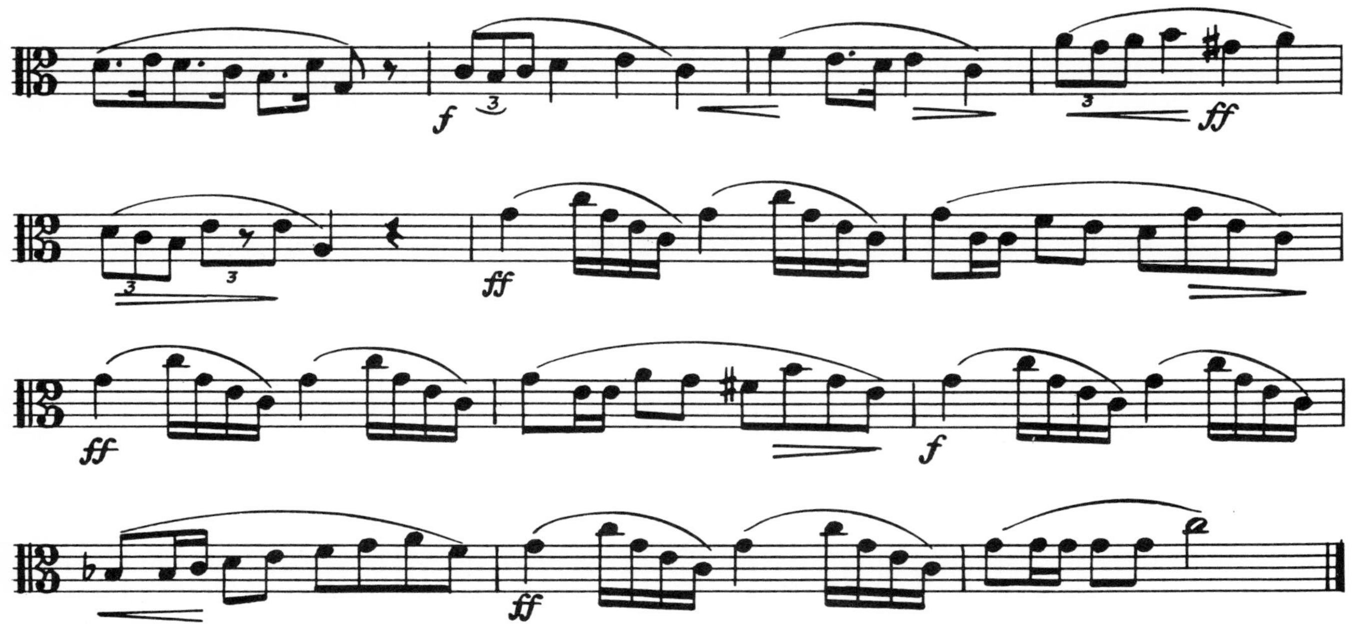

6. This meditation, called "The Dying Poet," is one of ninety piano pieces composed by Louis Gottschalk, noted pianist and composer of his day. Gottschalk was born in New Orleans in 1829 and died in Rio de Janeiro in 1869.

7. Perhaps the most thrilling choral music ever written is that of the "Hallelujah Chorus" from Handel's oratorio *The Messiah*.

7. **Allegro**

f *f* *f*

f *f* *f*

p *f*

p *f*

8. Miksa Hauser, a Hungarian composer, was born in 1822 and died in 1887. This "Cradle Song" is his most notable composition.

9. This *Gypsy Rondo* by Haydn is indicative of the happy mood of most of his music.

9. Presto

Fine

D.C. al Fine

10. Stephen Heller (1814-1888), Hungarian pianist and composer, is best known for his "Tarentelle." A tarentelle is a wild Italian dance in 6/8 time.

Tenor Clef

1. One of the most dearly loved works of Johann Sebastian Bach is his chorale prelude "Jesu, Joy of Man's Desiring," from Cantata No. 147. The melody appears against an elaborate instrumental background. This excerpt has been arranged to show both part of the chorale (not the triplet figures) and the instrumental accompaniment (the triplet figures).

1.

Andante

2. Adolf von Henselt (1814-1889), Bavarian pianist and composer, wrote a number of very difficult study pieces called "etudes." This etude is "La Gondola."

2. Allegro

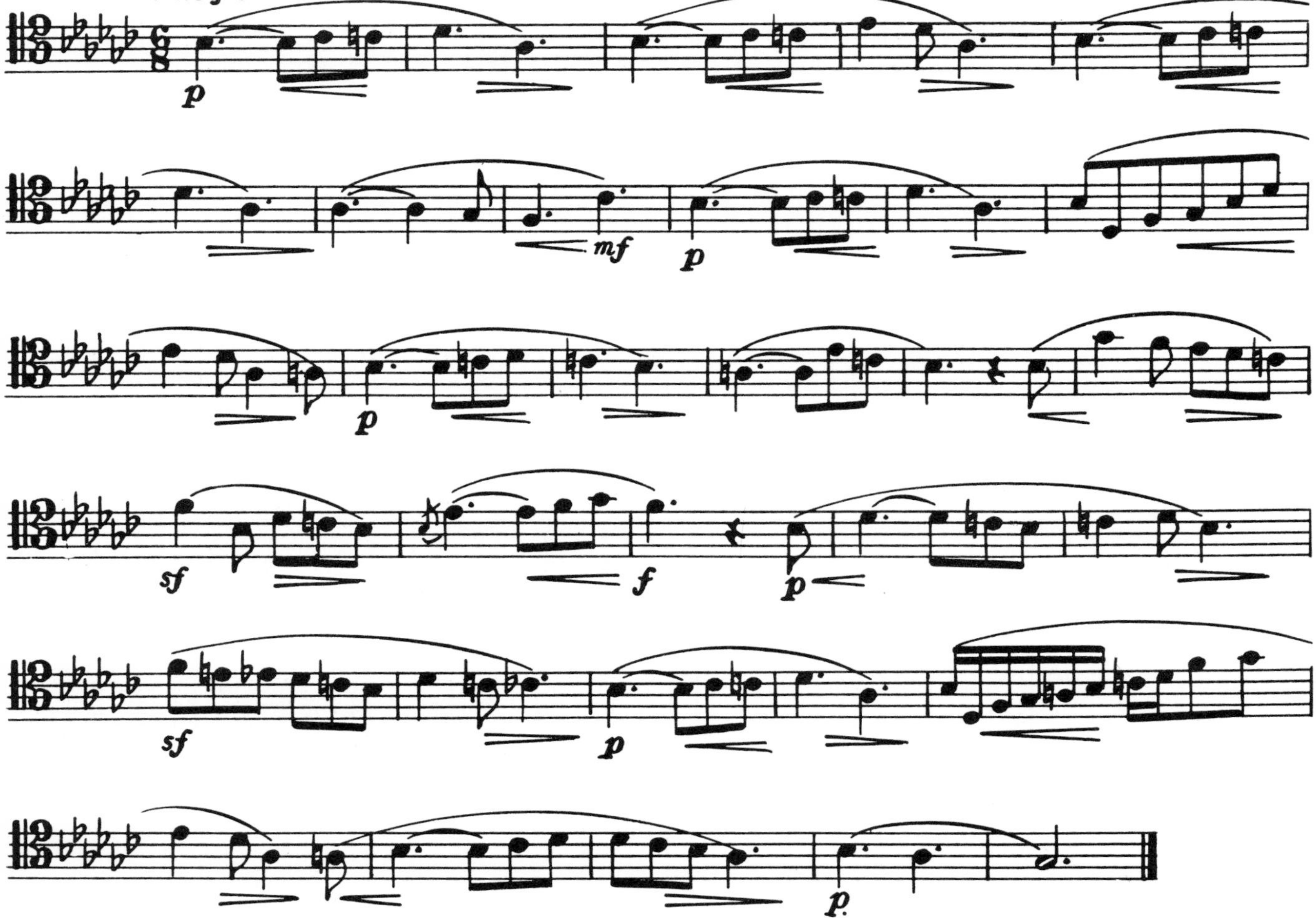

3. This is another of Henselt's piano compositions called "Melody" or "Love Song."

3. Allegro

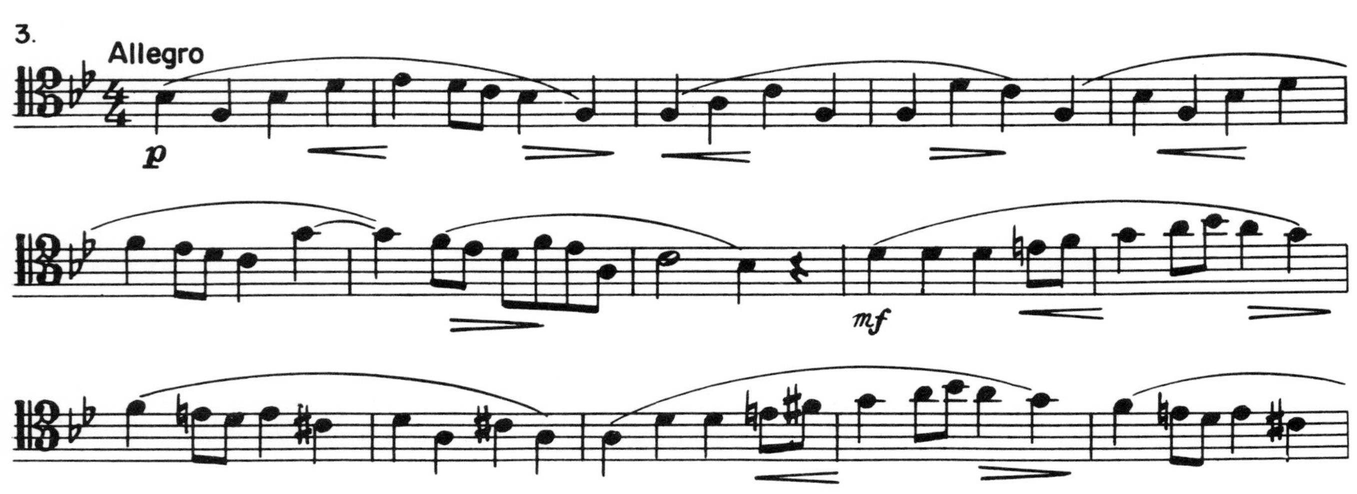

4. This melody, written by the German composer Frederick Himmel (1765-1814), was later transcribed by the German composer J. N. Hummel (1778-1837).

5. Gustav Lange (1830-1889), German pianist and composer, is best known for his piano work "The Flower Song." This type of composition was very popular near the turn of the century.

6. This berceuse, or cradle song, was written by the Norwegian composer Halfdan Kjerulf (1815-1868).

6.

Andante

7. "Last Night the Nightingale Woke Me" is the best-known work of Halfdan Kjerulf.

8. This is "Pure As Snow," another piano composition by Gustav Lange. Although Lange is not considered an outstanding composer, many of his compositions have an interesting melodic line that has assured their popularity for many years.

9. Franz Liszt wrote several short works for the piano known as "Consolations." Liszt, a famous pianist and composer of his day, was the father-in-law of Wagner. He was born in Hungary in 1811 and died at Bayreuth (where Wagner's operas were performed) in 1886.

9.

Andante

10. This is one of Mendelssohn's *Songs Without Words,* the very well known "Spring Song."

If the student wishes to learn the art of transposition fluently, he will find it profitable to write out all of the exercises in this book in each of the seven clefs. Any student who plays the piano and wishes to become an expert accompanist would do well to practice playing his piano literature with the right hand using one clef (other than the treble) and the left hand using another (other than the bass clef).

It is profitable for the student if the instructor plays recordings of the compositions excerpted above so that the student can become familiar with the themes in their original settings. Most of these works have been recorded. Similarly, if the student can afford it, he will be well rewarded musically if he includes some of these standard works in his own record collection.

MINOR KEYS

Treble Clef

1. This is the theme from the third movement of Schubert's Symphony No. 5 in B♭ major, adapted from the first violin and cello parts. The third movement is a minuet, a French dance in ¾ time that begins on the third beat of the measure with an accent on that beat. Haydn and Mozart used the minuet for the third movement of their symphonies. Beethoven usually called the third movement of his symphonies *scherzos* (Italian for "jest"), and they are heartier than the stately minuet.

2. This is the theme of "Bourrée No. 2" from *English Suite* No. 1 in A minor. The theme begins in A minor and modulates at the end of this section to E minor.

3. This is the theme of "Gavotte No. 1" of Bach's English Suite No. 3. If this theme seems too difficult to sing, even when taken slowly, the instructor should play it on the piano. The student should at least be familiar with the melody, since it is one of Bach's well-known compositions.

3. Largo

4. This is the theme of the last movement of Haydn's *Farewell Symphony*, played by the first violins.

5. This is the opening theme of Mozart's Symphony No. 40 in G minor, K. 550. The ending of the melody line has been altered to complete the theme in G minor rather than modulating to B♭ major as Mozart did. This is a first violin part.

6. This theme is from the minuet (third movement) of the same symphony. Played by the first violins, the theme begins in G minor and modulates to D minor.

7. Here is the opening theme to the fourth movement of the same symphony. It is found in the first violin part.

8. These themes appear at the beginning of Schubert's Symphony No. 8 in B minor *(Unfinished Symphony).* The cellos begin the theme and the first violins begin a sort of accompaniment theme until the oboe starts its theme. Other woodwind parts are added, and finally the first section comes to a close before the second theme, which is so lovely in the cello part, is played. This second theme appears earlier in this book in the sight-singing exercises for major keys.

9. This is the introduction and first theme of the second movement of Schubert's Symphony No. 7 in C major. The cellos carry the theme in the introduction, and the oboe states the first main theme.

9.

Andante

10. The second movement of Beethoven's *Eroica Symphony* is a funeral march. The first theme is played by the violins.

10.

Adagio

11. This is the melody of a Bach chorale whose title rendered in English is "Christ Lay in Death's Dark Prison." This is the chorale on which an Easter cantata (No. 158) is based. The chorale closes the cantata.

12. The title of this chorale might be translated as "Dawning Brought a Beautiful Day." It is the closing chorale in Cantata No. 145.

13. This chorale, the final number in Cantata No. 28, has an English title "Help Me God's Goodness to Praise."

14. This is the middle section, in the tonic minor key, of *A Loure,* by J. S. Bach. The first section appears earlier (treble clef, No. 18, in the major melodies). This particular section modulates to B♭ major—which is the relative major—and to D minor, a closely related key to B♭ major.

15. This is the bourrée from Bach's Violin Sonata No. 2 in A minor. It begins in F minor and modulates to the relative major key, A♭ major.

16. Here is a rondo by Philipp Emanuel Bach, son of Johann Sebastian Bach. P. E. Bach (1714-1788) was often referred to as the "Hamburg Bach." He is often credited with the founding of the modern school of piano playing.

17. This is "The Tambourin," by J. Philippe Rameau. A tambourin is a dance which derives its name from the instrument used to accompany it, the tambourine. Rameau (1683-1764) was an eminent French composer, theorist, and organist.

18. These sections, in a minor key, are from Haydn's *Gypsy Rondo*. The major section of the composition appears earlier in this book (alto clef, No. 9).

19. This delightful little "Moment Musical" by Franz Schubert is another example of a gay melody in a minor key. There are six compositions in the set, which Schubert entitled *Moment Musicaux,* Op. 94.

19. **Allegro**

20. A beautiful and popular melody is this art song "Serenade" by Franz Schubert. The yearning melody expresses the emotions of the serenader as he sings to his lady.

20. **Moderato**

Bass Clef

1. This, the closing chorale in Bach's Cantata No. 36, bears the English title "Come Now, Saviour of the People."

2. This very popular Bach chorale is "Jesus Christ Our Saviour."

3. The title of this Bach chorale might be translated as "Ah, Dear Christian, Be Consoled."

4. This chorale by Bach is "I Have Transgressed, Lord."

5. Apparently Bach was very fond of this melody, for he harmonized it in many different ways. A translation of the title might be "Jesus, Saviour of My Soul."

6. This Bach chorale is entitled in English "Ah, What Must I, a Sinner, Do?"

7. This Bach chorale, from Cantata No. 65, bears the English title "Whatever God Wills, May It Come to Pass."

8. "Come Here to Me, Speaks the Son of God" is the English title for this final chorale in Bach's Cantata No. 108.

9. "Our Father Who Art in Heaven" is the title of this Bach chorale. It is the closing chorale of Cantata No. 102.

10. This chorale title might be translated as "Ah, How Empty, Ah, How Fleeting." It is the closing chorale in Bach's Cantata No. 26.

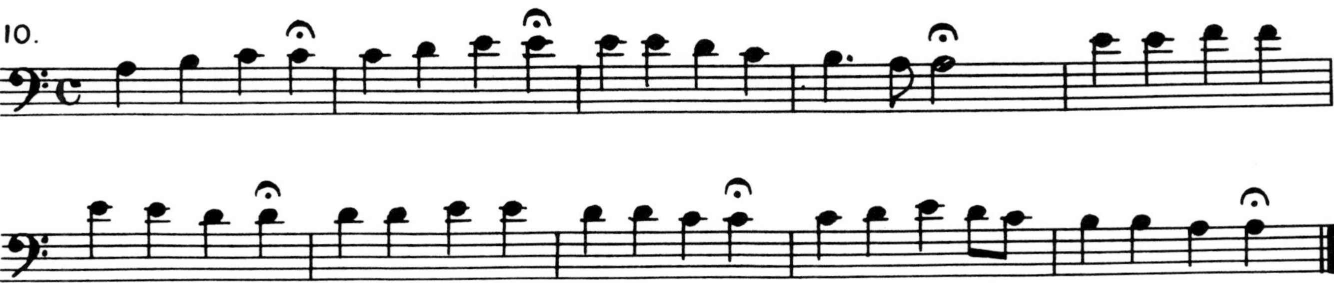

If the instructor wishes to use harmonizations of the above chorale melodies, after the chorales have first been sight-read, he will find them in any collection of the 371 chorales by Bach. Elvera Wonderlich's *Chorale Collection* (New York, Appleton-Century-Crofts, Inc.) is especially recommended. The German titles of the chorales illustrated above are:

Treble clef: No. 11—Christ lag in Todesbanden
12—Erschienen ist der herrlich' Tag

Bass clef: No. 1—Nun komm, der Heiden Heiland
2—Jesus Christus, unser Heiland
3—Ach lieben, Christen seid getrost
4—Herr, ich habe missgehandelt
5—Jesu, der du meine Seele
6—Ach was soll ich Sünder machen
7—Was mein Gott will, das g'scheh'
8—Kommt her zu mir, spricht Gottes Sohn
9—Vater unser im Himmelreich
10—Ach wie nichtig, ach wie flüchtig

11. This melody is taken from the second number in Mendelssohn's *Songs Without Words*. It begins in A minor and modulates to E minor.

12. Known as the "Venetian Gondola Song No. 1," this is the sixth number of *Songs Without Words*. Mendelssohn composed it about 1830.

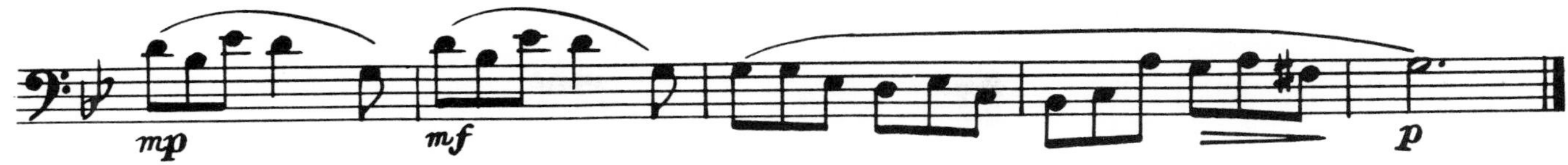

13. This is No. 14 in *Songs Without Words.*

13. Allegro

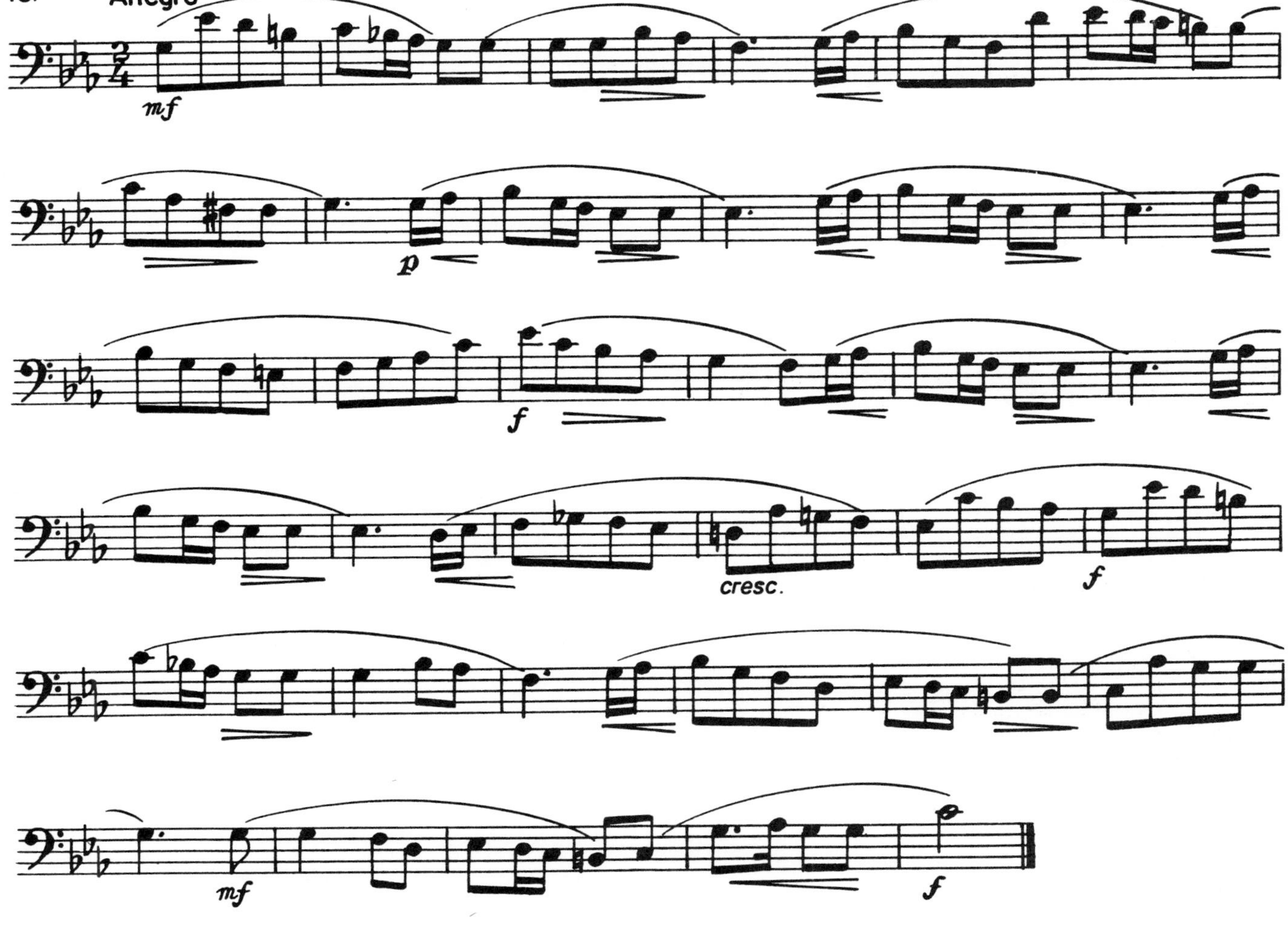

14. Mendelssohn composed this melody in 1843. It is known as the "Funeral March" and is No. 27 of *Songs Without Words.*

14. Andante

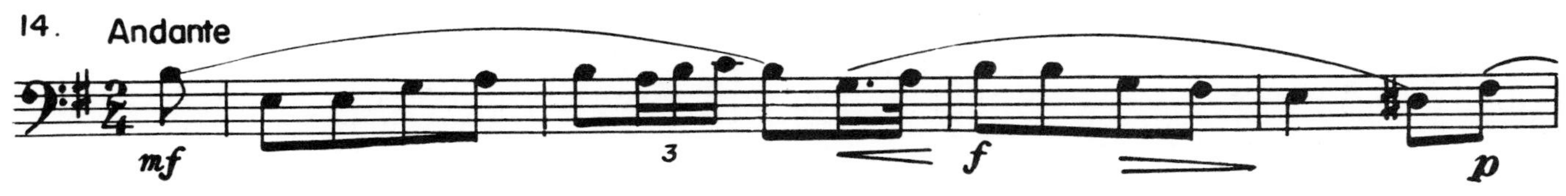

15. This melody, No. 35 in *Songs Without Words,* was written about 1844.

15. Moderato

16. This is the theme of the trio of the third movement of Beethoven's Sonata for Piano, No. 2 in A major, Op. 2, No. 2. It has been modified here to put it within singing range.

16. Allegro

17. This is the theme of the second movement of Beethoven's Sonata for Piano, No. 6 in F major, Op. 10, No. 2. This second movement is in F minor. This is the sixth sonata Beethoven wrote for the piano, and was composed about 1798.

17. Andante

mf f f

mf mp mf

mf f mf mp

mp

mf

18. This is the third and last movement of Beethoven's Sonata for Piano, No. 8 in C minor, Op. 13 *(Pathetique)*. The sonata was composed about 1799.

19. This is a prelude by Frederick Chopin. The word *prelude* has been applied to a composition of free and improvised character. Chopin wrote a set of 24 of these short pieces which together are known as *Preludes,* Op. 28. This is No. 20. Often all 24 preludes are played as part of a concert pianist's program.

20. This is No. 6 of Chopin's *Preludes,* Op. 28. The theme is played by the left hand; hence it appears in the bass clef in this composition.

For further reading in the alto and tenor clefs, see *Sight-Singing Manual* by A. I. McHose and R. N. Tibbs (New York, Appleton-Century-Crofts, Inc.).

LESSON 12

Exercises for Melodic Dictation

The following melodies, grouped by major and minor keys, are to be sung by the student using letter names and then the neutral syllable *loo*.

Next the exercises are presented in the form of melodic dictation, using this method:

1. The instructor sets the key of the molody (1) by stating it, or (2) by having the student listen to the melody.
2. The instructor in a similar fashion sets the time signature of the melody.
3. The instructor in similar fashion sets the beginning pitch with its proper note value.
4. The instructor plays through the exercise while the class or individual student listens.
5. The student now writes the actual pitches and note values of the melody he has heard.
6. After the instructor has sung the exercise to himself twice (to allow the student time to record), he plays it again for the class or student.
7. This process is repeated until the instructor feels that the student should have the exercise complete enough to warrant advancing to the next exercise. (Under no circumstances should the instructor play the melody more than four times. Playing more than four times neither develops the student's training in concentration nor his tonal memory, and these are aims in teaching dictation.)

To further develop skills in reading all clefs, it would be advisable for the student to take dictation in them all. Here we have presented them solely in the bass and treble clefs.

The instructor may dictate in

G, G♭ Major
1.
2.
3.
4.
5.
6.
7.
8.
9.
10.

D, D♭Major
1.
2.
3.
4.
5.
6.
7.
8.
9.
10.

A, A♭ Major

E, E♭ Major
1.
2.
3.
4.
5.
6.
7.
8.
9.
10.

B, B♭ Major
1.
2.
3.
4.
5.
6.
7.
8.
9.
10.

F♯, F Major
1.
2.
3.
4.
5.
6.
7.
8.
9.
10.

MINOR KEYS

The exercises are presented in all forms of the minor. In each key, numbers 1-3 are written in the natural minor; numbers 4-6 are written in the harmonic minor; and numbers 7-10 in the melodic minor.

G, G♯ minor
1.
2.
3.
4.
5.
6.
7.
8.
9.
10.

D, D♯minor

A, A♯, A♭ minor

1.

2.

3.

4.

5.

6.

7.

8.

9.

10.

E, E♭ minor
1.
2.
3.
4.
5.
6.
7.
8.
9.
10.

B, B♭ minor

1.

2.

3.

4.

5.

6.

F, F# minor
1.
2.
3.
4.
5.
6.
7.
8.
9.
10.

Name ....

Date ....

SAMPLE TEST NUMBER 1 FOR LESSON 12: Melodic Dictation

The instructor dictates any of the melodies in this lesson in both major and minor keys. He may prefer to use any other exercises in this book marked for dictation or he may choose to construct his own melodies. It is suggested that for each dictation test five melodies in each mode (major or minor) be used.

For further drill in learning the different clefs, the student may be asked to write what he hears in any clef designated by the instructor.

Name ....   Date ....

SAMPLE TEST NUMBER 2 FOR LESSON 12: Melodic Dictation

LESSON 13
Chord Construction

CONSTRUCTION OF MAJOR, MINOR, AUGMENTED, AND DIMINISHED CHORDS

Chords are generally built in intervals of a third. In some of our twentieth-century music, composers use chords built on the interval of the fourth. However, for the study of rudiments, it is necessary to study and learn about only those chords built on intervals of a third.

The lowest note of a three-note chord is called its *root;* the middle note is called the *third;* and the highest note is called the *fifth.*

CONSTRUCTING CHORDS BY THE USE OF THIRDS

A *major chord* is composed of a major third on the bottom and a minor third on the top.

Formula: $\frac{m3}{M3}$

Example: Given C as the root of a major chord:
A major third up from C is E.
A minor third up from E is G.
Result: C-E-G.

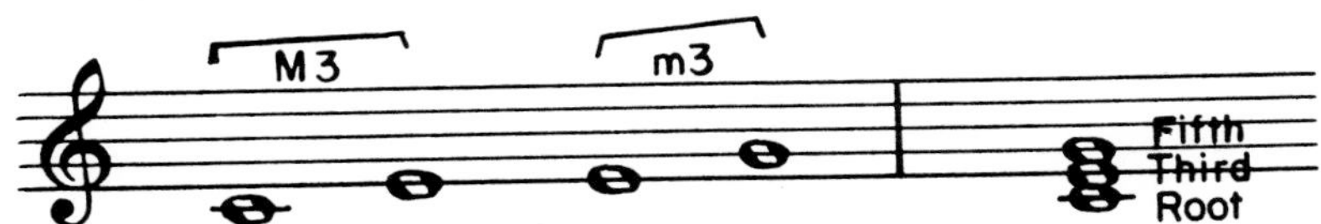

A *minor chord* is composed of a minor third on the bottom and a major third on top. (This is just the opposite of the major chord.)

Formula: $\frac{M3}{m3}$

Example: Given C as the root of a minor chord:
A minor third up from C is E♭.
A major third up from E♭ is G.
Result: C-E♭-G.

An *augmented chord* contains two major thirds, one above the other.

Formula: $\frac{\text{M3}}{\text{M3}}$

Example: Given C as the root of an augmented chord:
A major third up from C is E.
A major third up from E is G♯.
Result: C-E-G♯.

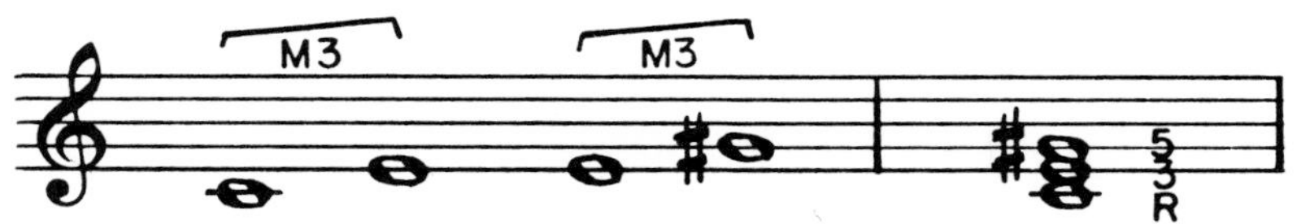

A *diminished chord* contains two minor thirds, one above the other.

Formula: $\frac{\text{m3}}{\text{m3}}$

Example: Given C as the root of a diminished chord:
A minor third up from C is E♭.
A minor third up from E♭ is G♭.
Result: C-E♭-G♭.

In addition to serving as the root of any chord, any note may also be the *third* of any chord. The same formulas still apply, but now you must first build down the desired third and then build up the desired third, in each case starting with the middle note of the chord.

To construct a *major chord* starting with the *third*, build down a major third and then erect a minor third on top of the major third.

Example: Given C as the third of a major chord:
Build down a major third from C to A♭.
Build up a minor third from C to E♭.
Result: A♭-C-E♭.

To construct a *minor chord* starting with the *third,* build down a minor third and then erect a major third on top of the minor third.

Example: Given C as the third of a minor chord:
Build down a minor third from C to A.
Build up a major third from C to E.
Result: A-C-E.

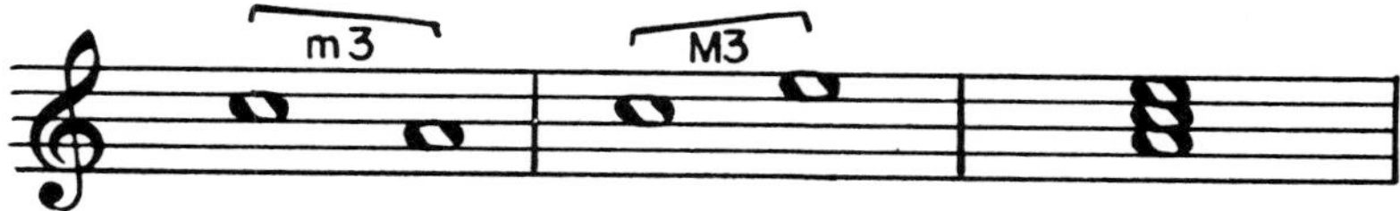

To construct an *augmented chord* starting with the *third,* build down a major third and then erect a major third on top of the first major third.

Example: Given C as the third of an augmented chord:
Build down a major third from C to A♭.
Build up a major third from C to E.
Result: A♭-C-E.

To construct a *diminished chord* starting with the *third,* build down a minor third and then erect a minor third on top of the first minor third.

Example: Given C as the third of a diminished chord:
Build down a minor third from C to A.
Build up a minor third from C to E♭.
Result: A-C-E♭.

In addition to serving as the root or third of any chord, any note may also be the *fifth* of any chord. Now, starting with the highest note of a chord, we must build down the desired third to reach the middle note and then build down again to reach the root.

To construct a *major chord* starting with the *fifth,* build down a minor third and then build down a major third below the minor third.

Example: Given C as the fifth of a major chord:
Build down a minor third from C to A.
Build down a major third from A to F.
Result: F-A-C.

To construct a *minor chord* starting with the *fifth*, build down a major third and then build down a minor third below the major third.

Example: Given C as the fifth of a minor chord:
Build down a major third from C to A♭.
Build down a minor third from A♭ to F.
Result: F-A♭-C.

To construct an *augmented chord* starting with the *fifth*, build down a major third and then build down a major third beneath the top major third.

Example: Given C as the fifth of an augmented chord:
Build down a major third from C to A♭.
Build down a major third from A♭ to F♭.
Result: F♭-A♭-C.

To construct a *diminished chord* starting with the *fifth*, build down a minor third and then build down a minor third beneath the top minor third.

Example: Given C as the fifth of a diminished chord:
Build down a minor third from C to A.
Build down a minor third from A to F♯.
Result: F♯-A-C.

Although there are other methods for constructing chords, as we shall see later in this lesson, the method outlined above is advocated in this book, for it is perhaps the simplest for beginners. This method requires the employment of only *two* intervals. These are a major third or a minor third, down or up from *any* note of the scale. In order to use this method, the student must drill himself *thoroughly* in spelling major thirds and minor thirds up and down from any pitch, so that this information is always at his fingertips. Although speed is imperative in the constructing of chords, accuracy must not be sacrificed to speed. One's motto should be *accuracy with speed.*

CONSTRUCTING CHORDS BY THE USE OF THIRDS AND FIFTHS

A second method of spelling chords uses the intervals of thirds and fifths.

Using any note as the *root* of the chord, the following formulas apply:

A *major chord* has a major third and a perfect fifth, both measured from the root of the chord.

Example: Given C as the root of a major chord:
A major third from C is E.
A perfect fifth from C is G.
Result: C-E-G.

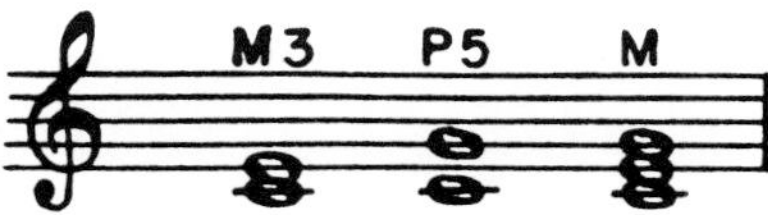

A *minor chord* has a minor third and a perfect fifth, both measured from the root of the chord.

Example: Given C as the root of a minor chord:
A minor third from C is E♭.
A perfect fifth from C is G.
Result: C-E♭-G.

An *augmented chord* has a major third and an augmented fifth, both measured from the root of the chord.

Example: Given C as the root of an augmented chord:
A major third from C is E.
An augmented fifth from C is G♯.
Result: C-E-G♯.

A *diminished chord* has a minor third and a diminished fifth, both measured from the root of the chord.

Example: Given C as the root of a diminished chord:
A minor third from C is E♭.
A diminished fifth from C is G♭.
Result: C-E♭-G♭.

If you are given any note as the *third* of a chord, the major, minor, augmented, and diminished chords can be constructed by using the following formulas:

To obtain a *major chord,* build down a major third to find the root, and then build up a perfect fifth from the root.

Example: Given C as the third of a major chord:
Build down a major third from C to A♭.
Build up a perfect fifth from A♭ to E♭.
Result: A♭-C-E♭.

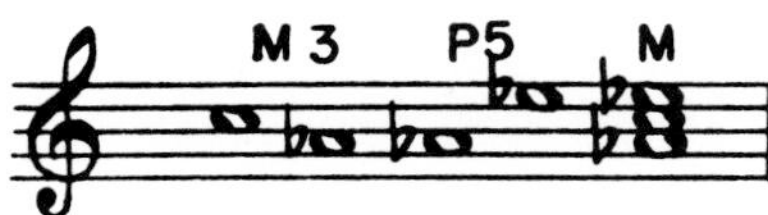

To obtain a *minor chord,* build down a minor third to find the root, and then build up a perfect fifth from the root.

Example: Given C as the third of a minor chord:
Build down a minor third from C to A.
Build up a perfect fifth from A to E.
Result: A-C-E.

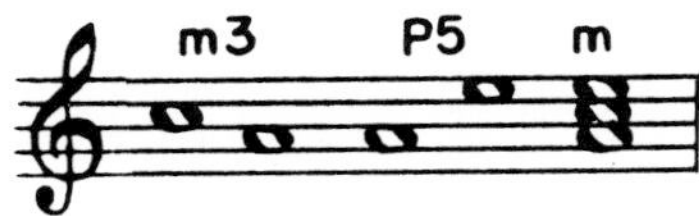

To obtain an *augmented chord,* build down a major third to find the root, and then build up an augmented fifth from the root.

Example: Given C as the third of an augmented chord:
Build down a major third from C to A♭.
Build up an augmented fifth from A♭ to E.
Result: A♭-C-E.

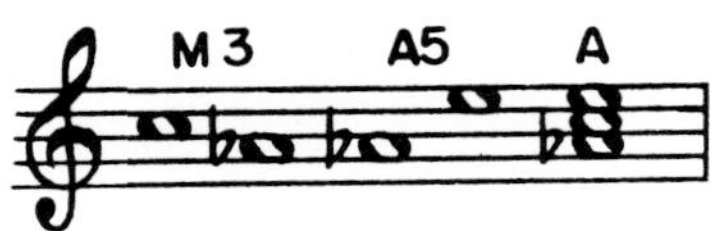

To obtain a *diminished chord,* build down a minor third to find the root, and then build up a diminished fifth from the root.

Example: Given C as the third of a diminished chord:
Build down a minor third from C to A.
Build up a diminished fifth from A to E♭.
Result: A-C-E♭.

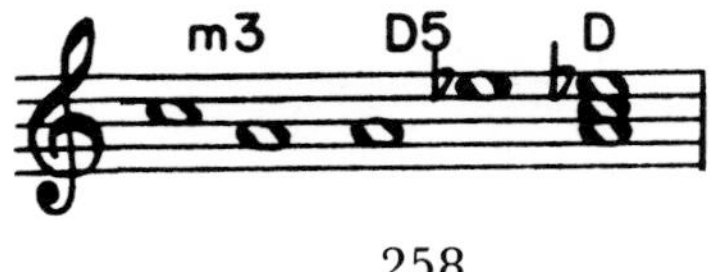

To construct the major, minor, augmented, and diminished chords, when you are given any note as the *fifth* of the chord, use these formulas:

To obtain a *major chord,* build down a perfect fifth to find the root, and then build up a major third from the root.

Example: Given C as the fifth of a major chord:
Build down a perfect fifth from C to F.
Build up a major third from F to A.
Result: F-A-C.

To obtain a *minor chord,* build down a perfect fifth to find the root, and then build up a minor third from the root.

Example: Given C as the fifth of a minor chord:
Build down a perfect fifth from C to F.
Build up a minor third from F to A♭.
Result: F-A♭-C.

To obtain an *augmented chord,* build down an augmented fifth to find the root, and then build up a major third from the root.

Example: Given C as the fifth of an augmented chord:
Build down an augmented fifth from C to F♭.
Build up a major third from F♭ to A♭.
Result: F♭-A♭-C.

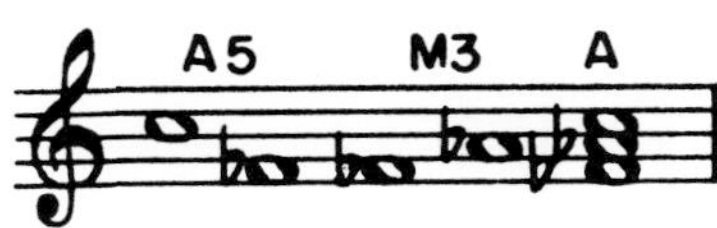

To obtain a *diminished chord,* build down a diminished fifth to find the root, and then build up a minor third from the root.

Example: Given C as the fifth of a diminished chord:
Build down a diminished fifth from C to F♯.
Build up a minor third from F♯ to A.
Result: F♯-A-C.

Whereas the first method required only the use of the major and minor thirds, this second method requires the use of those intervals plus the perfect fifth, augmented fifth, and diminished fifth.

CONSTRUCTING CHORDS BY THE USE OF CHORD QUALITY

A third method of chord construction depends upon (1) memorizing the quality of the chords whose roots are the degrees of the C major scale, and (2) a knowledge of how to alter these chords to achieve the chord you wish to build.

Chord Quality

In C major, as in any major scale, the chords erected on the first, fourth, and fifth degrees (the I, IV, V chords) are major in quality. The chords erected on the second, third, and sixth degrees (II, III, VI chords) are minor in quality. The chord erected on the seventh degree of the scale (the VII chord) is diminished in quality.

Summary:
- I is a major chord
- II is a minor chord
- III is a minor chord
- IV is a major chord
- V is a major chord
- VI is a minor chord
- VII is a diminished chord

Parallel Chords

If you select a chord whose quality is known (major, minor, etc.) and shift all notes in the chord either a half-step up or a half-step down, it is obvious that the new chord will have the same quality as the original chord. For example, the I, IV, and V chords in the C major scale (C-E-G; F-A-C; G-B-D) are major in quality. If we shift *all* the notes in each of these chords up a half-step, we secure the following chords: C♯-E♯-G♯; F♯-A♯-C♯; and G♯-B♯-D♯. All of these chords are major in quality. Likewise, if we shift *all* of the notes in the original chords down a half-step, we secure these chords: C♭-E♭-G♭; F♭-A♭-C♭; and G-♭B-♭D♭. These chords are also major in quality.

We have learned that the II, III, and VI chords (D-F-A; E-G-B; A-C-E) in the C major scale are minor in quality. If we shift all the notes in each of these chords up a half-step, we secure the following chords: D♯-F♯-A♯; E♯-G♯-B♯; and A♯-C♯-E♯. Since these chords retain the quality of the original chords, they are minor chords. Likewise, if we shift all of the notes in the original chords down a half-step, we secure these chords: D♭-F♭-A♭; E♭-G♭-B♭; and A♭-C♭-E♭. These chords are also minor in quality.

We have learned that the VII chord (B-D-F) in the C major scale is diminished in quality. If we shift all the notes in this chord up a half-step, we secure B♯-D♯-F♯. Since this chord retains the quality of the original chord, it is a diminished chord. Likewise, if we shift all of the notes in this chord down a half-step, we secure B♭-D♭-F♭. This chord is also diminished in quality.

Using the harmonic minor scale, we find the following chords in the minor key. (Note that the quality of the chords on each step of the scale is *not* the same in the major and the minor keys):

I	is a minor chord
II	is a diminished chord
III	is an augmented chord
IV	is a minor chord
V	is a major chord
VI	is a major chord
VII	is a diminished chord

We have discussed above the method of constructing chords parallel to major, minor, and diminished chords. There remains only to construct parallel chords for the *augmented* chord, which occurs naturally only as the III chord in a minor scale.

As our example, we will use the III chord in A minor: C-E-G♯. If we shift all the notes in this chord up a half-step, we secure C♯-E♯-G𝄪. Since this chord retains the quality of the original chord, it is an augmented chord. Likewise, if we shift all the notes in the original chord down a half-step, we secure the chord C♭-E♭-G♮. This chord is also augmented in quality.

Altering Chords

The quality of any chord may be changed by altering the third, the fifth, or both the third and the fifth.

To change a *minor chord* to a *major chord,* raise the third of the minor chord a half-step. The following example illustrates (1) the alteration of the II, III, and VI chords in C major from minor to major; and (2) a similar alteration of the parallel chords one half-step removed from the original chords.

To change a *major chord* to a *minor chord,* lower the third of the major chord a half-step. The example below illustrates (1) the alteration of the I, IV, and V chords in C major from major to minor; and (2) a similar alteration of the parallel major chords:

To change a *major chord* into an *augmented chord,* raise the fifth of the major chord a half-step. The example shows (1) how to alter the I, IV, and V chords of C major from major to augmented; and (2) a similar alteration for the parallel major chords:

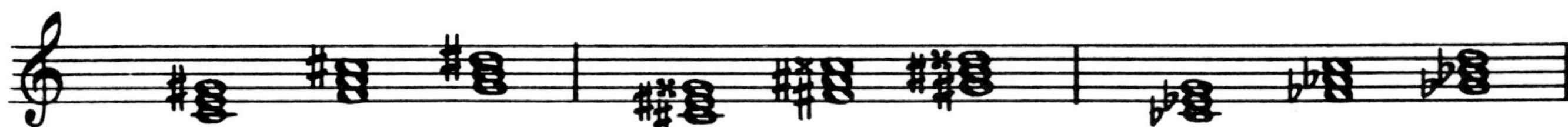

To change a *major chord* into a *diminished chord,* lower both the third and the fifth of the major chord a half-step. The following example shows (1) the alteration of the I, IV, and V chords of C major from major to diminished: and (2) a similar alteration for the parallel major chords:

To change a *minor chord* into a *diminished chord,* lower the fiifth of the minor chord a half-step. The example below shows (1) how to alter the II, III, and VI chords in C major from minor to diminished and (2) a similar alteration for the parallel minor chords:

To change a *minor chord* into an *augmented chord,* raise both the third and the fifth of the minor chord a half-step. The example shows (1) how to alter the II, III, and VI chords in C major from minor to augmented; and (2) a similar alteration for the parallel minor chords.

To change a *diminished chord* into a *major chord,* raise both the third and the fifth of the diminished chord a half-step.

To change a *diminished chord* into a *minor chord,* raise the fifth of the diminished chord a half-step.

To change a *diminished chord* into an *augmented chord,* raise the third of the diminished chord a half-step and the fifth a whole step.

These alterations of the VII chord in C major are shown in the example below:

To change an *augmented chord* into a *major chord,* lower the fifth of the augmented chord a half-step.

To change an *augmented chord* into a *minor chord,* lower both the third and the fifth of the augmented chord a half-step.

To change an *augmented chord* into a *diminished chord,* lower the third of the augmented chord a half-step and the fifth a whole step.

To exemplify the three alterations of the augmented chord, we take the III chord in A minor (C-E-G♯):

CHART OF CHORD ALTERATIONS

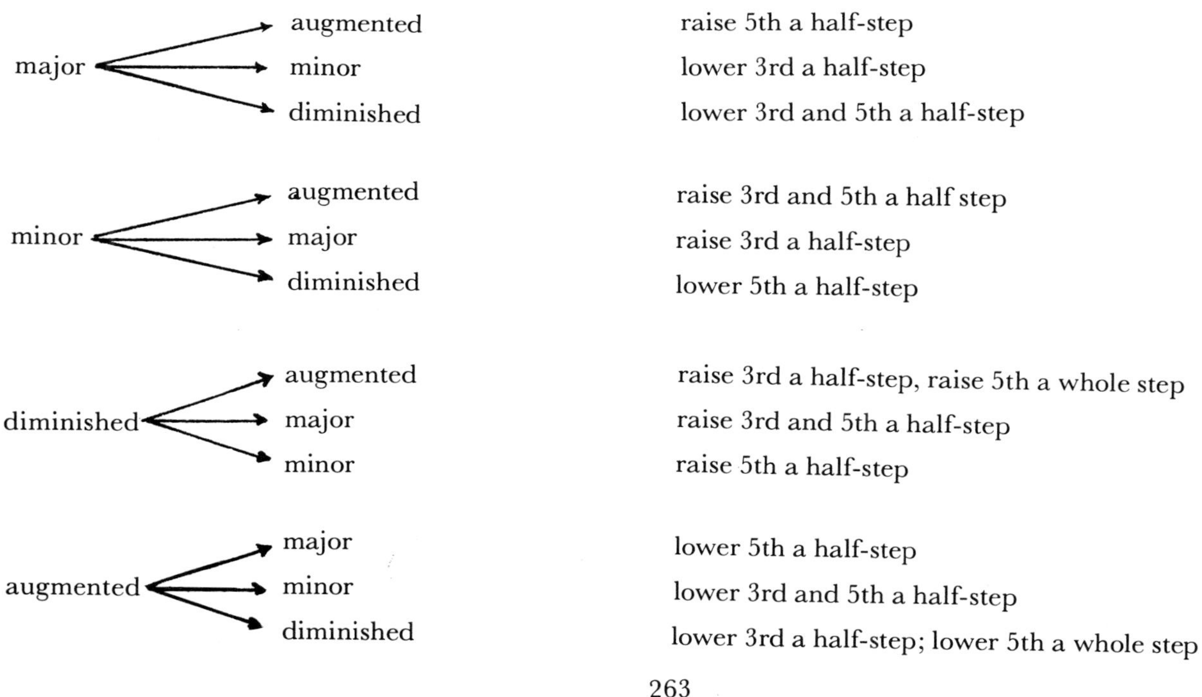

From	To	Alteration
major	augmented	raise 5th a half-step
	minor	lower 3rd a half-step
	diminished	lower 3rd and 5th a half-step
minor	augmented	raise 3rd and 5th a half step
	major	raise 3rd a half-step
	diminished	lower 5th a half-step
diminished	augmented	raise 3rd a half-step, raise 5th a whole step
	major	raise 3rd and 5th a half-step
	minor	raise 5th a half-step
augmented	major	lower 5th a half-step
	minor	lower 3rd and 5th a half-step
	diminished	lower 3rd a half-step; lower 5th a whole step

Rule for Chord Construction

With the foregoing background knowledge of (1) the quality of the chords based on the degrees of the C major scale; (2) adjacent parallel chords; and (3) methods for altering chord quality, we can deduce a rule for erecting any kind of chord when the root is given.

The rule is this: Given the root and the quality of the chord desired, find in the C major scale that chord which bears the same letter designation. If the root of the desired chord is contained in the C major scale, merely alter the selected triad in C major to produce the desired chord quality.

Problem: To construct a major chord with A as its root.

Solution: 1. Find the chord in the C major scale which has A as its root. This is the VI chord, A-C-E, which is minor in quality.

2. Alter the minor chord A-C-E to a major chord by raising the third from C to C♯.

3. Result: The major chord with A as its root is spelled A-C♯-E.

If the root of the desired chord contains a sharp or a flat, and hence does not occur in the C major scale, select the chord in the C major scale whose root bears the same letter designation, and construct from that chord a parallel chord on the desired root. If the parallel chord does not have the quality desired, alter the parallel chord.

Problem: To construct the augmented chord on G♭.

Solution: 1. Find the chord in the C major scale which has G as its root. This is the V chord, G-B-D, which is major in quality.

2. Construct a chord on G♭ which will parallel the V chord. This will be G♭-B♭-D♭. Because it is parallel to the V chord, it will be similar in structure and therefore will be major in quality.

3. Alter the parallel major chord G♭-B♭-D♭ to an augmented chord by raising the fifth from D♭ to D♮.

4. Result: The augmented chord with G♭ as its root is G♭-B♭-D♮.

Any of these three methods outlined in the lesson may be chosen by the student for learning the spelling of chords, and perhaps the student may use a combination of the methods. Also the student may use one method to check another, in order to determine if he has the correct spelling for the chord desired. It is essential that the student learns to spell chords quickly and accurately, for upon this knowledge his four-part writing will be based.

SINGING THE MAJOR CHORDS AND MINOR CHORDS

In singing the major chords, three formulas are used:

1. Starting from the root of the chord, sing, as you have already done, 1-3-5-8-5-3-1.
2. Starting with the third of the chord, sing 3-1-5 or 3-5-1.
3. Starting with the fifth of the chord, sing 5-3-1.

For examples, we will use the C major chord. The student should use the formulas with all major and minor chords. Do not use augmented or diminished chords in singing just yet, for these chords will not be needed for the first few lessons in four-part writing.

Using C as the root of the chord, sing:

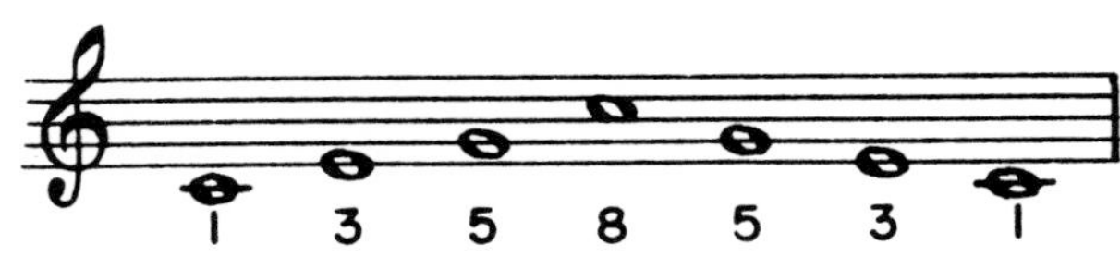

Using the third of the C major chord, which is E, sing:

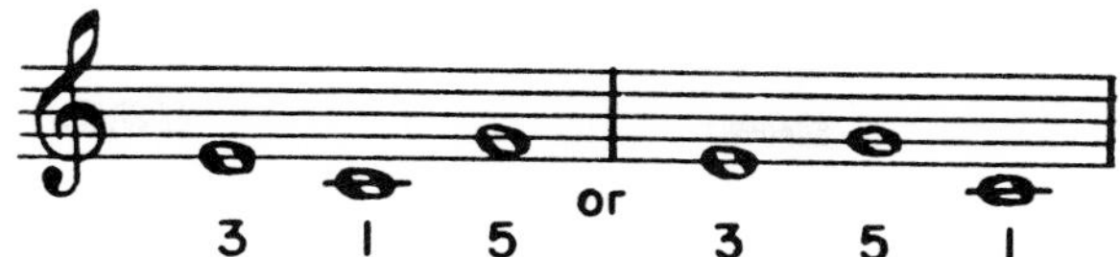

Using the fifth of the C major chord, which is G, sing:

Using C as the third of a major chord, sing:

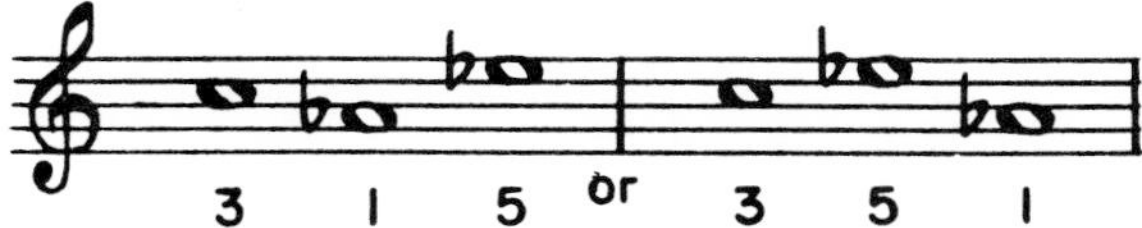

Using C as the fifth of a major chord, sing:

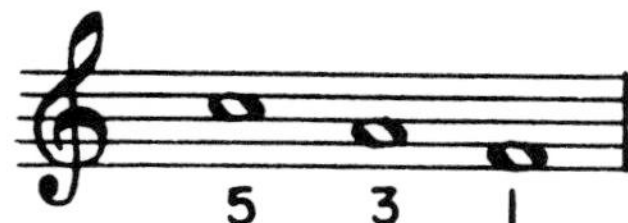

These formulas are drilled on by the entire class, sung by individuals, and finally the student records on paper whether he hears the root, the third, or the fifth of the chord in the top voice of the chord when the instructor plays the chord.

For example:

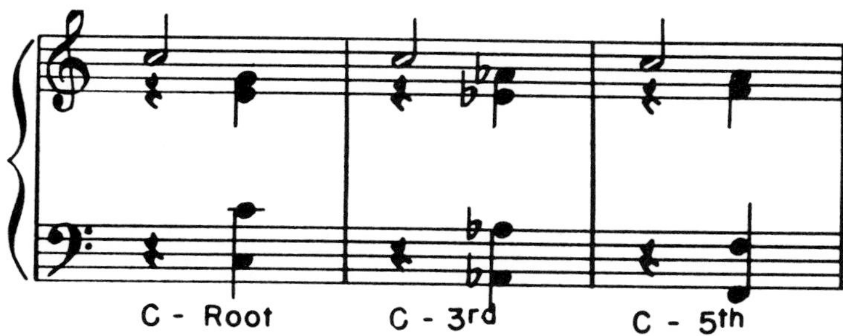

The instructor now plays any chord in the form just illustrated, placing the root, third, or fifth in the soprano (top) voice. The student is asked to designate the correct formula (1-3-5-8-5-3-1; 3-1-5; or 5-3-1) and then sings it while the instructor plays the chord. This is not too easy for some students and will require a great deal of drill.

After some proficiency has been attained in singing the correct formulas, they then may be dictated in groups of 20 chords as in the following example. The note recorded is the one heard in the *soprano* voice. In example I, the first soprano note heard was the root which is recorded as 1.

I.		II.	
	1-3-5-3-1		5-3-1-3-5
	3-1-5-5-1		1-3-1-5-1
	5-5-3-1-3		1-3-5-5-1
	1-1-5-3-3		3-1-5-3-1

After the student has heard all 20 chords, the instructor should check with the student, and any incorrect answers should be drilled on at once, singing the formula the student should have heard.

Considerable practice should be devoted to taking any note and singing it as the root of the chord, then using the same note successively as the third and the fifth of the chord. First use the note in major chords, singing the formulas; and then in the minor chords.

For example:

Although the student will not be singing the diminished and augmented chords, it is well for him to be able at this time to distinguish in hearing the quality of these chords.

The instructor will play the four kinds of chords and the student will take them down in groups of 20 as follows:

I.	II.
M-m-M-D-m	M-m-D-D-A
A-m-M-D-m	m-D-a-M-m
D-M-m-A-m	A-M-M-m-m
A-M-M-m-D	D-M-m-A-M

(Key: M is major; m is minor; A is augmented; D is diminished.)

KEYBOARD DRILL ON CHORDS

1. The student plays all four types of chords, using any note as the root. These should be played with the right hand only.
2. The student plays any major or minor chord, using any note as the root third, or fifth of the chord. The right-hand fingering of the C major chord is:

C	E	G	C	G	E	C
1	2	3	5	3	2	1

This same fingering will fit most of the chords.

DICTATION DRILL ON CHORDS

1. While the instructor plays the chords using root, third, or fifth in the soprano, the student records what he has heard in groups of 20 chords each, as shown above.

2. As the instructor plays the four different kinds of chords, the student records what he hears in groups of 20 chords each, as shown above.

Name .... Date ....

WORKSHEET FOR LESSON 13: Chord Construction

Construct the chords requested.

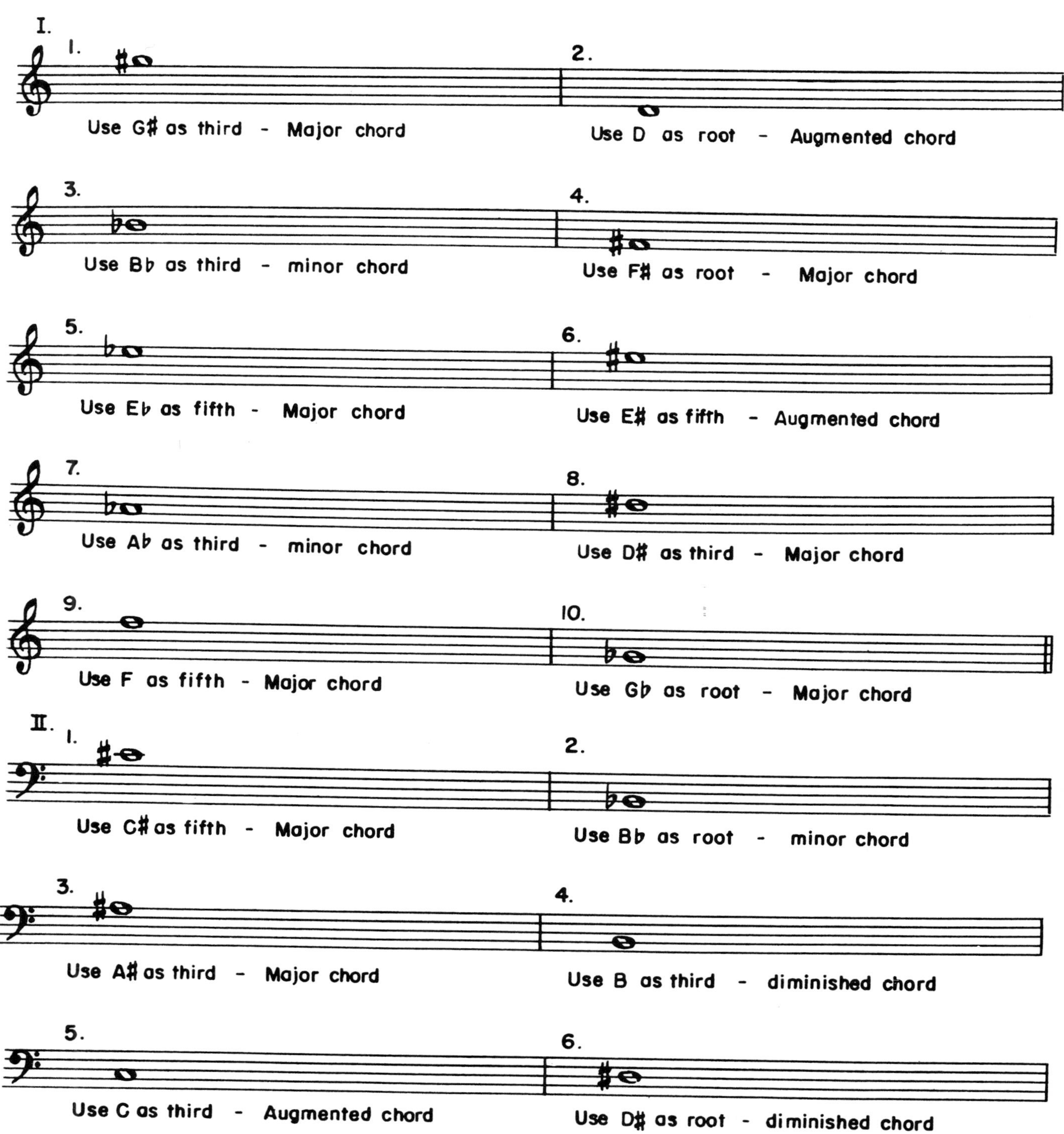

7.
Use E♭ as third - minor chord
8.
Use F♭ as root - Major chord
9.
Use G as third - Major chord
10.
Use A♭ as fifth - minor chord

Name .... Date ....

SAMPLE TEST FOR LESSON 13: Chord Construction

Construct the chords requested.

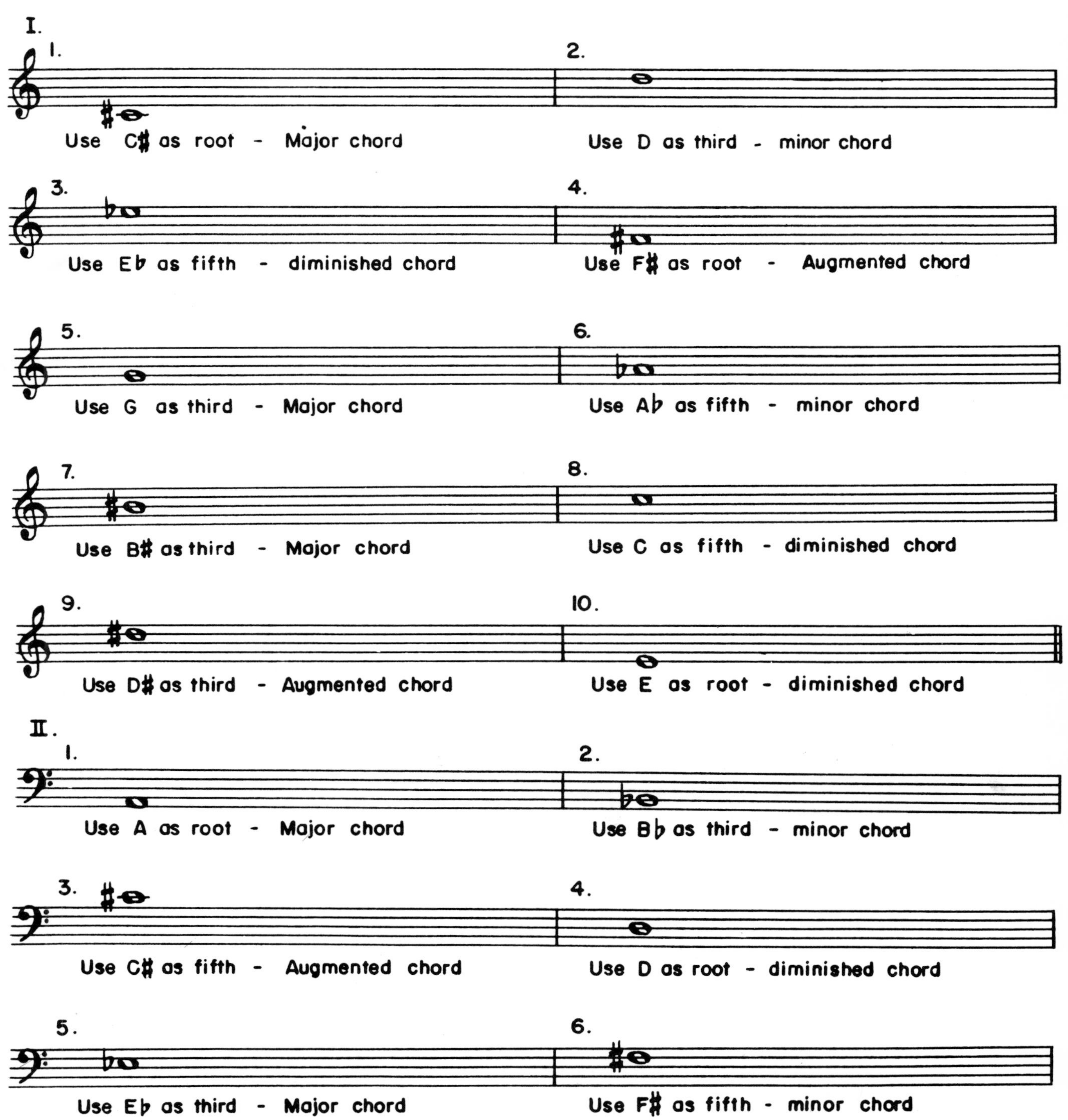

7.
Use G as root - Augmented chord
8.
Use A♭ as third - minor chord
9.
Use B as fifth - Major chord
10.
Use C as root - Augmented chord

THE NAMES OF THE STEPS OF THE SCALE

Each step of the scale has a specific name. We have already learned that the keynote is called the *tonic*. If we were to study the science of music, we would learn from the "overtone series" that next to the tonic, the most important step in any scale is the fifth step of the scale. Something that is very outstanding and important is said to be dominant. So in music we call this fifth step of the scale *dominant*. "Sub" means something under, so the first tone under the dominant is called the subdominant. Therefore the fourth step of the scale is the *subdominant*. Halfway between two points is the middle, for which we will use the term mediant. Therefore, halfway between the tonic and the dominant is the *mediant,* which is the third step of the scale. Likewise, between the tonic and the subdominant will be the *submediant,* the sixth step of the scale. Something that is placed above is called super. Therefore, the note above the tonic will be called the *supertonic,* which is the second step of the scale. If you should play the scale ascending, starting on the tonic, and stop on the seventh step of the scale, you would feel a very strong tendency to take this tone on up to the tonic. Therefore we say this tone leads into the tonic and give to it the name, *leading tone*.

The various steps of the scale, placed on the staff, look like this:

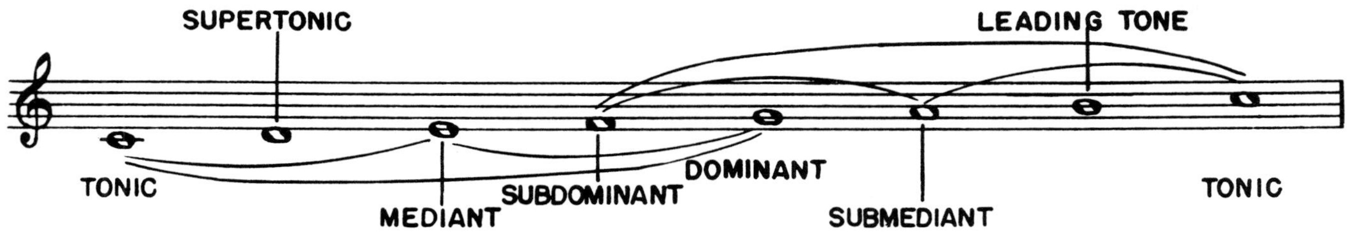

As we have seen, any pitch may be used as any step of a major scale. Using A as each step of a major scale, we have:

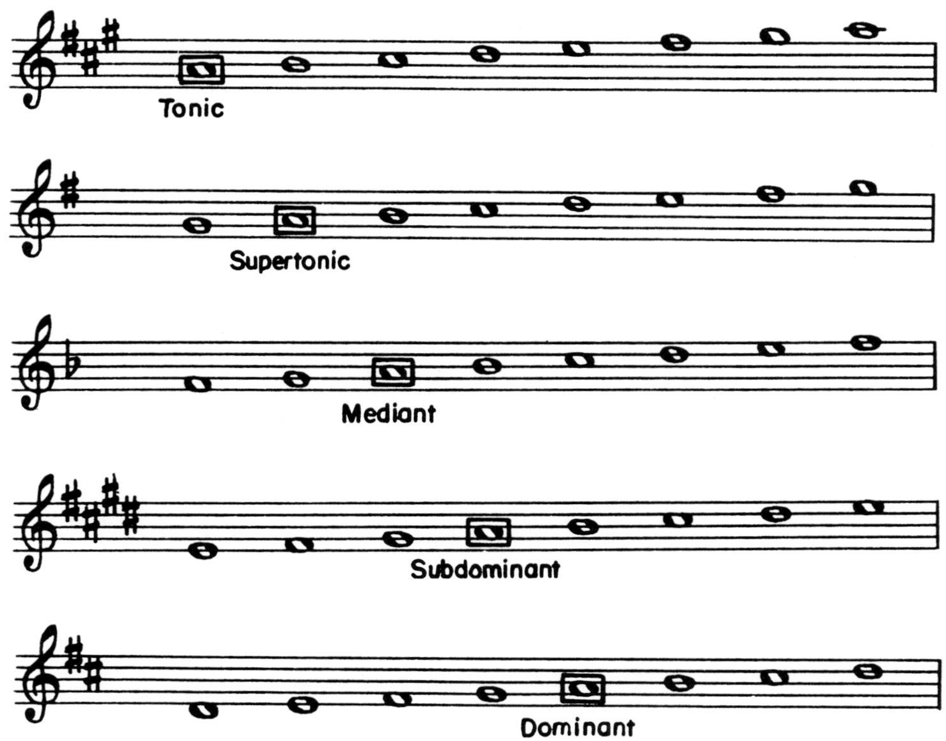

NAMES OF THE CHORDS BUILT ON THE STEPS OF THE SCALE

Just as each step of the scale has a specific name, so every chord built on a scale step has a specific name. This applies to major or minor scales.

I	is the tonic chord
II	is the supertonic chord
III	is the mediant chord
IV	is the subdominant chord
V	is the dominant chord
VI	is the submediant chord
VII	is the leading tone chord

DETERMINING THE KEY OF A COMPOSITION

Usually we can determine the key in which a composition is written by examining the first and last chords of the composition. Generally a work begins on some form of the tonic chord and ends on the tonic. If it begins on an up-beat, some form of the dominant chord might be used. If the key is minor, you will have to study through the composition to determine which form of the minor scale has been used.

For example, the following exercise is written in the key of C minor. It could not be C major because of the E♭. The first measure outlines the tonic chord in C minor: C-E♭-G. We know this is a melodic minor because in the next to the last measure, both the submediant (sixth step) and the leading tone (seventh step) are raised.

In the following example, the ending indicates that the key is A♭. We know the key is not A♭ minor because a C♮ occurs in the composition, whereas in A♭ minor there would be a C♭. If we add up the flats that occur, we find four: B♭, E♭, A♭, D♭. These four flats are the signature of A♭ major, so we know the composition is in that key.

LESSON 14

Sample Final Examination Covering the Entire Book

Ear-training
Sight-singing
Keyboard
Written rudiments

SAMPLE FINAL EXAMINATION in Ear-Training

1. Name the following intervals heard. The instructor dictates in any order desired, or may choose any other intervals of the same level of difficulty.

2. Distinguish hearing the difference between major, minor, diminished, and augmented chords.
   Example:

(1)	(2)
M-m-D-A-M	m-M-A-D-m
m-M-A-D-M	M-m-D-A-m
A-D-M-M-m	D-M-M-m-M
D-A-m-m-M	A-D-m-A-M

3. The instructor dictates the following in any order desired, or substitutes other exercises of equal difficulty. The student writes these as whole notes upon the staff.

4. The instructor chooses from any of the following exercises for melodic dictation.

5. The instructor dictates the following groups of 20 chords and the student identifies the soprano voice as containing the root, the third, or the fifth.

(1) Major chords	(2) Minor chords
1-3-5-1-3	5-3-5-3-5
5-1-3-5-1	5-1-3-5-1
3-5-1-3-5	3-5-1-1-3
1-3-1-5-3	1-3-5-5-3

6. The instructor plays the two following groups of 20 chords and the student writes the appropriate chord quality.

(1)	(2)
m-m-D-M-A	D-A-M-m-M
M-D-A-m-D	m-M-m-D-M
D-A-M-m-A	D-A-M-M-m
A-M-m-D-m	A-M-D-m-M

SAMPLE FINAL EXAMINATION in Sight-Singing

The instructor may choose any of the melodies (major, minor, or both) that have appeared in this book, or he may choose any other material that is of the same level of difficulty. In choosing from the material presented in Lesson 11, he might give an examination to include the following:

a.	$\frac{3}{8}$	F major	Beethoven	Symphony No. 1, second movement (melody No. 2 in major—treble clef)
b.	$\frac{4}{4}$	C major	Brahms	Symphony No. 1, last movement (No. 7 in major—treble clef)
c.	$\frac{2}{4}$	B♭ major	Schubert	Symphony No. 5, last movement (No. 16 in major—treble clef)
d.	$\frac{6}{8}$	D major	Haydn	Symphony 101, first movement (No. 13 in major—bass clef)
e.	$\frac{2}{4}$	G major	Haydn	*Surprise Symphony,* last movement (No. 17 in major—bass clef)
f.	$\frac{4}{4}$	A minor	Bach	Bourrée No. 2 from *English Suite No. 1* (No. 2 in minor—treble clef)
g.	$\frac{4}{4}$	G minor	Mozart	Symphony No. 40, first movement (No. 5 in minor—treble clef)
h.	$\frac{6}{8}$	G minor	Mendelssohn	*Songs Without Words,* No. 6 (No. 12 in minor—bass clef)
i.	$\frac{4}{4}$	C minor	Beethoven	Sonata for Piano No. 8 *(Pathétique)* (No. 18 in minor—bass clef)
j.	$\frac{3}{4}$	F minor	Beethoven	Sonata for Piano No. 6, Op. 10, No. 2 (No. 17 in minor—bass clef)

If the instructor has given sufficient drill on exercises in the clefs other than treble and bass, these exercises may also be included in this examination.

SAMPLE FINAL KEYBOARD EXAMINATION

1. With the right hand, play the A♭ major scale, ascending and descending.
2. With the left hand, play the E major scale, ascending and descending.
3. Use F♯ as the fourth degree of a major scale, resolve it, and name the key to which it belongs.
4. Use G as the second degree of a major scale, resolve it, and name the key to which it belongs.
5. Use B♭ as the sixth degree of a major scale, resolve it, and name the key to which it belongs.
6. Use D♯ as the seventh degree of a major scale, resolve it, and name the key to which it belongs.
7. With the right hand, play the F♯ minor scale in the melodic form, ascending and descending.
8. With the left hand, play the G minor scale in the harmonic form, ascending and descending.
9. With the right hand, play the rest tones (tonic chord) in G♭ major.
10. With the right hand, play the rest tones in B♭ minor.
11. Play the perfect intervals from E (right hand only).
12. Play the major intervals from A♭ (right hand only).
13. Play the minor intervals from D (right hand only).
14. Use F as the root of a major chord, and play the correct formula for it (1-3-5-8-5-3-1).
15. Use G as the third of a major chord and play the correct formula for it.
16. Use C as the fifth of a minor chord and play the correct formula for it.
17. Use B♭ as the root of a minor chord and play the correct formula for it.
18. Use E as the root of a diminished chord and play the chord.
19. Use A as the third of an augmented chord and play the chord.
20. Use D as the fifth of a minor chord and play the correct formula for it.

Name .... Date ....

SAMPLE FINAL EXAMINATION on Written Rudiments

1. Name the following intervals:

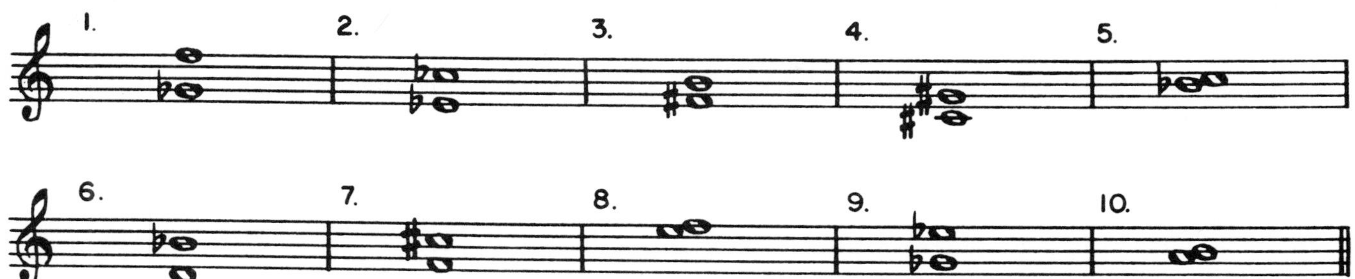

2. Name these intervals:

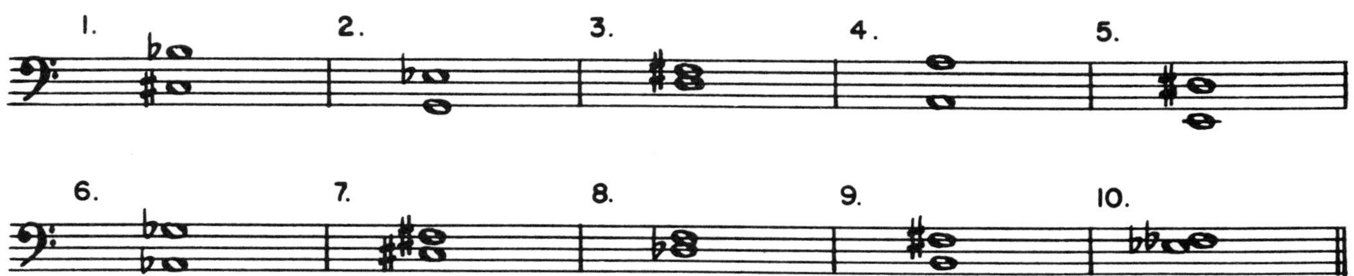

3. Name these melodic intervals:

4. Name these melodic intervals:

5. Write the following signatures and scales:

(1) F minor, melodic form

(2) Tonic minor of E♭ major, harmonic form

2.

(3) Relative minor of D♭ major, melodic form

(4) Tonic major of E minor

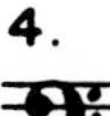

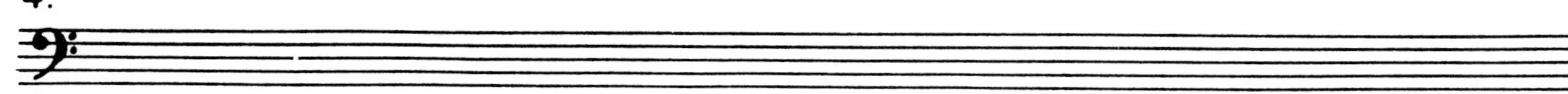

(5) Relative major of A♭ minor

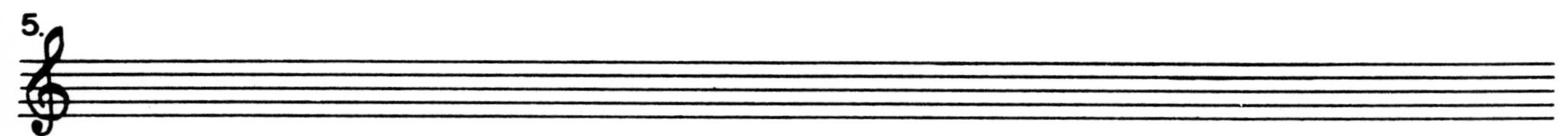

6. In what harmonic minor scale are the following? Just state the key.

7. In what major scale are each of the following? Just state the key.

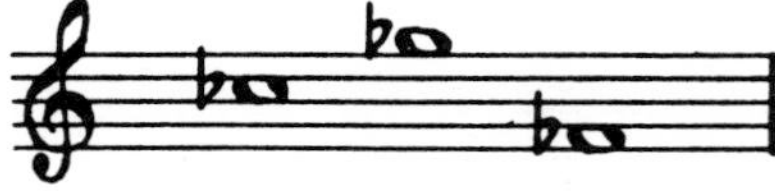

Name .... Date ....

8. State the key of each four-measure exercise. If in minor, state the form used.

9. In what major keys is C♯ respectively:

1. Subdominant 2. Submediant 3. Tonic 4. Mediant 5. Dominant

10. Spell the following chords, in the treble clef only:

1. C as the fifth of a minor chord:

2. F as the third of a minor chord:

3. D♯ as the root of a diminished chord:

4. E as the third of a major chord:

5. E♭ as the root of a major chord:

6. B as the third of a major chord:

7. F as the fifth of a major chord:

8. G as the fifth of a diminished chord:

9. G♯ as the root of an augmented chord:

10. A as the root of an augmented chord: